W9-AVC-560

AFRICAN AMERICAN BREAKTHROUGHS

500 Years of Black Firsts

AFRICAN AMERICAN BREAKTHROUGHS

500 Years of Black Firsts

Jay P. Pederson and Jessie Carney Smith, *Editors*

An imprint of Gale Research Inc.,
an International Thomson Publishing Company

NEW YORK • LONDON • BONN • BOSTON • DETROIT • MADRID
MELBOURNE • MEXICO CITY • PARIS • SINGAPORE • TOKYO
TORONTO • WASHINGTON • ALBANY NY • BELMONT CA • CINCINNATI OH

AFRICAN AMERICAN BREAKTHROUGHS

500 YEARS OF BLACK FIRSTS

Jay P. Pederson and Jessie Carney Smith, *Editors*

Staff

Sonia Benson, *U•X•L Associate Developmental Editor*
Kathleen Witman, *U•X•L Assistant Developmental Editor*
Carol DeKane Nagel, *U•X•L Developmental Editor*
Thomas L. Romig, *U•X•L Publisher*

Margaret A. Chamberlain, *Permissions Supervisor (Pictures)*

Mary Kelley, *Production Associate*
Evi Seoud, *Assistant Production Manager*
Mary Beth Trimper, *Production Director*

Mary Krzewinski, *Cover and Page Designer*

Cynthia Baldwin, *Art Director*

∞™ This book is printed on acid-free paper that meets the minimum requirements of American National Standard for Information Sciences–Permanence Paper for Printed Library Materials, ANSI Z39.48-1984.

ISBN 0-8103-9496-0

Printed in the United States of America

Published simultaneously in the United Kingdom

I(T)P™ Gale Research Inc., an International Thomson Publishing Company.
ITP logo is a trademark under license.

ADVISORY BOARD

READER'S GUIDE

AFRICAN AMERICAN REFERENCE LIBRARY

African American Breakthroughs: 500 Hundred Years of Black Firsts provides fascinating details on hundreds of milestones involving African Americans. The volume is arranged in subject categories, and entries summarize events and include brief biographies of the people involved. *African American Breakthroughs* features illustrations, a bibliography, a timeline of key historical events, a calendar of firsts, and a thorough index.

A Note about Researching Firsts

History is occasionally skewed by any number of human factors. Sometimes the modesty and reluctance of some pioneers to call attention to themselves and their achievements result in an unrecorded milestone. At other times people triumphantly trumpet word of their pioneering while maintaining only a passing familiarity with accuracy. While compiling *African American Breakthroughs,* we were sometimes convinced of a probable first that we could not include for lack of the final bits of proof. Occasionally, established sources attributed firsts to significant national figures in African American history rather than to the real pioneers on the local or regional level.

Many discrepancies in our research arose from inaccuracies and ambiguities in our sources. Beyond general error, differences among sources often occur when there is uncertainty about the date to use or the criteria for claiming a first. Does a politician, for example, achieve a first in the year of the election or the year of the inauguration? Did Laurian Rugambwa become the first black Roman Catholic cardinal in modern times when the pope named him, when the College of Cardinals concurred, or when he was officially raised to the rank? Three black women were the first to earn Ph.D.'s in 1921.

One finished her requirement first, but another's graduation ceremony was earlier. Who was first? (We choose to list all three.)

In our research we found many instances of information in published sources that is quite simply wrong. Once published, the errors tend to persist. Not all mistakes are due to conscious fabrication. Some people genuinely believe that they are the first to do something, overlooking an earlier claim about which they know nothing. Their beliefs creep into interviews and so into biographies.

In *African American Breakthroughs* we have tried to be as careful as possible to avoid these pitfalls, dealing with our sources critically and honestly to present the most accurate list of firsts by black Americans possible.

Related reference sources:

African American Almanac features a comprehensive range of historical and current information on African American life and culture. Organized into twenty-six subject chapters, including Civil Rights, The Family and Health, and Science, Medicine, and Invention, the volumes contain more than three hundred black-and-white photographs and maps, a selected bibliography, and a cumulative subject index.

African American Biography profiles three hundred African Americans, both living and deceased, prominent in their fields, ranging from civil rights to athletics, politics to literature, entertainment to science, religion to the military. A black-and-white portrait accompanies each entry, and a cumulative subject index lists all individuals by field of endeavor.

African American Chronology explores significant social, political, economic, cultural, and educational milestones in black history. Arranged by year and then by month and day, the chronology spans from 1492 to modern times and contains more than one hundred illustrations, extensive cross references, and a cumulative subject index.

African American Voices presents full or excerpted speeches, sermons, orations, poems, testimony, and other notable spoken works of African Americans. Each entry is accompanied by an introduction and boxes explaining terms and events to which the speech alludes, as well as several pertinent illustrations.

Comments and Suggestions

We welcome your comments on *African American Breakthroughs* as well as your suggestions for topics to be featured in future editions. Please write: Editors, *African American Breakthroughs,* U•X•L, 835 Penobscot Bldg., Detroit, Michigan 48226-4094; call toll-free: 1-800-877-4253; or fax: 313-961-6348.

TABLE OF CONTENTS

CALENDAR OF FIRSTS

Timeline of Important African American Events

1787
The U.S. Constitution provides for a male slave to count as three-fifths of a person in determining representation by state.

1777
Vermont is the first state to ban slavery.

1619
Twenty Africans arrive in Jamestown, Virginia, as indentured servants, the first black settlers of colonial America.

1641
Massachusetts is the first colony to make slavery legal.

1600 · · · · 1650 · · · · 1700 · · · · 1750 · · · ·

1620
Mayflower lands at Plymouth Rock

1692-95
Salem witch trials

1775-81
Revolutionary War

1831
The Nat Turner revolt, one of the bloodiest uprisings in African American history, takes place in Southampton County, Virginia.

1808
The federal law banning the importation of African slaves goes into effect but is largely disobeyed.

1849
Harriet Tubman escapes from slavery, then returns to the South at least 20 times to lead more than 300 slaves to freedom.

1800 • • • **1810** • • • **1820** • • • **1830** • • • **1840** • • • •

1803
Louisiana Purchase

1812-14
War of 1812

1838
Cherokee relocated on Trail of Tears

1845
United States annexes Texas

Timeline of Important African American Events

1857
The U.S. Supreme Court's *Dred Scott* decision denies blacks citizenship and denies the power of Congress to restrict slavery in any federal territory.

1863
The Emancipation Proclamation frees the slaves in those states rebelling against the Union.

1865
The 13th Amendment, outlawing slavery in the United States, is passed.

1868
The 14th Amendment, affirming citizenship rights for all persons born or naturalized in the United States, is passed.

1870
The 15th Amendment, which secures voting rights for all male U.S. citizens, is passed.

1850
Fugitive Slave Laws are passed, requiring northerners to aid in the capture and return of runaway slaves. Abolitionist Frederick Douglass opens his home in northern New York as a hiding place for slaves trying to reach Canada.

1896
The Supreme Court's decision in *Plessy* v. *Ferguson* upholds the concept of "separate but equal" public facilities.

1850 · · · 1860 · · · 1870 · · · 1880 · · · 1890 · ·

1861-1865
American Civil War

1876
Sioux defeat Custer's troops at Little Bighorn

1890
National American Women's Suffrage Association founded

1922

The Harlem Renaissance, a golden age of African American literature and arts, begins. One of the leading figures of the literary movement is writer and folklorist Zora Neale Hurston.

1905

The Niagra Movement, which leads to the National Association for the Advancement of Colored People (NAACP), is established. W.E.B Du Bois is instrumental in organizing both groups.

1937

Joe Louis defeats James J. Braddock, becoming heavyweight boxing champion of the world.

1936

Jesse Owens wins four gold medals at the Summer Olympics in Berlin, Germany.

1947

Jackie Robinson joins the Brooklyn Dodgers, becoming the first black player in major league baseball.

1900 · · · **1910** · · · **1920** · · · **1930** · · · **1940** · · ·

1903
Henry Ford founds the Ford Motor Company

1914-18
World War I

1920
19th Amendment guarantees vote to women

1929
Great Depression begins

1939-45
World War II

Timeline of Important African American Events

1955
Rosa Parks refuses to change seats on a Montgomery, Alabama, bus, beginning a boycott of the bus system by blacks that eventually leads to the U.S. Supreme Court's outlawing bus segregation in the city.

1954
In *Brown* v. *Board of Education*, the Supreme Court overturns *Plessy* v. *Ferguson*, ruling unanimously that racial segregation in public schools is unconstitutional.

1963
Martin Luther King, Jr., delivers his "I Have a Dream" speech at the March on Washington, the largest civil rights demonstration in American history.

1965
Malcom X is assassinated in New York City.

1968
King is assassinated in Memphis, Tennessee, sparking at least 125 riots around the country.

1950 • • • • **1955** • • • • **1960** • • • • **1965** • • • • •

1950-53
Korean War

1963
President John F. Kennedy assassinated

1969
Neil Armstrong becomes first astronaut to walk on moon

1993
Toni Morrison becomes the first black woman to win the Nobel prize in literature.

1988
Jesse Jackson receives 1,218.5 delegate votes at the Democratic National Convention, losing the nomination to Michael Dukakis.

1977
The final episode of the ABC-TV epic miniseries based on Alex Haley's novel *Roots* receives the highest ratings in TV history.

1974
Henry Aaron hits his 715th home run, breaking Babe Ruth's long-standing record.

1989
General Colin L. Powell is named chairman of the U.S. Joint Chiefs of Staff.

1970 • • • • **1975** • • • • **1980** • • • • **1985** • • • • **1990** • •

1973
United States withdraws from Vietnam War

1979-80
52 Americans held hostage at U.S. Embassy in Iran

1990-91
Persian Gulf War

African American Breakthroughs

500 Years of Black Firsts

Business and Labor

Advertising • Automobile Industry • Banking • Food • Insurance
Labor Unions • Manufacturing • Miscellaneous Industries • Publishing
Real Estate • Retailing • Stock Brokerage
Transportation, Shipping, and Sailing

Advertising

1893 ◆ **Nancy Green** (1831–1898), a former slave from Montgomery County, Kentucky, was the first Aunt Jemima and the world's first "living trademark." She made her debut at age 59 serving pancakes at the Columbian Exposition in Chicago. The Aunt Jemima Mills Company distributed a souvenir button featuring her photograph and the caption "I'se in town honey." The slogan later became part of the company's promotional campaign. Green was the official trademark for three decades.

Sources: *Black Ethnic Collectibles,* p. 18; Reasons, *They Had a Dream,* vol. 3, p. 29.

1956 ◆ Vince Cullers Advertising, Inc., was the first African American advertising agency in the United States. It was founded by Vincent T. Cullers.

Sources: *Black Enterprise* 1 (February 1971), pp. 15–22; *Ebony Success Library,* vol. 1, p. 82; *Who's Who Among Black Americans, 1992–1993,* p. 329.

Automobile Industry

1916 ◆ **Frederick Douglass Patterson** (?–1932) was the first African American car manufacturer. Between 1916 and 1919 Patterson built some 30 Greenfield-Patterson cars in Greenfield, Ohio.

Source: Reasons, *Reasons They Had a Dream,* vol. 3, p. 48.

Maggie Lena Walker

1967 ♦ **Albert William Johnson** (1921–) was the first African American Oldsmobile dealer. Jackson's franchise was located in a primarily African American area of Chicago. Less than four years later, he opened a Cadillac dealership.

Sources: Black Enterprise 8 (June 1978), pp. 98–102; *Ebony Success Library,* vol. 1, p. 175; *Who's Who Among Black Americans, 1992–1993,* pp. 747–48.

1987 ♦ **Barbara J. Wilson** (1940–) was the first African American woman automobile dealer. She received the Candace Award as Businesswoman of the Year in 1987. Wilson is president of Ferndale Honda, Ferndale, Michigan (1984–) and Porterfield's Marina Village, Detroit (1989–).

Sources: Jet 72 (6 July 1987), p. 51; *Who's Who Among Black Americans, 1992–1993,* p. 1543.

Banking

1888 ♦ The True Reformers' Bank of Richmond, Virginia, and the Capital Savings Banks of Washington, D.C., were the first African American-created and African American-run banks. The True Reformers' Bank was chartered on March 2 and opened for business on April 3. The Capital Savings Bank was organized on October 17 and was the first African American bank with no fraternal, or mutual aid, connections.

Sources: Bennett, *Before the Mayflower,* p. 650; Kane, *Famous First Facts,* p. 93; *Negro Year Book, 1913,* p. 230.

1903 ♦ **Maggie Lena Walker** (1865–1934) was the first African American woman bank president. She founded the Saint Luke Penny Savings Bank in Richmond, Virginia. The bank began as an insurance society in which Walker became active at the time of her marriage in 1886. She retired because of poor health in 1933, but the bank was strong enough to survive the Depression and is still in existence.

Sources: *Encyclopedia of Black America,* pp. 152, 830; *Negro Almanac,* pp. 231, 1394; *Notable Black American Women,* pp. 1188–93.

1953 ♦ **James Del Rio** (1924–) was the first African American licensed mortgage banker in the United States and established one of the first African American mortgage companies in the country. Del Rio was a successful real estate broker in Detroit. He later served eight years in the Michigan legislature and then became a Detroit Recorder's Court judge.

Sources: Ebony 18 (February 1963), pp. 55–60, 29 (June 1974), pp. 90–92; *Ebony Success Library,* vol. 1, p. 93.

The Sivart Mortgage Company, Chicago, Illinois, was the first African American mortgage banking firm. The firm was established by Dempsey J. Travis (1920–), a Chicago business-man. In 1961 the company became the first African American-owned firm approved by the Federal Housing Administration and the Veterans Administration.

Sources: Alford, *Famous First Blacks,* p. 16; *Ebony Success Library,* vol. 2, pp. 256–59; *Who's Who Among Black Americans, 1992–1993,* p. 1411.

Reginald F. Lewis

1970 ♦ **Thomas A. Wood** (1926–) was the first African American to serve on the board of a major bank not run by African Americans, Chase Manhattan. Wood took a B.S. degree in electrical engineering at the University of Michigan and in 1968 founded TAW International Leasing, a New York–based firm that conducts business mainly in Africa.

Sources: Ebony 27 (March 1972), pp. 88–96; *Ebony Success Library,* vol. 2, pp. 302–5; *Encyclopedia of Black America,* p. 867.

Food

1987 ♦ **Reginald F. Lewis** (1942–1993) completed the first leveraged buyout of a Fortune 500 company by an African American. (A leveraged buy-out, or LBO, is a purchase that is heavily financed by a bank or other lender.) The company, food giant TLC Beatrice International Holdings, is the largest ever African American-owned corporation. (TLC stands for "The Lewis Company.") After developing a successful law firm during the 1970s, Lewis entered the larger business world in 1984 when he purchased the down-and-out McCall's Pattern Company through a newly formed investment firm. The risky purchase ($1 million plus the assumption of $24 million in debt) paid off. By the time of his bid for Beatrice in 1987, Lewis had sold McCall's for a $70 million profit. The Beatrice purchase price was a staggering $985 million, which Lewis financed through what was then the largest LBO deal ever.

When Lewis died unexpectedly in January 1993, he left his family with over 50% ownership of the $1.6 billion-in-sales corporation. Lewis, who may prove to be the most important African American businessman of the twentieth century, had an estimated net worth of $415 million at the time of his death.

Sources: Estell, ed., *African American Almanac,* 6th ed., pp. 678–679; Pederson, ed., *African American Almanac,* U·X·L ed., p. 325.

Insurance

1810 ◆ The African Insurance Company of Philadelphia was the first known African American insurance company. Its president was Joseph Randolph.

Sources: Kane, *Famous First Facts,* p. 322; *Negro Year Book, 1913,* p. 300; *Negro Year Book, 1916–1917,* p. 318.

1893 ◆ The North Carolina Mutual Life Insurance Company, founded this year in Durham, North Carolina, was the first African American insurance company to reach $100 million in assets. It is still the largest African American-owned insurance company. The success of the company was largely due to the abilities of Charles Clinton Spaulding (1874–1952), who became general manager of the company in 1900 and was president from 1923 until his death.

Sources: Alford, *Famous First Blacks,* p. 16; *Dictionary of American Negro Biography,* pp. 567–68; *Encyclopedia of Black America,* pp. 207, 806.

1932 ◆ **Asa T. Spaulding** (1902–1990) was the first African American actuary, or statistical expert, in the United States. After earning a magna cum laude degree in accounting from New York University in 1930 and an M.A. from the University of Michigan in 1932, Spaulding went to work for the North Carolina Mutual Life Insurance Company of Durham, North Carolina. He became president of the company in 1959 and retired in 1968. He was also the first African American to serve on the board of directors of a major non-African American corporation, W. T. Grant (1964), and the first African

American elected to the Durham County Board of Commissioners. He is a member of the state Business Hall of Fame.

Sources: Ebony Success Library, vol. 1, p. 289; *Encyclopedia of Black America,* p. 806; *Jet* 78 (24 September 1990), p. 15; *Who's Who Among Black Americans, 1992–1993,* p. 1610.

1957 ◆ **Cirilo A. McSween** (1929–) was the first African American to represent a major white-owned insurance company, New York Life Insurance Company, and the first African American to sell a million dollars worth of life insurance for any company in one year. McSween later became the first African American to sell a million dollars of insurance in one month.

Sources: Ebony 20 (May 1965), pp. 207–8; *Ebony Success Library,* vol. 1, p. 213; *Who's Who Among Black Americans, 1992–1993,* p. 974.

1977 ◆ The E. G. Bowman Company was the first African American-owned insurance firm on Wall Street. It was founded in 1953 by Ernesta G. Procope. She named it for her husband, who had died the previous year. Her present husband is editor and publisher of the *Amsterdam News*.

Sources: Notable Black American Women, pp. 885–86; *Who's Who Among Black Americans, 1992–1993,* p. 1152.

Labor Unions

1850 ◆ In July 1850 in New York, **Samuel Ringgold Ward** (1817–1864) became the first president of the American League of Colored Workers; Frederick Douglass was a vice-president. Ward is known mainly as a lecturer and the author of *The Autobiography of a Fugitive Negro* (1855). The American League focused on industrial education for its workers.

Sources: Dictionary of American Negro Biography, pp. 631–32; Foner, *Organized Labor and the Black Worker,* p. 11; *Negro Almanac,* pp. 13, 1017.

1858 ◆ In July 1858 the Association of Black Caulkers in Baltimore, Maryland, became the first black labor organization on record. Earlier organizations (such as the American League of Colored Workers) were more mutual aid societies than labor unions. The Association was formed to prevent white workers from driving blacks out of a trade blacks had typically controlled.

Sources: Encyclopedia of Black America, p. 491; Foner, *Organized Labor and the Black Worker,* p. 11.

A. Philip Randolph

1925 ◆ **A. Philip Randolph** (1889–1979) founded the Brotherhood of Sleeping Car Porters, the first major nationwide black union. It would take 10 years of struggle and new federal labor laws before the union established a bargaining agreement with the Pullman Palace Car Company. Thus the union became the first official bargaining agent for black workers on October 1, 1935. In 1957 Randolph became the first black vice-president of the American Federation of Labor and Congress of Industrial Organizations (AFL-CIO); he served until 1968.

Sources: Bennett, *Before the Mayflower*, pp. 366, 525, 532; *Encyclopedia of Black America*, pp. 727–28; Foner, *Organized Labor and the Black Worker*, pp. 177–87; *Jet* 81 (13 April 1992), p. 32; *Negro Almanac*, p. 560.

1936 ◆ The opening of the National Negro Congress, the first attempt at a united front organization to try to better the conditions of black workers, was on February 14, 1936. A. Philip Randolph was its first president.

Sources: Bennett, *Before the Mayflower*, pp. 361, 531; Foner, *Organized Labor and the Black Worker*, pp. 213–14.

1938 ◆ **Ferdinand C. Smith** (1894–1961) was a founder of the National Maritime Union, and in 1938 became its first black vice-president. When that office was abolished in 1939, he became the first black national secretary. In 1943 he became the first black member of the National CIO Executive Board. He was influential in recruiting the mixed crew for Hugh Mulzac, who set sail as the first black captain of a merchant ship on October 20, 1942. (*See also* **Miscellaneous: Various, 1942.**) A native of Jamaica and an alleged traitor because of his Communist ties, Smith was arrested and deported as an undesirable alien in 1948.

Sources: *Dictionary of American Negro Biography*, pp. 562–64; Foner, *Organized Labor and the Black Worker*, pp. 227, 231, 285.

1962 ◆ **Nelson Jack Edwards** (1917–1974) was the first black member of the International Executive Board of the United Auto Workers. In 1970 he became the first black vice-president of the union.

Sources: *Ebony Success Library*, vol. 2, pp. 68–71; *Encyclopedia of Black America*, p. 352; *Negro Almanac*, pp. 1405–6.

As a member of the National Executive Board of the Amalgamated Meat Cutters and Butcher Workmen, Addie Wyatt (1924–) was the first black woman labor executive.

Sources: *Ebony* 32 (August 1977), p. 70, 39 (March 1984), p. 104; Lee, *Interesting People,* p. 196; *Who's Who Among Black Americans, 1992–1993,* p. 1577.

1981 ◆ **Barbara B. Hutchinson** was the first black woman member of the AFL-CIO Executive Council. Hutchinson was director of women's affairs for the American Federation of Government Employees.

Sources: *Jet* 61 (10 December 1981), p. 8, 64 (21 March 1983), p. 9.

1988 ◆ **John Nathan Sturdivant** (1938–) was the first black president of the American Federation of Government Employees and so the first African American to head a major mixed ethnic group AFL-CIO.

Sources: *Jet* 75 (3 October, 1988), p. 10; *Who's Who Among Black Americans, 1992–1993,* p. 1351.

Manufacturing

1798 ◆ **James Forten, Sr.** (1766–1842) established the first major black-owned sailmaking shop in Philadelphia. His financial worth soon reached $100,000. Forten was a leader in the radical abolitionist movement. An organizer of the American Antislavery Society (1833), he also supported the women's suffrage (right to vote) and temperance (anti-liquor) movements. He inspired his daughters Margaretta, Sarah, and Harriet, and his granddaughter, writer and educator Charlotte Forten Grimké, in their efforts on behalf of blacks.(*See also* **Science, Medicine, and Invention: Inventions and Patents, 1798.**)

Sources: *Dictionary of American Negro Biography,* pp. 234–35; *Encyclopedia of Black America,* p. 391–92; *Negro Almanac,* pp. 234, 808.

1818 ◆ **Thomas Day** (c. 1800–1860) was the first widely recognized black furniture maker in the Deep South. He worked in Milton, North Carolina, and his workshop, the Yellow Tavern, is a National Historical Landmark.

Sources: Cantor, *Historic Landmarks of Black America,* p. 231; *Dictionary of American Negro Biography,* pp. 162–63; *Negro Almanac,* pp. 221–22.

1885 ◆ **D. Watson Onley** built the first steam saw and planing mill owned and operated entirely by blacks, in Jacksonville, Florida. After the mill was destroyed by arson, Onley worked for Florida State Normal and Industrial

Madame C. J.
Walker

College, attended Howard University School of Dentistry, and established a practice in Washington, D.C.

Source: Culp, *Twentieth Century Negro Literature,* opposite p. 347.

1910 ♦ **Madame C. J. Walker** (1867–1919) is believed by some to be the first black woman millionaire. This is disputed by supporters of Annie Turnbo Malone (1869–1957). Both women produced hair care products for black women and were developing their businesses at the same time; it is claimed that Walker worked as a salesperson for Malone products. Both became very wealthy by around 1910, but Malone's business began to run into difficulties due to poor management after 1927.

Sources: Dictionary of American Negro Biography, p. 621 (Walker); *Encyclopedia of Black America,* p. 545 (Malone), p. 830 (Walker); *Negro Almanac,* pp. 1393–94 (Walker); *Notable Black American Women,* pp. 724–27 (Malone), 1184–93 (Walker).

1962 ♦ **Harvey Clarence Russell, Jr.** (1918–) was the first black vice-president in a leading national corporation, Pepsico. He became vice-president in charge of special markets in 1962, vice-president in charge of planning in 1965, and vice-president for community affairs in 1969.

Sources: Black Enterprise 2 (September 1971), pp. 15–18; *Ebony* 17 (June 1962), pp. 25–32; *Encyclopedia of Black America,* p. 737; *Who's Who Among Black Americans, 1992–1993,* p. 1232.

1970 ♦ **Clarence C. Finley** (1922–) was the first black division president of a major white firm, Charm-Tred-Monticello, a branch of Burlington Industries. Finley had begun to work for Charm-Tred Company as a file clerk in 1942.

Sources: Alford, *Famous First Blacks,* pp. 16–17; *Ebony* 26 (February 1971), pp. 58–65; *Ebony Success Library,* vol. 2, pp. 72–75.

1990 ♦ **Bertram M. Lee** (1939–) was the first black member of the board of directors of Reebok International. Lee has a B.A. from North Central College. He is president of Kellee Communications Group (1986–) and the Denver Nuggets (1989–), and is active in many other businesses. Lee and Peter Bynoe became secondary partners of the Denver Nuggets in 1989.

Sources: Jet 78 (1 October 1990), p. 35; *Who's Who Among Black Americans, 1992–1993,* p. 855.

Miscellaneous Industries

1846 ◆ **William Leidesdorff** (1810–1848) opened the first hotel in San Francisco. He is also credited with organizing the first horse race, operating the first steamboat (1847), and becoming the first black American millionaire. In April 1848 he became chair of the board of education, which opened California's first public school. Leidesdorff was born in the Virgin Islands, the son of a Danish man and an African woman. He came to California in 1841 and became a Mexican citizen in 1846 in order to acquire vast land holdings. When he became a U.S. subconsul in 1845, he was probably the first black to hold a diplomatic post in U.S. history.

Sources: Cantor, *Historic Landmarks of Black America,* p. 294; *Dictionary of American Negro Biography,* pp. 392–93; Katz, *The Black West,* pp. 117–19.

1959 ◆ **Ruth J. Bowen** (1930–) was the first black woman to establish a successful booking and talent agency in New York City. She has represented such artists as Dinah Washington, Sammy Davis, Jr., Aretha Franklin, and Ray Charles. Bowen began in 1959 with an initial $500 investment, and within 10 years became the largest black-owned agency in the world.

Sources: *Black Women in White America,* p. 151; *Encyclopedia of Black America,* p. 188; *Negro Almanac,* pp. 1375–76; *Who's Who Among Black Americans, 1992–1993,* p. 135.

1972 ◆ On May 16, 1972, the Johnson Publishing Company headquarters was dedicated. The 11-story building was the first built by African Americans in downtown Chicago since the time of Jean Baptiste Pointe Du Sable.

Source: *Ebony Success Library,* vol. 2, p. 1355.

1993 ◆ **Pearline Motley** was the first African American honored as American Business Woman of the Year. She received the award from the American Business Women's Association for 1993. Motley was the manager of the Federal Women's Program of the Agricultural Stabilization and Conservation Service in Kansas City, Missouri.

Source: *Jet* 83 (28 December 1992), p. 20.

Publishing

1938 ◆ **John H. Johnson** (1918–), the founder of the first successful magazines devoted to black topics, *Ebony* (1945) and *Jet* (1951), was the first black named as one of the country's "Ten Outstanding Young Men" by the

John H. Johnson

U.S. Junior Chamber of Commerce. This was the first of many awards won by Johnson for his success in publishing. In 1972 he became the first black to receive the Henry Johnson Fisher Award of the Magazine Publishers Association, the highest honor in that field. (*See also* **Media: Periodicals, 1942.**)

Sources: *Ebony Success Library*, vol. 2, p. 132–37; *The Negro Almanac*, pp. 1261–62; *Who's Who Among Black Americans, 1992–1993*, p. 760.

1960 ◆ As editor at Doubleday, **Charles F. Harris** (1935–) established Zenith Books, the first series to present minority histories for the general and educational markets. In 1971 Harris joined Howard University Press.

Sources: *Ebony* 20 (March 1965), p. 6; *Ebony Success Library*, vol. 1, p. 143; *Who's Who Among Black Americans, 1992–1993*, p. 605.

Real Estate

1866 ◆ **Biddy Mason** (1818–1891) was the first known black woman property owner in Los Angeles, California. Born into slavery in Georgia or Mississippi, she and her master went first to the Utah Territory and then to California, where Mason legally gained her freedom on January 21, 1856. She worked as nurse and midwife, and her savings and careful investment became the foundation that enabled her grandson Robert to be called the richest black in Los Angeles around 1900. A very religious and charitable woman, Mason opened her house for the establishment of the first African Methodist Episcopal church in the city in 1872. She is also said to have opened the first daycare for homeless community children.

Sources: Katz, *The Black West*, pp. 129–30; *Notable Black American Women*, pp. 732–34; *Sepia* (April 1960), p. 71.

1890 ◆ **Thomy Lafon** (1810–1893) was one of the first black men reputed to be a millionaire (the other was William Leidesdorff). He was a New Orleans real estate speculator and moneylender. His estate was valued at nearly half a million dollars. Lafon was noted for philanthropy, and he left the bulk of his estate to charity.

Sources: Dictionary of American Negro Biography, pp. 379–80; Dictionary of Black Culture, p. 261; Efforts for Social Betterment Among Negro Americans, pp. 40–41.

1905 ◆ **Phillip A. Payton, Jr.** (1876–?) was the first black to open Harlem to black residents. He persuaded developers who had built a surplus of apartments to rent to blacks. By 1908 Payton controlled more than a half million dollars worth of property in New York City. He also spent money as quickly as he made it, and he went broke in 1908.

Sources: Black Enterprise 6 (June 1976), pp. 126–27; Encyclopedia of Black America, p. 417; Lewis, When Harlem Was in Vogue, pp. 25–26.

Biddy Mason

Retailing

1834 ◆ **David Ruggles** (1810–1849) was the first known black bookseller. His New York City shop was burned out by a white mob in September 1835. An active abolitionist and worker on the Underground Railroad, Ruggles was also noted as the first black hydrotherapist. (See also **Science, Medicine, and Invention: Medicine, 1846**.)

Source: Dictionary of American Negro Autobiography, pp. 536–38.

1968 ◆ **Leon Howard Sullivan** (1922–) developed the first major black-sponsored shopping center, Progress Plaza, in Philadelphia, Pennsylvania. This Baptist minister was very active in developing black business. On January 4, 1971, he became the first African American to sit on the board of General Motors.

Sources: Current Biography, 1969, pp. 419–21; Ebony Success Library, vol. 2, pp. 248–51; Encyclopedia of Black America, p. 811; Hornsby, Jr., Chronology of African-American History, pp. 158, 250–51; Negro Almanac, pp. 61, 618, 1417; Who's Who Among Black Americans, 1992–1993, p. 1353.

1975 ◆ **Wally "Famous" Amos** (1937–) opened the first black cookie-only retail store. He went from mail clerk to executive vice-president at the William Morris Agency, which made him their first black talent agent. The company he launched, Famous Amos Chocolate Chip Cookies, eventually grossed $80 million a year, but by the early 1990s financial problems caused Amos to lose both his company and the rights to use his name commercially. His newest venture is The Uncle Noname Cookie Company.

Sources: Jet 72 (30 March 1987), p. 6; Parade (22 May 1994), pp. 4–6; Sepia 27 (June 1978), pp. 22–28; Time 109 (13 June 1977), pp. 72, 76; Who's Who Among Black Americans, 1992–1993, p. 29.

1982 ◆ **Sybil Collins Mobley** (1925–) became the first black woman member of the board of Sears, Roebuck & Company. An educator with a Ph.D. from the University of Illinois, she taught in the business school of Florida Agricultural, and later Mechanical University, where she became a dean in 1974.

Sources: Jet 62 (30 August 1982), p. 38; Who's Who Among Black Americans, 1992–1993, p. 1005.

1983 ◆ **Ben F. Branch** (1924–1987) became president of the nation's first black-owned soft drink company, Dr. Branch Products, in Chicago, Illinois. Branch was also a civil rights activist and a musician. He combined these interests by organizing the SCLC-Operation Breadbox Orchestra, the world's only gospel orchestra.

Source: Jet 72 (14 September 1987), p. 55.

Stock Brokerage

1970 ◆ On February 13, 1970, **Joseph L. Searles III** (1940–) became the first black member of the New York Stock Exchange.

Sources: Black Enterprise 1 (October 1970), p. 19; Jet 37 (19 February 1970), p. 20, 69 (17 February 1986), p. 22; Negro Almanac, p. 1430; Statistical Record of Black America, p. 474.

1971 ◆ On June 24, 1971, the firm of Daniels and Bell became the first black company to serve as a New York Stock Exchange member. The firm was founded by Willie L. Daniels (1937–) and Travers Bell, Jr.

Sources: Ebony Success Library, vol. 1, p. 86; Negro Almanac, 1976, p. 1024; Sepia 21 (June 1972), pp. 67–70.

Johnson Products became the first black firm listed on a major stock exchange when it joined the American Stock Exchange in 1971. The firm was founded by George Ellis Johnson (1927–) in 1954.

Sources: Ebony Success Library, vol. 2, pp. 126–31; Encyclopedia of Black America, p. 473; Jet 69 (18 November 1985), p. 16; Who's Who Among Black Americans, 1992–1993, p. 757.

1972 ✦ **Jerome Heartwell Holland** (1916–1985) was the first African American to serve on the board of the New York Stock Exchange. Holland was an all-American football player at Cornell University, New York, where he took his B.S. (1939), and M.S. (1941) degrees. He was the first black player on the Cornell football team. After receiving a Ph.D. from the University of Pennsylvania in 1950, Holland served as president of Delaware State College from 1953 to 1960, and of Hampton Institute from 1960 to 1970, when he became ambassador to Sweden.

Sources: *Ebony Success Library,* vol. 2, pp. 104–7; *Encyclopedia of Black America,* p. 443; *Jet* 68 (6 May 1985), p. 54.

Transportation, Shipping, and Sailing

1784 ✦ **Paul Cuffe** (or Cuffee, 1759–1818), was the first African American to sail his own ship. Born near Bedford, Massachusetts, Cuffe went to sea at a young age and became involved in coastal trade. He later developed trade with Sierra Leone, where he encouraged missionary work and colonization. (*See also* **Explorers, Pioneers, and Wild West Heroes, 1811**).

Sources: *Dictionary of American Negro Biography,* pp. 147–48; *Encyclopedia of Black America,* pp. 280, 296; *Negro Almanac,* pp. 9, 209, 234.

1831 ✦ **John Mashow** was the first African American to establish a major shipbuilding firm. He was active in South Dartmouth, Massachusetts, until shortly before the Civil War.

Source: James, *The Real McCoy,* p. 33.

1840s ✦ **A. F. Boston** was the first known African American to command an American whaling ship, the *Loper*. The officers and most of the ship's crew were African American, and the ship made at least one successful trip.

Source: James, *The Real McCoy,* p. 35.

1971 ✦ **James O. Plinton, Jr.** (1914–) was the first black top executive of a major airline, Eastern Airlines. Plinton became a pilot instructor for the U.S. Army Air Corps in 1935, and was the first African American to complete the Air Corps' Central Instructors School, in 1944. He was also the first African American to co-organize an airline outside the United States; Quisqueya Lte. in Port-au-Prince, Haiti, was established in 1948. He joined

Trans World Airlines in 1950, and became vice-president for marketing affairs for Eastern in 1971.

Sources: Black Enterprise 10 (September 1979), pp. 59–60; *Ebony Success Library,* vol. 1, p. 250; *Encyclopedia of Black America,* pp. 146, 678; *Who's Who Among Black Americans, 1992–1993,* pp. 1130–31.

1979 ◆ The Kent-Barry-Eaton Connection Railway Company was the first minority-owned company to operate a railroad. The line ran 42 miles between Grand Rapids and Vermontville, Michigan.

Source: Jet 56 (23 August 1979), p. 24.

1987 ◆ **Vander Brown, Jr.,** was the first African American to head a division of Greyhound Lines, Western Greyhound, one of the four regional divisions.

Source: Jet 72 (29 June 1987), pp. 38–39.

Civil Rights and Protest

1502 ◆ Portuguese explorers delivered their first shipment of black slaves to the New World.

Source: Hornsby, Jr., and Straub, *African American Chronology*, p. 1.

1526 ◆ The first group of African Americans to set foot on what is now the United States arrived in South Carolina. They were brought by a Spanish explorer to help build a settlement but they soon escaped and went to live among Native North Americans.

Source: Hornsby, Jr., and Straub, *African American Chronology*, p. 1.

1619 ◆ Twenty Africans arrived in Jamestown, Virginia, in August, transported by a Dutchman, who sold them as indentured servants. They were the first black colonial settlers.

Sources: Bennett, *Before the Mayflower*, p. 441; Kane, *Famous First Facts*, p. 598; *Negro Almanac*, p. 2.

1622 ◆ **Anthony and Mary Johnson** and family were the first known free African Americans. They lived in Old Accomack, later Northampton County, in the Virginia colony. In 1651 Anthony Johnson, John Johnson, and John Johnson, Sr., were the first black landowners in Virginia, receiving grants totaling 850 acres. Anthony Johnson and his wife were among the 23 black servants in the 1624–25 census of the colony. In 1653 Anthony Johnson became the first African American on record as a slave owner. (*See also* **Religion, 1623.**)

Sources: Bennett, *Before the Mayflower*, pp. 35–38; *Encyclopedia of Black America*, p. 37; *Negro Year Book, 1921–1922*, pp. 126–27.

1630 ◆ Massachusetts passed the first law protecting slaves who fled brutal treatment by their masters.

Source: *Negro Almanac*, p. 2.

1640 ◆ The first known black to have passed from indentured servitude into slavery was **John Punch**. Punch attempted to escape from servitude with two fellow white servants. All three were whipped. The service terms of the whites were extended five years, while Punch's contract was increased to life.

Source: Negro Year Book, 1921–1922, p. 126.

1641 ◆ The first colony to legalize slavery and to forbid use of "unjust violence" in the capture of slaves was Massachusetts.

Sources: Hornsby, Jr., Chronology of African-American History, p. 3; Negro Year Book, 1921–1922, p. 126.

1642 ◆ The colony of Virginia was the first to pass a fugitive slave law. After a second escape attempt, slaves were branded. The law probably applied to servants.

Sources: Negro Almanac, p. 2; Negro Year Book, 1921–1922, p. 127.

1652 ◆ The first law regulating black servitude was passed by the Rhode Island General Court of Election on May 18, 1652. This law placed African Americans on the same footing as white bondservants; they were to be free after completing their term of service of 10 years.

Source: Kane, Famous First Facts, p. 598.

1663 ◆ The first major conspiracy between black slaves and indentured servants occurred in Gloucester County, Virginia, September 13, 1663. The conspiracy was betrayed by an indentured servant.

Sources: Alford, Famous First Blacks, p. 27; Hornsby, Jr., Chronology of African-American History, p. 3; Negro Almanac, p. 3.

1688 ◆ The Mennonite Quakers at Germantown, Pennsylvania, adopted and signed the first formal antislavery document in United States history. After the Society of Friends declared that slavery violated the rights of man and was in opposition to Christianity, the Mennonite Antislavery Resolution was approved by the group on February 18.

Sources: Garrett, Famous First Facts About Negroes, p. 1; Hornsby, Jr., Chronology of African-American History, p. 4; Kane, Famous First Facts, p. 598; Negro Almanac, p. 3.

1712 ◆ The first major slave revolt in the North occurred in New York City on April 7, 1712. As a result, 21 African Americans were executed and 6 others committed suicide. The men had met about midnight, April 6, to take revenge for their masters' abuse. Some were armed with firearms, swords, knives, and hatchets. Paul Cuffe set fire to his master's house, which attracted

---

DATES OF EMANCIPATION IN THE NORTHERN STATES

1777   Vermont
1780   Pennsyvania[1]
1783   Massachusetts
1783   New Hampshire
1784   Rhode Island
1799   New York[1]
1804   New Jersey[2]

Notes: [1]Gradually instituted. [2]Gradually instituted; abolition completed by statute in 1846.

Source: Hornsby, Jr., *Chronology of African-American History,* p. 8.

---

a crowd of townspeople. The revolt grew as the rebels discharged their firearms on the crowd, killing 9 whites and wounding 5 or 6 more.

Sources: Hornsby, Jr., *Chronology of African-American History*, p. 4; Johnson, *Black Manhattan*, pp. 7–8; *Negro Almanac*, p. 4; *Negro Year Book, 1921–1922*, p. 149.

1739 ◆ The first serious slave revolt in the South took place in South Carolina, when a slave named Cato led an uprising at Stono, about 20 miles west of Charleston. After killing 2 warehouse guards and securing arms and ammunition, the slaves headed south, hoping to reach Florida. As they marched to drum beats, they killed about 20 to 30 whites who attempted to interfere. Armed whites captured all but a dozen slaves, and more than 30 African Americans, who were alleged participants, were killed.

Source: Hornsby, Jr., *Chronology of African-American History,* p. 4.

1774 ◆ On March 8, 1774, the Massachusetts General Assembly passed the first act banning the importation of black slaves. It was suspended by the governor the following day. Rhode Island passed similar legislation on June 13. Slaves brought into the colony were to gain their freedom immediately.

Sources: Kane, *Famous First Facts*, p. 598; *Negro Almanac*, p. 811.

1775 ◆ The Pennsylvania Society for Promoting the Abolition of Slavery was the first antislavery society. It was organized on April 14, 1775, with John Baldwin as its first president.

Sources: Encyclopedia of Black America, p. 789; Hornsby, Jr., *Chronology of African-American History*, p. 7; Kane, *Famous First Facts*, p. 1; *Negro Almanac*, pp. 5, 812.

Harriet Tubman

1777 ◆ Vermont became the first colony to abolish slavery on July 2, 1777. Although the results were gradual, by 1804 all states north of Delaware had taken action to abolish slavery.

Sources: Bennett, *Before the Mayflower,* p. 446; Hornsby, Jr., *Chronology of African-American History,* p. 8.

1783 ◆ **Paul Cuffe** (1759–1818) and his brother John were the leaders in a lawsuit that gave African Americans civil equality in Massachusetts by permitting them to vote. In 1780 they were the first African Americans to protest the denial of suffrage when they refused to pay taxes. This protest developed into a petition drive and a court case. The courts decided in 1783 in their favor.

Source: Dictionary of American Negro Biography, p. 147.

1786 ◆ The first Underground Railroad activities were carried out by a group of Quakers in Philadelphia. Between 1812 and the Civil War, the necessarily secret organizations became more widespread and more effective. From 1830 to 1860 it is estimated that some 9,000 fugitives passed through Philadelphia, and some 40,000 through Ohio. One of the most famous conductors was **Harriet Tubman** (c. 1820–1913), who within a 10-year period made at least 10 trips from the North into Southern states and led over 200 slaves to freedom.

Sources: Negro Year Book, 1921–1922, pp. 153–54; *Notable Black American Women,* pp. 1151-55.

1787 ◆ On July 13, 1787, the Continental Congress prohibited slavery in the Northwest Territory, the area north of the Ohio River and east of the Mississippi River. This was the first law forbidding slavery in territories.

Sources: Bennett, *Before the Mayflower,* p. 448; Kane, *Famous First Facts,* p. 598; *Negro Almanac,* p. 6.

1797 ◆ On January 30, 1797, the first recorded antislavery petition was presented to Congress—and rejected. The petition by North Carolina African Americans sought "redress against a North Carolina law which requires that slaves, although freed by their Quaker masters, be returned to the state and to their former condition."

Sources: Hornsby, Jr., *Chronology of African-American History,* p. 12; *Negro Almanac,* p. 8.

Nat Turner's capture

1822 ◆ The first recorded leader of a major slave revolt was **Denmark Vesey** (1767–1822), who on May 30, 1822, organized an uprising in Charleston, South Carolina. As many as 5,000 African Americans were prepared to take part in the revolt, originally set for July that year, but authorities foiled the plan and Vesey and nearly 50 others were executed. After the insurrection, South Carolina and other states passed laws to control free African Americans and to tighten the reins on slaves. Another well-known leader of a slave revolt was Gabriel Prosser (c. 1775–1800), who planned an uprising for August 30, 1800, which subsequently failed.

Sources: Bennett, *Before the Mayflower,* pp. 127–31; Hornsby, Jr., *Chronology of African-American History,* pp. 15–16; *Negro Almanac,* p. 10.

1830 ◆ The first National Negro Convention met at Mother Bethel Church in Philadelphia September 20–24, 1830, "to devise ways and means for bettering of our condition," to fight oppression, promote universal education, and inspire other pursuits. Richard Allen presided. After the Civil War the conventions focused on voting, fair employment, education, citizenship rights, and the overturning of discriminatory laws.

Sources: Baer and Singer, *African-American Religion in the Twentieth Century,* p. 26; *Encyclopedia of Black America,* p. 834; Hornsby, Jr., *Chronology of African-American History,* p. 18.

1831 ◆ In Southampton County, Virginia, during August 1831 **Nat Turner** (1800–1831) led the first slave revolt of magnitude. The revolt was crushed, but only after Turner and his band had killed some 60 whites and threw the South into panic. After hiding out, Turner was captured and hanged. Thirty other African Americans suffered the same fate. It was not until John Brown's raid on Harpers Ferry, Virginia, in 1859 that another slave revolt or conspiracy became known.

Sources: Bennett, *Before the Mayflower,* pp. 131–39; Hornsby, Jr., *Chronology of African-American History,* p. 18; *Negro Almanac,* p. 11.

1832 ◆ A group of "females of color" in Salem, Massachusetts, formed the first black women's antislavery society in the United States, on February 22, 1832. The abolitionist press documents the existence of a variety of women's antislavery societies during this period. Free black women actively participated in the racially mixed societies.

Sources: Black Women in America, vol. 1, p. 8; Salem, *We Are Your Sisters,* p. 113; Yee, *Black Women Abolitionists,* pp. 6, 87.

1838 ◆ The first known African American regular lecturer in the antislavery cause and the first major black abolitionist was **Charles Lenox Remond** (1810–1873). After a triumphant tour of England, his fame soared. He became one of the 17 members of the New England Anti-Slavery Society.

Sources: Bennett, *Before the Mayflower,* 161–62; *Dictionary of American Negro Biography,* pp. 520–22; Robinson, *Historical Negro Biographies,* pp. 115-16.

1839 ◆ A group of Africans launched the first revolt at sea that resulted in the legal freedom of the rebels. They seized the slaveship *Amistad* and brought it into Montauk, Long Island, New York. The ship came into American custody on August 26, 1839. Joseph Cinque (c. 1811–1878), the young African leader, and his followers were tried in court and defended by former U.S. president John Quincy Adams. The Supreme Court decision to free them was handed down on March 9, 1840. The 35 surviving Africans were returned to Africa on November 25, 1841.

Sources: Bennett, *Before the Mayflower,* p. 457; Hornsby, Jr., *Chronology of African-American History,* p. 1838; *Negro Almanac,* p. 12.

Maria W. Stewart (1803–1879), women's rights activist, journalist, and educator, was the first American-born woman to speak publicly on political themes to a mixed audience of men and women. On September 21, 1833, she was perhaps the first black woman to lecture in defense of women's rights. Her public speeches, delivered in Boston during a two-year period, also made her the first black woman to lecture on antislavery issues. Abolitionist William Lloyd Garrison published the text of her four public speeches in 1835.

Sources: *Black Women in America*, vol. 2, pp. 1113–14; *Notable Black American Women*, pp. 1083–87; Yee, *Black Women Abolitionists*, p. 26.

1842 ◆ **Frederick Douglass** (1817–1895) published his first article as he sought the freedom of George Latimer, an escaped slave. Latimer had been captured, leading to the first of several famous fugitive slave cases. Latimer's freedom was later purchased by the Boston abolitionists. George Latimer was the father of inventor Lewis H. Latimer. (*See also* **Literature: Short Stories, 1853**; **Politics: National, 1872; Science, Medicine, and Invention: Inventions and Patents, 1882.**)

Sources: *Dictionary of American Negro Biography*, p. 385; *Negro Almanac*, p. 12; *The Real McCoy*, pp. 96–97.

1854 ◆ The first successful suit to end segregation in street cars was won this year. Until that time African Americans in New York were restricted to certain cars marked "Colored People Allowed in This Car." A black woman, who was a public school teacher and protester, was dragged out of her seat. She took her case to court, with Chester A. Arthur (who later became president) as one of her lawyers.

Source: Johnson, *Black Manhattan*, p. 46.

1857 ◆ **Dred Scott** (1795–1858), a Virginia slave, sued for his freedom after becoming a resident living on free soil in Missouri. The Dred Scott decision (*Dred Scott v. Sanford*) rendered this year was the first clear decision by the Supreme Court denying African Americans U.S. citizenship, even though they might be citizens of their states. The doctrine of dual citizenship remained important as it resurfaced in the post-Civil War attack on black rights. The Supreme Court in 1873 affirmed again the doctrine of dual citizenship, federal and state, and suggested that most civil rights fell under state citizenship and so were not protected under the Fourteenth Amendment.

Sources: Bennett, *Before the Mayflower*, pp. 178, 262, 463; *Dictionary of American Negro Biography*, pp. 548–49; *Negro Almanac*, pp. 332-33.

1862 ◆ Slavery was abolished in the District of Columbia when "an act for the release of certain persons held to service or labor in the District of Columbia" was enacted April 16, 1862. The law stated that persons held "by reason of African descent are hereby discharged and freed from all claim to such service or labor" and "neither slavery nor involuntary servitude ... shall hereafter exist in said district." Slave owners were compensated, and $100,000 was appropriated to support emigration of former slaves from the United States. A law passed on April 2, 1862, offering compensated emancipation to the border slave states found no takers.

Sources: Hornsby, Jr., *Chronology of African-American History*, p. 34; Kane, *Famous First Facts*, p. 598; *Negro Year Book 1921–1922*, p. 134.

1866 ◆ Citizenship was first granted to African Americans by the Civil Rights Bill, an "Act to Protect all Persons in the United States in their Civil Rights and Furnish the Means of Their Vindication." The bill also gave African Americans "the same right, in every State and territory ... as is enjoyed by white citizens." Enacted during the first session of the 39th Congress on April 9, 1866, the bill passed over President Andrew Johnson's veto.

Sources: Bennett, *Before the Mayflower*, p. 476; Hornsby, Jr., *Chronology of African-American History*, p. 41; Kane, *Famous First Facts*, p. 170.

1867 ◆ Black males were first granted the right to vote by the act of January 8, 1867, which was "to regulate the elective franchise in the District of Columbia." The right was given to every male at least 21 years old, except those who were paupers, under guardianship, convicted of infamous crimes, or who had freely comforted rebels. President Andrew Johnson vetoed the bill on January 5, 1867, but both the Senate and the House of Representatives voted to override the veto, and the bill became law.

Sources: Clayton, *The Negro Politician*, pp. 23–24; Hornsby, Jr., *Chronology of African-American History*, p. 40; Kane, *Famous First Facts*, p. 234; *Negro Almanac*, p. 17.

1868 ◆ Black Americans were granted citizenship and equal protection under the law for the first time with the passage of the Fourteenth Amendment on July 28, 1868.

Sources: Bennett, *Before the Mayflower*, pp. 260–61, 483; Hornsby, Jr., *Chronology of African-American History*, p. 42; *Negro Almanac*, p. 17.

1870 ◆ **Thomas Mundy Petersen** (Petersen-Munday), a school custodian of Perth Amboy, New Jersey, became the first black person to vote as a result of the adoption of the Fifteenth Amendment on March 31, 1870, one day after the ratification of the amendment to the U.S. Constitution. The special election was held to ratify or reject a city charter. Petersen was appointed to the committee to revise the charter, which was adopted in the election. He later became a delegate to the country's Republican convention.

Sources: Cantor, *Historic Landmarks of Black America,* p. 87; *Jet* 58 (3 April 1980), p. 20; 72 (6 April 1987); Kane, *Famous First Facts,* p. 233.

1881 ◆ Tennessee was the first state to require the separation of the races in railway cars. This is usually considered the beginning of "Jim Crow" laws and a legally defined system of segregation in the South. The test of a similar 1890 law in Louisiana led to the U.S. Supreme Court decision in *Plessy v. Ferguson* on May 18, 1896. The court's doctrine of "separate but equal" became the legal underpinning of segregation for the next 60 years.

Sources: Bennett, *Before the Mayflower,* p. 267; Hornsby, Jr., *Chronology of African-American History,* pp. 50, 55; *Negro Almanac,* pp. 150–52; *Negro Year Book, 1921–1922,* p. 171.

Marcus Garvey

1914 ◆ Black nationalist **Marcus Garvey** (1887–1940) formed the first black mass movement organization, the United Negro Improvement Association (UNIA). The UNIA aimed to unite African Americans under the motto "One God! One Aim! One Destiny!" Garvey was born in St. Ann's Bay, Jamaica, traveled to England in 1912, and returned to Jamaica in 1914. He came to America on March 23, 1916, and one year later established a branch of the UNIA in Harlem. This branch immediately became the headquarters of Garvey's international movement.

In 1918 he founded a weekly newspaper titled *Negro World* to spread his gospel of nationalism and self-help. By mid-1919 he had launched the Black Star Shipping Line to help create economic opportunities for African Americans, who bought stock in the line. Later Garvey and his stockholders expanded the business to form a cross-continent steamship trade. In 1923 he was convicted and jailed for mail fraud. He was pardoned and deported in 1927, then he moved to London. He wrote extensively about his movement and race philosophy. With more than a million followers, he built one of the largest and most powerful black mass movements in American history.

Sources: Black Leaders of the Twentieth Century, pp. 104–38; *Contemporary Black Biography,* vol. 1, pp. 75–78; *Dictionary of American Negro Biography,* pp. 254–56; Garrett, *Famous First Facts About Negroes,* p. 167; Katz, *Eyewitness: The Negro in American History,* pp. 399–400.

1935 ♦ **Charles Hamilton Houston** (1895–1950) became the first full-time paid special counsel for the NAACP. He devised a strategy at the NAACP that ultimately led to school desegregation. The campaign against discrimination in education took two decades, after Houston's death, when the *Brown v. Board of Education* decision of 1954 declared segregation in public schools unconstitutional. During his career Houston helped prepare civil rights cases in lower federal and state courts and argued such cases before the U.S. Supreme Court. He was the first African American to serve on the editorial board of the *Harvard Law Review*. In 1929 he became dean of Howard University Law School, Washington, D.C., and led the school into full approval by the American Bar Association. Civil rights groups acknowledged him for his work at Howard and his philosophy of social engineering. For his pioneering work in developing the NAACP legal campaign, he was awarded the Spingarn Medal on September 27, 1950.

Sources: Bennett, *Before the Mayflower,* pp. 363, 546; *Black Leaders of the Twentieth Century,* pp. 220–40; *Dictionary of American Negro Biography,* pp. 328–30.

1947 ♦ The first known freedom ride occurred April 9, 1947, when the Congress of Racial Equality (CORE) and the Fellowship of Reconciliation tested the South's compliance with the court's decision of June 3, 1946, which banned segregation on interstate buses. CORE sent 23 black and white riders through the South. This was the first challenge to segregation on interstate buses. The freedom rides of May 1961 were more widely publicized. They led to a firm policy on desegregation of interstate travel.

Sources: Bennett, *Before the Mayflower,* p. 542; Hornsby, Jr., *Milestones in Twentieth-Century African-American History,* p. 44; *Negro Almanac,* p. 27.

1957 ♦ The first nonviolent civil rights organization dedicated to protest and change was the Southern Christian Leadership Conference (SCLC), formed in 1957 after the success of the 1955–56 Montgomery bus boycott. Leaders of the SCLC included Martin Luther King, Jr., Bayard Rustin, and Ralph Abernathy.

Sources: Alford, *Famous First Blacks,* p. 26; *Contemporary Black Biography,* vol. 1, pp. 132–33; *Encyclopedia of Black America,* pp. 804–5; *Negro Almanac,* p. 30.

1958 ♦ The first sit-ins to win concessions in a Southern state in modern times occurred in restaurants in Oklahoma City on August 19, 1958. The NAACP Youth Council members sat at lunch counters and were served without incident or publicity.

Sources: Alford, *Famous First Blacks,* p. 25; Bennett, *Before the Mayflower,* p. 556.

1960 ♦ The first sit-in movement to achieve major results began February 1, 1960, when four students from North Carolina Agricultural and Technical College sought service at an F.W. Woolworth store's lunch counter reserved for whites. The students were Ezell Blair, Franklin McCain, David Richmond, and Joseph McNeil. The movement, patterned after the passive resistance techniques of Mahatma Gandhi, gained momentum, and by February 10, 1960, had spread to 15 Southern cities in 5 states. On March 16, 1960, San Antonio, Texas, became the first city to integrate its lunch counters as result of the movement.

Sources: Alford, *Famous First Blacks,* p. 25; Bennett, *Before the Mayflower,* pp. 383–84, 557; Cantor, *Historic Landmarks of Black America,* pp. 229–31; Hornsby, Jr., *Milestones in Twentieth-Century African-American History,* pp. 63, 66.

1963 ♦ **Medgar Evers** (1925–1963) became the first major black martyr of the contemporary civil rights movement. In 1954 Evers was appointed the first field secretary for the NAACP in Mississippi. He worked for black voting rights and for enforcement of *Brown v. Board of Education,* the 1954 Supreme Court decision that outlawed school segregation. Despite repeated threats of violence following his controversial speeches, Evers devoted himself to the civil rights struggle. On June 12, 1963, he was assassinated outside his home while returning from an NAACP strategy session. White supremacist Byron de la Beckwith was placed on trial twice for the murder of Evers in 1964. However, the all-white juries failed to reach a verdict either time. Mississippi authorities reopened the case in 1989 and discovered enough new evidence to arrest and charge Beckwith again. Finally, in February 1994, a jury of eight African Americans and four whites found Beckwith guilty. He was sentenced to life in prison.

Sources: Estell, ed., *African American Almanac,* 6th ed., pp. 383–84; Pederson, *African American Almanac,* U·X·L ed., p. 266.

1964 ♦ The first wave of large riots in a black urban neighborhood of the 1960s occurred in the Harlem section of New York in July. The riots then spread to the Bedford-Stuyvesant section of Brooklyn; Rochester, New York; and Jersey City and Paterson, New Jersey.

Sources: Bennett, *Before the Mayflower,* p. 571; Hornsby, Jr., *Milestones in Twentieth-Century African-American History,* p. 78; *Negro Almanac,* p. 32.

Martin Luther
King, Jr.

Civil rights activist **Stokely Carmichael** (1941–) was the first person to popularize the phrase "Black Power" as a slogan during James Meredith's voter registration drive through Mississippi. In 1966 he became head of the Student Nonviolent Coordinating Committee and changed its focus from nonviolence to black liberation (the group was later renamed the Student National Coordinating Committee).

Sources: Alford, *Famous First Blacks,* p. 24; *Encyclopedia of Black America,* p. 215; *Negro Almanac,* pp. 240–42, 284.

1984 ◆ The first Black Family Summit was held at Fisk University, Tennessee, in May 1984.

Source: Negro Almanac, pp. 258–59.

1989 ◆ The first memorial to the civil rights movement of the 1960s was dedicated in Montgomery, Alabama, in 1989. This is perhaps the first wide recognition of little-known martyrs of the civil rights movement, along with the famous. The memorial consists of two simple black granite pieces, a circular stone that lists 40 civil rights martyrs, and a wall of rushing water.

Source: Cantor, *Historic Landmarks of Black America,* p. 132–33.

1993 ◆ For the first time since Martin Luther King Day became an official federal holiday, all 50 states marked its observance on January 18, even longtime holdouts New Hampshire and Arizona. President Ronald Reagan signed the bill establishing the holiday in 1983. The holiday, scheduled to begin in 1986 on the third Monday in January, was the first such honor ever extended to any African American in United States history.

Source: Hornsby, Jr., and Straub, *African American Chronology,* pp. 235, 331.

Education

Awards and Honors • College Administrators • College Buildings
College Degrees • College Faculty • College Foundings
College Fund-Raising • College Integration • Honorary Degrees
Schools

Awards and Honors

1907 ✦ **Alain Leroy Locke** (1885–1954), educator, interpreter, and promoter of black culture, was the first black Rhodes scholar. From 1907 to 1910 he studied at Oxford (England) and from 1910 to 1911 at the University of Berlin (Germany). It was not until 1960 that the second black Rhodes scholar, Joseph Stanley Sanders (1942–), was selected.

Sources: Alford, *Famous First Blacks,* p. 35; Bennett, *Before the Mayflower,* p. 642; *Dictionary of American Negro Biography,* pp. 398–404; Hornsby, Jr., *Milestones in Twentieth-Century African-American History,* pp. 8–9.

1928 ✦ **Charlotte Hawkins Brown** (1883–1961) became the first black member of the Twentieth Century Club of Boston. Membership in the club included persons distinguished in education, art, science, and religion. On October 10, 1902, she founded Alice Freeman Palmer Institute in Sedalia, North Carolina. On November 23, 1907, the school was renamed and incorporated as Palmer Memorial Institute.

Sources: Encyclopedia of Black America, p. 194; *Notable Black American Women,* pp. 109–14; Robinson, *Historical Negro Biographies,* pp. 167–68; *Who's Who Among Black Americans, 1927,* pp. 25–26.

1990 ✦ The first building named in honor of an African American at Louisiana State University, Baton Rouge, was Alexander Pierre Tureaud, Sr., Hall. Tureaud (1899–1972) was recognized for his dedication to civil rights. His legal work had opened the doors of the university to black students 40 years earlier. He was the only black practicing attorney in the state from 1938

Alain Leroy Locke

to 1947 and became known for initiating dozens of desegregation suits before the 1964 Civil Rights Act.

Source: Jet 78 (28 May 1990), p. 24.

College Administrators

1863 ◆ Historian, educator, and African Methodist Episcopal (AME) minister **Daniel A. Payne** (1811–1893) was the first black president of a black college in the Western world—Wilberforce University (Ohio). On Payne's advice, the AME Church purchased Wilberforce, which in 1856 had been founded by the Methodist Episcopal Church. The university was officially transferred on March 30, 1863. Payne turned to writing in his later years and produced several works. His most important are *The History of the African Methodist Episcopal Church* (1891) and *Recollections of Seventy Years* (1888).

Sources: Bennett, *Before the Mayflower*, pp. 173, 463; *Dictionary of American Negro Biography*, pp. 484–85; *Negro Almanac*, p. 1010; Simmons, *Men of Mark*, pp. 1078–85.

1926 ◆ **Mordecai Wyatt Johnson** (1890–1976) became the first black president of Howard University, Washington, D.C., on June 20, 1926. Martin Luther King, Jr., heard Johnson lecture on a trip to India, in which Johnson spoke of Mohandas Gandhi's life and teachings. This led King to expand his understanding of Gandhi and to become committed to nonviolent resistance.

Sources: Bennett, *Before the Mayflower*, p. 526; *Encyclopedia of Black America*, p. 475; Katz, *Eyewitness*, pp. 507–8.

1937 ◆ **Dwight Oliver Wendell Holmes** (1877–1963) became the first black president of Morgan State College (now University), where he guided the transition of the school from Methodist to state control. He served until 1948, when he retired. He is known also for his book *Evolution of the Negro College,* published in 1934. Through his career and his writings, he significantly influenced black higher education.

Sources: Dictionary of American Negro Biography, pp. 320–21; *Encyclopedia of Black America*, p. 443; *Who's Who in America, 1946-1947*, p. 1106.

1946 ♦ **Charles Spurgeon Johnson** (1893–1956), sociologist, editor, writer, and educational statesman, became the first black president of Fisk University, Nashville, Tennessee, on September 1, 1946. Johnson was also connected with the Harlem Renaissance through his post as editor of *Opportunity*, a magazine that became an important outlet for black writers and artists of the 1920s.

Sources: Dictionary of American Negro Biography, pp. 347–49; Hornsby, Jr., Milestones in Twentieth-Century African-American History, pp. 45–46.

1953 ♦ **Albert Edward Manley** (1908–) became the first black president of Spelman College. He served until 1976, when he became president emeritus (honorary president).

Sources: Ebony Success Library, vol. 1, p. 215; Who's Who Among Black Americans, 1992–1993, p. 909.

Daniel A. Payne

1960 ♦ **James Madison Nabrit, Jr.** (1900–) and **Samuel Milton Nabrit** (1905–) became the first black brothers to hold simultaneously the presidencies of two of the largest black universities. James was president of Howard University, Washington, D.C., from 1960 to 1969, while Samuel was president of Texas Southern University, Houston, from 1955 to 1966. (*See also* **Politics: Federal Appointments and Diplomacy, 1965,** and **Science, Medicine, and Invention: Atomic Energy Commission, 1966.**)

Sources: Encyclopedia of Black America, pp. 611–12; Who's Who Among Black Americans, 1992–1993, p. 1045; Wormley, Many Shades of Black, pp. 61, 159.

1970 ♦ The first black president of a major American university in the twentieth century was **Clifton Reginald Wharton, Jr.** (1926–), who on January 2, 1970, became head of Michigan State University in East Lansing. He was named chancellor of the State University of New York in 1977. (*See also* **Politics: Federal Appointments and Diplomacy, 1993.**)

Sources: Encyclopedia of Black America, pp. 851–52; Garrett, Famous First Facts About Negroes, pp. 61–62; Who's Who Among Black Americans, 1992–1993, p. 650.

1972 ♦ The first black woman elected to the Yale University Corporation was **Marian Wright Edelman** (1939–), lawyer, children's rights activist, and head of the Children's Defense Fund, an agency that she founded

Johnnetta Betsch
Cole

in 1973. In 1980 she became the first African American (and the second woman) to head the Spelman College Board of Trustees.

Sources: Black Women in America, vol. 1, pp. 377–78; Encyclopedia of Black America, p. 331; Notable Black American Women, vol. 1, pp. 309–12.

1981 ◆ **Jewell Plummer Cobb** (1924–) became president of California State University at Fullerton. She was the first black woman appointed in the system and believed to be the first to head a major public university on the West Coast.

Sources: Black Women in America, vol. 1, pp. 257–58; Jet 60 (13 August 1981), p. 25; Notable Black American Women, pp. 195–98; Who's Who Among Black Americans, 1992–1993, p. 279.

1984 ◆ The first woman of any race to become president of Wilberforce University was **Yvonne Walker-Taylor**. Her father, D. Ormond Walker, was president there for nearly 50 years. Walker-Taylor had served as provost and interim president of Wilberforce, and she later became presidential professor at Central State University (Oklahoma).

Sources: Jet 66 (12 March 1984), p. 23; Who's Who Among Black Americans, 1992–1993, p. 1448.

The first black chancellor of California's 106 community colleges was **Joshua L. Smith** (1934–), former president of Manhattan Borough Community College.

Sources: Jet 69 (13 January 1986), p. 11; Who's Who Among Black Americans, 1992–1993, p. 1305.

1987 ◆ Educator and anthropologist **Johnnetta Betsch Cole** (Robinson) (1936–) became the first black woman president of Spelman College, Atlanta, Georgia. She is affectionately called "sister president," a label she gave herself in 1987. Her landmark book, *All American Women,* published in 1986, broke new ground in women's studies for its emphasis on race, culture, and class.

Sources: Black Women in America, vol. 1, pp. 260–61; Negro Almanac, pp. 97, 1081; Notable Black American Women, pp. 198–201; Who's Who Among Black Americans, 1992–1993, p. 203.

1989 ◆ The first black chancellor of Los Angeles Community Colleges was **Donald Gayton Phelps** (1929–). He was inaugurated in May 1989 to head the nine-campus school, the largest community college in the world.

Sources: Jet 76 (17 April 1989), p. 37; Who's Who Among Black Americans, 1992–1993, p. 1119.

1990 ◆ **Marguerite Ross Barnett** (1942–1992) took office as the first woman and first black president of the University of Houston on September 1, 1990. In 1968 she was the first black woman president of the University of Missouri, St. Louis.

Sources: Black Women in America, vol. 1, pp. 89–90; Jet 78 (21 May 1990), p. 36; Notable Black American Women, pp. 55–56.

College Buildings

1881 ◆ Allen Hall, located on the Huston-Tillotson College campus in Austin, Texas, is believed to be the first building in Texas (and the first west of the Mississippi) to educate African Americans. The college was founded in 1876, when Sam Huston College and Tillotson College merged.

Source: Encyclopedia of Black America, p. 457–58.

College Degrees

1823 ◆ **Alexander Lucius Twilight** (1795–1857), educator, preacher, and legislator, became the first-known African American to graduate from an American college, when he received his B.A. degree from Middlebury College (Vermont). Other African Americans who graduated from college during this early period were Edward A. Jones (1808?–1865), who received his degree from Amherst College (Massachusetts), and John Brown Russwurm (1799–1851), first black graduate from Bowdoin College (Maine). Both graduated in 1826, with Jones some few days ahead of Russwurm. By 1860 only about 28 African Americans had received bachelor's degrees from American colleges.

Sources: Bennett, Before the Mayflower, p. 172; Bowles and DeCosta, Between Two Worlds, pp. 12–13; Dictionary of American Negro Biography, p. 613.

1850 ◆ The first black woman to graduate from college was **Lucy Ann Stanton** (Mrs. Levi N. Sessions, ?–1910). She completed the two-year women's course and received a Bachelor of Literature degree from Oberlin College (Ohio) on December 8, 1850. She taught school in the South during Reconstruction. Two other women have been called the first black woman college graduates. Grace A. Mapps was the first black woman to obtain a degree from a four-year college in the United States—Central College, McGrawville, New York. Mary Jane Patterson (1840–94) was the first black woman to earn a B.A. degree from the four-year men's course at Oberlin College (Ohio) in 1862.

Sources: Dictionary of Black Culture, p. 399; Jackson-Coppin, *Reminiscences of School Life, and Hints on Teaching,* p. 149; Kane, *Famous First Facts,* p. 118; Lane, *William Dorsey's Philadelphia and Ours,* pp. 137, 139; *Women in American Protest and Religion, 1800–1930,* p. 202.

1865 ◆ **Patrick Francis Healy** (1834–1910), a Jesuit priest and scholar, passed his final examination on July 26, 1865, and received a Ph.D. degree from Louvain University, Belgium, to become the first black American to receive an earned doctorate. He became America's first black president of a mainly white university when he was installed on July 31, 1871, as president of Georgetown University, Washington, D.C., the oldest Catholic university in America. He resigned the position in 1884. (*See also* **Religion: Catholics, 1854.**)

Sources: Bennett, *Before the Mayflower,* pp. 474, 641; *Dictionary of American Negro Biography,* pp. 304–5; *Encyclopedia of Black America,* p. 433.

1870 ◆ **Richard Theodore Greener** (1844–1922) was the first black graduate of Harvard University. In October 1873 he became a philosophy professor at the University of South Carolina. In addition to his main teaching duties, he assisted in the departments of Latin, Greek, mathematics, and constitutional history. He also served as acting librarian, arranging the university's rare book collection of 27,000 volumes and beginning preparation of a catalog. During this same time Greener studied law. In 1876 he graduated from the university's law school. He was admitted to the Supreme Court of South Carolina in 1877, and the next year practiced at the District of Columbia bar. He remained at South Carolina until March 1877, when the legislature abruptly closed the door of the university to black students. He headed the law school at Howard University and developed a considerable reputation as a speaker and writer.

Sources: Bennett, *Before the Mayflower,* p. 642; *Blacks at Harvard,* pp. 36–41; *Dictionary of American Negro Biography,* pp. 267–68; Garrett, *Famous First Facts About Negroes,* p. 52; Robinson, *Historical Negro Biographies,* pp. 83–84; Simmons, *Men of Mark,* pp. 326–35.

1874 ◆ **Edward Alexander Bouchet** (1825–1918) became the first African American to receive a doctorate from an American university when he graduated from Yale in November 1874. His graduate work in physics was supported by the Institute for Colored Youth of Philadelphia, the institution with which he was associated for 26 years as a teacher of chemistry and physics.

Sources: Dictionary of American Negro Biography, pp. 50–51; Encyclopedia of Black America, p. 187; Lane, William Dorsey's Philadelphia and Ours, p. 144.

1893 ◆ **Harriet (Hattie) Aletha Gibbs Marshall** (1869–1941) was the first black graduate of the Oberlin Conservatory of Music (Ohio). In 1903 she established the Washington Conservatory of Music in Washington, D.C., which she directed until 1923. She moved to Haiti with her husband that year, where she founded an industrial school and collected folk music. She returned to the United States in 1936 and established a National Negro Music Center in association with the Washington, D.C., conservatory. Born in Vancouver, British Columbia, the daughter of newsman and judge Mifflin Gibbs, she was a pioneer in her efforts to bring black concert artists from all over the nation to Washington.

W. E. B. Du Bois

Sources: Dictionary of American Negro Biography, p. 426; Encyclopedia of Black America, p. 546; Southern, Biographical Dictionary of Afro-American and African Musicians, pp. 264–65.

1895 ◆ The first African American to receive a Ph.D. from Harvard University was **William Edward Burghardt (W. E. B.) Du Bois** (1868–1963). He was also the first African American to earn a Ph.D. in history. (*See also* **Literature: History, 1896** and **Organizations: Academic and Intellectual Societies, 1943.**)

1897 ◆ **Anita Hemmings** was the first African American to graduate from Vassar College, Poughkeepsie, New York. Since she was very light-skinned, her declaration of her racial identity upon graduation attracted the sensational press and caused "dismay" for the college administration.

Source: Lane, William Dorsey's Philadelphia and Ours, p. 273.

1921 ◆ **Eva Beatrice Dykes** (1893–1986), **Sadie Tanner Mossell Alexander** (1898–1989), and **Georgianna R. Simpson** (1866–1944) were the first three black American women to earn Ph.D. degrees. They all received their degrees in 1921. Dykes was the first to complete the requirements, in English, at Radcliffe College (Massachusetts) on March 21, 1921, yet her June 22 commencement was the latest of the three women. Simpson's degree, in

Eva Beatrice Dykes

German, was awarded June 14 by the University of Chicago, making her the first ever to receive the degree. The University of Pennsylvania awarded Alexander's degree on June 15, when she became the first black American to receive a Ph.D. in economics. In 1927 Alexander became the first black woman to receive a law degree from the School of Law at the University of Pennsylvania. Later that year she became the first black woman to enter the bar and practice law in Pennsylvania.

Sources: Bennett, *Before the Mayflower*, p. 523; *Black Women in America*, vol. 1, pp. 17–19, vol. 2, pp. 1038–39; *Encyclopedia of Black America*, p. 98; Lee, *Interesting People*, p. 59; *Notable Black American Women*, pp. 5–8, 304–6.

1973 ◆ **Shirley Ann Jackson** (1946–) received a Ph.D. in physics and became the first black woman in the United States to receive a doctorate from Massachusetts Institute of Technology (MIT). Since 1976 she has been at AT&T Bell Laboratories, where she conducts research on topics relating to theoretical material sciences.

Sources: *Negro Almanac*, pp. 106, 1084; *Notable Black American Women*, pp. 565–66; *Who's Who Among Black Americans, 1992–1993*, p. 725.

College Faculty

1849 ◆ The first black faculty member on a white college campus was at Central College, McGrawville, New York. **Charles Lewis Reason** (1818–1893), reformer and writer, was named professor of mathematics, belles lettres (literature), and French in October 1849. In 1852 he became principal of the Institute for Colored Youth in Philadelphia. Another early black faculty member was William G. Allen, professor of Greek and German languages, rhetoric, and belles lettres. Allen married one of his white students and later was forced to flee with her to England. The third African American in this early group was George Boyer Vashon (1824–1878), who joined the McGrawville faculty in 1854.

Sources: *Dictionary of American Negro Biography*, pp. 516–517; Jackson, *A History of Afro-American Literature*, vol. 1, p. 126; Lane, *William Dorsey's Philadelphia and Ours*, p. 137; Woodson, *The Education of the Negro Prior to 1861*, p. 280.

1946 ◆ **Allison Davis** (1902–1983) was the first black professor at the University of Chicago, where in 1970 he became the first John Dewey Distinguished Service Professor of Education. He was the first in education from any race to become a fellow in the American Academy of Arts and Sciences, and one of the first to challenge the accuracy of the IQ test for "measuring accurately the educational potential of children from low-income families."

Sources: Encyclopedia of Black America, p. 302; Garrett, *Famous First Facts About Negroes,* pp. 62, 185; *Jet* 65 (12 December 1983), p. 15; *Who's Who in America, 1982–1983,* p. 766.

1969 ◆ **Derrick Bell** (1930–) became the first black law professor at Harvard Law School and in 1971 became the first black tenured professor. Twenty-three years later he began an unpaid leave of absence to protest Harvard's hiring policies. He was dismissed in 1992, when he exceeded the two-year limit on leaves of absence.

Sources: Blacks at Harvard, pp. 467–73; *Jet* 72 (29 June 1982), p. 28, 78 (14 May 1990), p. 25, 82 (20 July 1992), p. 22, 82 (27 July 1992), p. 56.

The first chairperson of Harvard University's Department of Afro-American Studies was **Ewart Guinier** (1911–1990). His daughter, Lani Guinier, gained national recognition in 1993 when President Bill Clinton nominated her to head the U.S. Department of Justice's civil rights division. He later withdrew the nomination.

Sources: Jet 84 (21 June 1993), pp. 4–7; *Who's Who Among Black Americans, 1988,* p. 282.

College Foundings

1833 ◆ The first college in the United States founded with a mission to educate African Americans was Oberlin College (Ohio). One of the original sponsors of Oberlin was Lane Seminary in Cincinnati, Ohio. When many of the students converted to abolitionism, it became expedient to move to northern Ohio and join the nucleus of students and instruction already established there. By the time of the Civil War, one-third of the student body was African American.

Sources: Negro Almanac, p. 11; Woodson, *The Education of the Negro Prior to 1861,* pp. 275–76, 300.

1839 ◆ Cheyney State College, sometimes referred to as the oldest black college in the United States, had its beginning in 1832. Richard Humphreys, a Philadelphia Quaker, willed $10,000 to a board of trustees to establish a school for African Americans. A school for black boys was eventually established in 1839 and incorporated in 1842. The school became known in 1852 as the Institute for Colored Youth. It reorganized in 1902 and moved to Cheyney, Pennsylvania. Here it was renamed, became a teacher training school in 1914, and a normal school in 1921, when it was purchased by the state. Since 1932 Cheyney State College has been a degree-granting institution.

Sources: American Colleges and Universities, 1983, p. 1565; Bowles and DeCosta, Between Two Worlds, pp. 23–24; Lane, William Dorsey's Philadelphia and Ours, p. 338; Woodson, The Education of the Negro Prior to 1861, pp. 268–70.

1854 ◆ Lincoln University (Pennsylvania) and Wilberforce University (Ohio) are the oldest historically black colleges established in America. Unlike Cheyney State, which had its origin in 1832, these institutions were the first to remain in their original location, indicate their aim to award bachelor's degrees, and develop fully into degree-granting institutions. Lincoln University, the outgrowth of Ashmun Institute, was incorporated January 1, 1854, and opened its doors to young black men on August 30, 1856. Wilberforce University was incorporated in 1856 and awarded its first B.A. degree in 1857. Beginning in 1862 the college came under black control, making it the oldest college controlled by African Americans.

Sources: Bennett, Before the Mayflower, pp. 457, 462–63, 641; Bowles and DeCosta, Between Two Worlds, p. 20; Woodson, The Education of the Negro Prior to 1861, pp. 268–72.

1867 ◆ The first black college founded in Tennessee and still in existence is Fisk University. Work on the founding of the school began in October 1865, and it incorporated August 22, 1867, under the sponsorship of the American Missionary Association. The institution opened on January 9, 1866. It was named in honor of General Clinton B. Fisk of the Freedmen's Bureau.

Sources: Fisk University Bulletin, 1986–1989, p. 4; Richardson, A History of Fisk University 1865–1946.

On January 8, 1867, Howard Theological Seminary changed its name to Howard University. On that date the university became the first black school to establish undergraduate, graduate, and professional schools. The school was established with the help of the Freedmen's Bureau and named in honor of General Oliver O. Howard, who headed the Bureau.

Sources: Encyclopedia of Black America, p. 455; Hornsby, Jr., Chronology of African-American History, p. 40; Jet 81 (13 January 1992), p. 38.

1874 ◆ Alabama State University was founded at Salem as the State Normal School and University for Colored Students and Teachers. It was the first state-supported institution in the United States to train black teachers. The institution moved to its present site in Montgomery in 1887.

Sources: Bowles and DeCosta, *Between Two Worlds,* p. 292; *Encyclopedia of Black America,* p. 95.

1881 ◆ Spelman College, Atlanta, Georgia, was the first institution of higher education established to educate black women. Sponsored by philanthropist John D. Rockefeller, the school opened on April 11, 1881, as the Atlanta Baptist Female Seminary. In 1884 the name Spelman was adopted in honor of Mrs. John D. Rockefeller's parents. (*See also* **Education: College Fund-Raising, 1992.**)

Sources: Black Women in America, pp. 1091–95; *Encyclopedia of Black America,* p. 807; Hornsby, Jr., *Chronicle of African-American History,* p. 50; Read, *The Story of Spelman College.*

1929 ◆ The first and only black college alliance, the Atlanta University System was founded in 1929. John Hope (1868–1936) became the first president of the system when Atlanta University (a co-educational institution), Spelman College (an undergraduate college for women), and Morehouse College (an undergraduate college for men), entered a partnership arrangement. Later Clark and Morris Brown colleges and the Interdenominational Theological Seminary (all co-educational) joined to form the largest educational center in the world for African Americans. Atlanta and Clark merged in 1988 to become Clark Atlanta University, which remains a part of the Center.

Sources: Encyclopedia of Black America, p. 144; Hornsby, Jr., *Chronology of African-American History,* p. 82; Hornsby, Jr., *Milestones in Twentieth-Century African-American History,* p. 30; *Jet* 52 (2 June 1977), p. 15.

College Fund-Raising

1981 ◆ Lou Rawls' Parade of Stars, a national fundraiser to benefit the United Negro College Fund (UNCF), began in 1976 and in 1981 became the first nationally televised benefit for education. Co-hosted with Marilyn McCoo, the show received pledges from all over the country to support the 42 historically black member institutions. UNCF was founded on April 24, 1944, to coordinate the fundraising efforts of private black colleges. (*See also* **Miscellaneous: Organizations, 1944.**)

Sources: Hornsby, Jr., *Milestones in Twentieth-Century African-American History,* pp. 41, 340; *Jet* 67 (21 January 1985), p. 22.

1988 ◆ Comedian and television star **Bill Cosby** (1937–) and his wife, **Camille,** donated $20 million to Spelman College. It was the first gift of its size in the 107-year history of the women's college and the largest such gift ever made by an African American.(*See also* **Film and Television: Television, 1965**.)

Sources: Herbert and Hill, *Bill Cosby*, p. 93; Hornsby, Jr., and Straub, *African American Chronology*, p. 264.

1992 ♦ Spelman College, Atlanta, Georgia, became the first black college to receive a single gift of $37 million, the largest gift ever made to a historically black college. The gift from the DeWitt Wallace/Spelman College fund was established in the New York Community Trust by the Reader's Digest Association.

Source: *Jet* 82 (25 May 1992), p. 22.

College Integration

1868 ♦ The University of South Carolina was first opened to all races on March 3, 1868. Elected to the Board of Trustees were B. A. Boseman and Francis L. Cardoza. The integrated student body seems to have ended in 1876. There was a long series of disturbances between July 8 and October 26, 1876, and federal troops were sent in. During this period Democratic as well as Republican state governments were established in South Carolina. The deal that elected Rutherford B. Hayes president of the United States was struck on February 26, 1877. Democrats took over South Carolina on April 10, 1877, when federal troops were withdrawn.

Source: Bennett, *Before the Mayflower*, p. 485.

1953 ♦ **Joseph A. Johnson, Jr.** (1914–) became the first black student at Vanderbilt University, Nashville, Tennessee, on May 2, 1953. By vote of the Board of Trustees, who said that "Christianity is not the exclusive possession of any one nation or race," he was admitted to the Divinity School. He was also the first African American to graduate and receive a Ph.D. from Vanderbilt, in 1958. He has since served on the school's board of trustees. The Shreveport native later became a presiding bishop in the Christian Methodist Church.

Sources: *Ebony Success Library*, vol. 1, p. 178; *Jet* 60 (7 May 1981), p. 18; 84 (3 May 1983), p. 32; *Who's Who Among Black Americans, 1980–1981*, p. 431.

1956 ♦ After three and a half years of legal efforts, **Autherine Juanita Lucy** (Foster) (1929–) was the first black student admitted to the University of Alabama, on February 3, 1956. A riot followed, and she was suspended that evening. She was expelled February 29 for making "false" and "outrageous" statements about the school. In 1989 she entered the university's graduate program in elementary education. She and her daughter, Grazia, graduated in the spring of 1992.

Sources: Bennett, *Before the Mayflower,* p. 552; *Black Women in America,* pp. 448–49; *Ebony* 11 (June 1956), p. 93, 12 (March 1957), pp. 51–54; Hornsby, Jr., *Milestones in Twentieth-Century African-American History,* p. 59; *Jet* 81 (18 November 1991), p. 10.

1961 ◆ **Charlayne Hunter-Gault** (1942–) and **Hamilton Earl Holmes** (1941–) were the first black students to enroll at the University of Georgia. Students rioted in protest of their admission, and they were temporarily suspended. Both students graduated from the school in 1963. Holmes became the first African American medical student at Emory University (Georgia) in 1967. Hunter-Gault received the George Foster Peabody Award from the University of Georgia School of Journalism in 1986. In 1961 Holmes became the first African American trustee of the University of Georgia Foundation.

Sources: Black Women in America, vol. 1, pp. 595–96; *Ebony Success Library,* vol. 1, p. 122; *Notable Black American Women,* pp. 535–36; *Who's Who Among Black Americans, 1992–1993,* p. 674 (Holmes), p. 704 (Hunter Gault).

The first African American admitted to the University of Mississippi was Air Force veteran **James Howard Meredith** (1933–), after being denied admission three times. Although the U.S. Supreme Court ordered Meredith's admission, Governor Ross R. Barnett defied the Court's decision. U.S. marshalls were called to escort him to classes and federal troops were called to quell campus disturbances. Meredith graduated in 1963.

Sources: Crisis 70 (January 1963), pp. 5–11; *Encyclopedia of Black America,* p. 553; Hornsby, Jr., *Milestones in Twentieth-Century African-American History,* p. 71; *Jet* 71 (1 December 1986), p. 8; Katz, *Eyewitness,* pp. 483, 496–97.

Honorary Degrees

1804 ◆ **Lemuel Haynes** (1753–1833) was the first African American to receive an honorary degree in the United States. Middlebury College (Vermont) at its second commencement in 1804 awarded Haynes an M.A. (*See also* **Military: Revolutionary War, 1775;** and **Religion: Congregationalists, 1785.**)

Source: Dictionary of American Negro Biography, pp. 300–301.

1896 ◆ Educator, school founder, and race leader **Booker T. Washington** (1856–1915) was the first black recipient of an honorary degree from Harvard University. He received an M.A. in 1896. (*See also* **Miscellaneous: Commemoratives and Monuments, 1940** and **1946.**)

Sources: Alford, *Famous First Blacks*, p. 35; *Dictionary of American Negro Biography*, pp. 633–38; Hornsby, Jr., *Chronology of African-American History*, p. 55.

1946 ◆ On February 21, 1946, **Mary McLeod Bethune** (1875–1955), educator and civic leader, became the first African American to receive an honorary degree from a white college in the South; she received the degree from Rollins College, Winter Park, Florida. (*See also* **Miscellaneous: Commemoratives and Monuments, 1974** and **Politics: Federal Appointments and Diplomacy, 1936.**)

Sources: Garrett, *Famous First Facts About Negroes*, pp. 59, 122–23, 161; *Jet* 82 (6 July 1992), p. 32; Kane, *Famous First Facts*, p. 216.

Booker T. Washington

1973 ◆ **B. B. (Riley B.) King** (1925–) became the first black musician to receive an honorary degree for his work in the blues when Tougaloo College (Mississippi) awarded him a doctorate of humanities. He was born in Indianola, Mississippi, and moved to Memphis, Tennessee, where he had his own radio show and in 1950–51 was a disc jockey. By the 1960s and 1970s he was a successful performer. In 1979 he was the first African American blues artist to perform in the USSR.

Sources: Current *Biography, 1970*, pp. 226–27; *Encyclopedia of Black America*, p. 489; Southern, *Biographical Dictionary of Afro-American and African Musicians*, p. 232.

Schools

1750 ◆ **Anthony Benezet** led the Philadelphia Quakers in opening the first free school for African Americans. It was an evening school taught by Moses Patterson. Benezet left money at his death to continue the school.

Sources: Garrett, *Famous First Facts About Negroes*, p. 48; *Negro Almanac, 1976*, pp. 528–29.

1787 ◆ The African Free School was the first free secular school in New York City. The free school for African Americans was opened on November 1, 1787, before any free school for whites, by the Manumission Society.

Sources: Hornsby, Jr., *Chronology of African-American History,* pp. 8–9; Horton, *Free People of Color,* pp. 59, 153; Johnson, *Black Manhattan,* pp. 20–23; *Negro Almanac, 1976,* p. 429.

1829 ◆ Saint Francis Academy, Baltimore, Maryland, was the first boarding school for black girls. The school was established by the Oblate Sisters of Providence and opened with 24 girls.

Sources: Black Women in America, p. 382; Garrett, *Famous First Facts About Negroes,* p. 49; *Notable Black American Women,* pp. 813–14.

1849 ◆ **Benjamin Roberts** filed the first petition to ban segregated schools. Roberts filed the school integration suit on behalf of his daughter against the city of Boston, which had a local ordinance requiring separate schools. The Massachusetts Supreme Court in *Roberts* v. *Boston* rejected the suit. Separate schools were abolished by state law in 1855, which resulted in Boston being the first major city to eliminate segregated schools.

Sources: Cantor, *Historic Landmarks of Black America,* p. 70; Garrett, *Famous First Facts About Negroes,* p. 49; *Negro Almanac, 1976,* p. 531.

1861 ◆ **Mary Smith Kelsick Peake** (1823–1862) a free woman of color, was the first teacher supported by the American Missionary Association for freed slaves. She began teaching children at Fort Monroe, Virginia, and on September 17, 1861, she opened a school in Hampton, Virginia, marking the beginning of the general education of African Americans in the South. The school started as a day school, giving elementary education to children. A night school for adults was soon added. Hampton Institute (later University) has its roots in this school. Peake's health gave out shortly after the establishment of the school, and she died of tuberculosis on February 22, 1862.

Sources: Cantor, *Historic Landmarks of Black America,* pp. 253–54; *Dictionary of American Negro Biography,* p. 486; *Negro Yearbook, 1921–1922,* pp. 230–31; *Notable Black American Women,* pp. 834–35.

1863 ◆ **Sarah J. (Smith) Thompson Garnet** (1831–1911) was the first black woman to be appointed principal in the New York public school system. Her second marriage occurred about 1879 to prominent abolitionist and Presbyterian minister Henry Highland Garnet (1815–1882). In 1892 Sarah Garnet and a number of prominent black women raised funds to replace the destroyed presses of Ida B. Wells's Memphis newspaper. Garnet was superintendent of the Suffrage Department of the National Association of Colored

Women. Her sister was the pioneer woman physician Susan Maria Smith McKinney Steward (1847–1918).

Sources: Black Women in America, vol. 1, p. 479; *Dictionary of American Negro Biography*, pp. 253–54; *Notable Black American Women*, pp. 388–91.

1865 ◆ **Francis Louis Cardoza** (1837–1903) was the first black principal of Avery Normal Institute, Charleston, South Carolina. Avery was aligned with the American Missionary Association and performed pioneer work in the education of the newly freed slaves. Born in Charleston of a Jewish father and a mother of mixed ancestry, Cardoza was educated abroad and was very active in Reconstruction politics. He served in several high governmental positions, including secretary of state in South Carolina; he later was principal of the Colored Prepatory High School and its successor, the M Street High School in Washington, D.C.

Sources: Dictionary of American Negro Biography, pp. 89–90; *Dictionary of Black Culture*, p. 81; *Encyclopedia of Black America*, p. 102.

1869 ◆ **Fanny Jackson** (Coppin) (1837–1913) became the first black woman to head a major educational institution for African Americans, the Institute for Colored Youth of Philadelphia. The Society of Friends founded the school in 1837, and when Coppin graduated from Oberlin College (Ohio) in 1865 she became principal of the Institute's female department. She was promoted to principal of the entire school in 1869. The Institute was a prestigious school with a faculty comprising some of the most highly educated African Americans of the period. She retired in 1902.

Sources: Black Women in America, vol. 1, pp. 281–83; Lane, *William Dorsey's Philadelphia and Ours*, pp. 135, 142–47; *Notable Black American Women*, pp. 224–28.

1879 ◆ **Josephine Silone Yates** (1859–1912) was the first black American certified to teach in the public schools of Rhode Island. In 1877 she had been the first African American to graduate from Rogers High School in Newport, Rhode Island. She later became an outstanding teacher at Lincoln Institute in Jefferson, Missouri, and president of the National Association of Colored Women.

Sources: Black Women in America, vol. 2, pp. 1297–98; *Notable Black American Women*, p. 1286–87.

1895 ◆ **Mary Church Terrell** (1863–1954) was the first black woman to serve on the Washington, D.C., Board of Education. She served from 1895 to 1901 and again from 1906 to 1911. (*See also* **Organizations: Civil Rights and Political Organizations, 1895.**)

Sources: Black Women in America, pp. 1157–59; Hornsby, Jr., *Milestones in Twentieth-Century African-American History*, pp. 49, 55; *Notable Black American Women*, pp. 1115–19.

1908 ♦ **Virginia Estelle Randolph** (1870–1958) was the first black Jeanes teacher. Anna T. Jeanes, a Philadelphia Quaker, provided $1 million to initiate a fund for teachers who worked with other teachers to encourage improvements in small black rural schools. Randolph was one of the most effective educators of her day. The Jeanes teacher program was fashioned after her notable practices in Henrico County, Virginia. Through the Jeanes movement, from 1908 to 1969, Randolph was instrumental in bringing about improvements in the lives of thousands of teachers, children, and community residents.

Sources: Black Women in America, vol. 2, pp. 962–63; Notable Black American Women, pp. 918–21; Who's Who in Colored America, 1937, p. 429.

1922 ♦ **Bessye Jeanne Banks Bearden** (1888–1943) was the first black woman member of the New York City Board of Education. Bearden was very dynamic in Democratic party politics; she founded and was the first president of the Colored Women's Democratic League. Bearden had a major role in political, civic, and social activities both in her community of Harlem and nationwide. Romare Bearden, renowned African American artist, was her son.

Sources: Black Women in America, pp. 97–98; Encyclopedia of Black America, p. 169; Notable Black American Women, pp. 70–72.

Mary Church Terrell

1936 ♦ **Gertrude Elise McDougald Ayer** (1884–1971) was the first black woman to have a full-time principalship in a New York City public school after the desegregation of the school system. (Sarah Garnet was the first black woman principal in 1863, in a black school.)

Sources: Notable Black American Women, pp. 29–31; Who's Who in Colored America, 1950, p. 585.

1953 ♦ **Rufus Early Clement** (1900–1967) was the first African American elected to a school board in the Deep South since Reconstruction. Clement was elected to the Atlanta Public School board by black and white citizens. In 1925 he was the youngest academic dean in America, at Livingstone College in Salisbury, North Carolina. He later became dean of Louisville Municipal College in Kentucky. In 1936 he became president of

Atlanta University and was instrumental in fostering their newly formed graduate school (1929), as well as enlarging the influence of the Atlanta University Center. In 1966 *Time* magazine chose Clement as one of the 14 most influential university presidents in America. He was always identified with organizations in the South directed toward the healing of race relations.

Sources: Bacote, *The Story of Atlanta University,* pp. 316–30, 344–82; *Dictionary of American Negro Biography,* p. 117; *Encyclopedia of Black America,* p. 275; Hornsby, Jr., *Chronology of African-American History,* p. 99; *Time* 87 (11 February 1966), p. 64.

1956 ◆ **John Henrik Clarke** (1915–) was the first African American licensed to teach African and African American history in New York State public schools. Best known as a critic, anthologist, and editor, he has also written short stories and poetry. Clarke was the co-founder of the *Harlem Quarterly,* book review editor of the *Negro History Bulletin,* and associate editor of *Freedomways: A Quarterly Review of the Negro Freedom Movement.*

Sources: Encyclopedia of Black America, p. 273; *Negro Almanac,* p. 985; *Who's Who Among Black Americans, 1992–1993,* p. 269.

1958 ◆ **Ernest Gideon Green** (1941–), investment banker and government worker, was the first black graduate from the Little Rock, Arkansas Central High School. Green was one of the "Little Rock Nine," the black students who integrated the Little Rock public schools under the watch of the federal troops called out by President Dwight D. Eisenhower in 1957. Along with the other students and adviser Daisy Bates, Green was the recipient of the Spingarn Medal in 1958.

Sources: Cantor, *Historic Landmarks of Black America,* pp. 147–48; Hornsby, Jr., *Chronology of African-American History,* p. 106; *Who's Who Among Black Americans, 1992–1993,* p. 556.

1969 ◆ **John W. Porter** (1931–) was the first black state superintendent of public instruction since Reconstruction. Porter was appointed to the position by Michigan governor William G. Millikin.

Sources: Ebony 14 (February 1959), p. 6; Garrett, *Famous First Facts About Negroes,* p. 61; *Who's Who Among Black Americans,* 1978, p. 723.

1981 ◆ **Ruth Burnett Love** (Holloway) (1935–) was the first African American and the first woman to serve as superintendent of the Chicago school system. She served from 1981 to 1984.

Sources: Notable Black American Women, pp. 685–87; *Who's Who Among Black Americans, 1990–1991,* p. 1157.

1990 ◆ **Gwendolyn Calvert Baker** (1931–) was the first black woman president of the New York City Board of Education. She is national executive director of the YWCA of America and president of the U.S. Committee for UNICEF Children's Fund.

Sources: Chicago Defender 13 July 1993; *Jet* 79 (1 April 1991), p. 31; *Who's Who Among Black Americans, 1992–1993,* p. 60.

Explorers, Pioneers, and Wild West Heroes

1492 ♦ **Pedro Alonzo Niño,** whom some historians think was black, arrived in the New World with explorer Christopher Columbus. Other blacks later sailed with Vasco Núñez de Balboa, Juan Ponce de Leon, Hernán Cortes, Francisco Pizarro, and Pedro Menéndez de Avilés on their travels to the Americas.

Source: Hornsby, Jr., and Straub, *African American Chronology,* p. 1

1538 ♦ Black explorer **Estevanico (or Esteban) Dorantez** (c. 1501–1539) was the first non-Native North American to discover what is now Arizona and New Mexico. Estevanico was born in Morocco, a country in North Africa. As a slave he was part of an expedition that left Spain in 1527 to explore the western coast of the Gulf of Mexico. But the explorers' ships were blown off course into what is now Tampa Bay, Florida. Sailing west they then became shipwrecked on Galveston Island off the Texas coast. Only four survivors, including Estevanico, were able to keep going.

He was an especially valuable member of the group because he related well to the Indians they met along the way. The explorers finally reached Mexico City around 1536. There they thrilled Spanish officials with tales they had heard from the Indians about seven golden cities to the northwest in a place called Cibola. In 1539 explorer Francisco Coronado set out to find Cibola and conquer it. Estevanico guided the advance party. Sent out alone ahead of the others, he was the first to see what would one day be Arizona and New Mexico. But he was killed at Hawikuh Pueblo, New Mexico, by Zuñi Indians—who feared he would try to conquer them—and the rest of the advance party went back to Mexico.

Sources: Cantor, *Historic Landmarks of Black America,* pp. 286, 320–21; *Dictionary of American Negro Biography,* p. 213; Garrett, *Famous First Facts About Negroes,* p. 68; Hornsby, Jr., and Straub, *African American Chronology,* pp. 1–2; *Negro Almanac,* p. 2; Pelz, *Black Heroes of the Wild West,* pp. 1–4; Westridge Young Writers Workshop, *Kids Explore America's African-American Heritage,* p. 32.

1565 ◆ St. Augustine, Florida, the center of the Spanish Florida colony, was the first permanent dwelling place for blacks in the present territory of the United States. It had both slaves and free blacks from its beginning.

Source: Davis, *The History of Black Catholics in the United States,* p. 30.

1619 ◆ Twenty Africans arrived in Jamestown, Virginia, in August, transported by a Dutchman who sold them as indentured servants. They were the first black colonial settlers.

Sources: Bennett, *Before the Mayflower,* p. 441; Kane, *Famous First Facts,* p. 598; *Negro Almanac,* p. 2.

1626 ◆ There were 11 blacks in New Amsterdam, now New York City, in 1626, the year of its founding. Four were the first named blacks there: Paul d'Angola, Simon Congo, Anthony Portuguese, and John Franciso.

Source: Johnson, *Black Manhattan,* p. 4.

1651 ◆ **Anthony Johnson,** a black man from Northampton County, Virginia, imported five servants and qualified for a 200-acre land grant along the Puwgoteague River in Virginia. Others soon joined Johnson and attempted to launch an independent African community. At its height, the settlement had 12 African homesteads with sizable holdings.

Source: Estell, ed., *The African-American Almanac,* 6th ed., p. 5.

c. 1700 ◆ Until 1763, escaped slaves formed the first settlement of free blacks, just north and east of St. Augustine, Florida.

Source: Davis, *The History of Black Catholics in the United States,* p. 30.

1781 ◆ Los Angeles, California, was the first major city founded with a majority black population. Of the 11 founding families who arrived from Mexico, more than half were black.

Source: Davis, *The History of Black Catholics in the United States,* pp. 33–34.

1790 ◆ **Jean Baptiste Pointe Du Sable** (1745–1818) bought property in what is now Chicago, Illinois. There he established a fur trading post, making him the area's first permanent settler. A native of St. Marc, Haiti, Du Sable was born in 1745. He was the son of a French businessman and a black slave. Du Sable went to school in France and later worked for his father in New Orleans, Louisiana. When the Spanish took over Louisiana from the French in 1765, Du Sable and a friend headed north for other French-settled areas along the Mississippi River. They stopped at what is now St. Louis, Missouri, where they carried on a successful fur trade with the Indians for two years before moving farther north.

In 1772 Du Sable decided to build a fur trading post on the Chicago River near Lake Michigan. It soon became a very busy trading center, and eventually the settlement of Chicago sprang up around the post. After the Illinois territory came under the control of the United States, Du Sable sold his property and returned to Missouri. He died there in 1818.

Source: Hornsby, Jr., and Straub, *African American Chronology,* p. 10

1804 ◆ **York** (c. 1770–1832) was the first black to reach the mouth of the Columbia River by land travel. He was a member of the (Meriwether) Lewis and (William) Clark Expedition, which explored the Missouri River and continued on to the Pacific Ocean. A slave, York excited the admiration of Indians because of his size, strength, and color; he became a valuable member of the expedition, both for his skills and his public relations value. He later returned to Kentucky and eventually gained his freedom, but he ran into difficulties in his attempts to establish a business.

Sources: Cantor, *Historic Landmarks of Black America,* pp. 313–14, 326–27; *Dictionary of American Negro Biography,* pp. 676–77; Garrett, *Famous First Facts About Negroes,* p. 68.

1811 ◆ **Paul Cuffe** (1759–1818) led the first organized attempt to return black Americans to their African homeland. In 1811 he transported 38 people to Sierra Leone, a West African country then under British colonial rule. (*See also* **Business and Labor: Transportation, Shipping, and Sailing, 1784.**)

Sources: Dictionary of American Biography, vol. 2, no. 2, p. 585; Robinson, *Historical Negro Biographies,* pp. 12–13; Simmons, *Men of Mark,* pp. 336–39.

1816 ◆ **Bob,** baptized as **Juan Cristobal** (1819), was the first black English-speaking settler in California.

Source: Encyclopedia of Black America, p. 78.

1826 ◆ **Peter Ranne** (or Ranee) was the first black to reach California by cross-country travel.

Source: Encyclopedia of Black America, p. 78.

1847 ◆ **Green Flake, Oscar Crosby,** and **Hank Lay** were the first blacks to settle in Salt Lake City, Utah. They accompanied the first Mormon party and may have been slaves at the time.

Source: Cantor, *Historic Landmarks of Black America,* p. 334.

1849 ◆ **Waller Jackson** was the first black miner to join the California gold rush. He dug gold at Downieville.

Source: Thum, *Hippocrene U.S.A. Guide to Black America,* p. 41.

1850 ♦ **James Pierson Beckwourth** (1798–1867) joined the California gold rush and while in the Sierra Nevadas discovered a mountain pass that still bears his name. He made the gap more passable, opened an inn, and by 1851 was guiding wagon trains through the pass. Beckwourth was one of the nineteenth-century pioneers known as "Mountain Men." In 1824 he joined a westward-bound fur trapping and trading expedition under the leadership of William Henry Ashley. Beckwourth soon became known as a man of many adventures and exploits. Although the basis of these stories is factual, many—with Beckwourth's approval—have been greatly exaggerated. Nevertheless, he undoubtedly symbolized the spirit of the legendary conquerors of the American West.

Source: Estell, ed., *The African-American Almanac,* 6th ed., pp. 1227–228.

Jim Beckwourth

1859 ♦ **Martin Robinson Delany** (1812–1885) was the first black American explorer in Africa. In spring 1859 Delany sailed to Africa and traveled in Liberia and the Niger Valley for nine months. Delany's *Official Report of the Niger Valley Exploring Party* appeared in 1861. (*See also* **Literature: Essay, 1852** and **Media: Periodicals, 1841.**)

Sources: Jackson, *A History of Afro-American Literature,* vol. 1, pp. 364-69; Logan and Winston, *Dictionary of American Negro Biography,* pp. 169-73; Simmons, *Men of Mark,* pp. 1007-15.

1861 ♦ The Pony Express was for the time the fastest mail service using a relay of horses between St. Joseph, Missouri, and Sacramento, California. The first black Pony Express riders were stagecoach driver and gold miner **George Monroe** (1843–1886) and **William Robinson.** Little else is known about their activities, though Monroe became a noted stage driver in whose honor Monroe Meadows in Yosemite National Park is named.

Sources: Katz, *Black West,* pp. 128–29; *Negro Almanac,* p. 213; Reasons, *They Had a Dream,* vol. 2, p. 41.

c. 1860s ♦ **Aunt Sally Campbell,** a Deadwood, South Dakota, miner, is believed to be the first non-American Indian woman to enter the Black Hills.

Source: Cantor, *Historic Landmarks of Black America,* pp. 316–17.

Clara Brown

c. 1860s ◆ A slave who came to California during the gold rush of 1849, **Alvin Aaron Coffey** (1822–1902) worked to save the $1,000 fee for his freedom, only to be betrayed by his master. He was forced to return to Missouri but pleaded successfully with his new master to allow him to return to California and earn the necessary money to free himself and his family. Upon earning the money, Coffey was able to live a contented life with his family as a farmer in Red Bluff, California. He was the first and only black man to become a member of the Society of California Pioneers.

Sources: Estell, ed., *The African-American Almanac,* 6th ed., p. 217; Thum, *Hippocrene U.S.A. Guide to Black America,* p. 41.

c. 1860s ◆ Born a slave in Tennessee, **Mary Fields** (?–1914) worked in western Montana as a cowgirl for the Ursuline nuns at the Saint Peter's Mission School. However, after becoming involved in a shoot-out with a man, she was ordered by the local bishop to leave the mission. The nuns then helped her find a job running a restaurant in the mining town of Cascade, Montana. After the restaurant failed, Fields found her true calling as a U.S. mail coach driver. She became the first black woman, and the second woman ever, to serve in this position. By her later years "Stagecoach Mary" was already a legend. She had a reputation for smoking cigars and spending time in the saloon, not to mention fighting on a par with men. Yet she is remembered as one of Cascade's leading citizens and a truly colorful character of the Wild West.

Sources: Pelz, *Black Heroes of the Wild West,* pp. 43–46; Thum, *Hippocrene U.S.A. Guide to Black America,* pp. 48, 208.

c. 1862 ◆ **Clara Brown** (c. 1803–1877), a former slave from Missouri, is credited with opening the first laundry and the first Sunday school in the Colorado Territory. She became a wealthy, leading citizen of Central City, Colorado, and devoted herself to charitable causes, including locating and transporting 38 of her relatives to the West. Brown was buried with honors from the Colorado Pioneers Association and is remembered with a memorial chair at the Central City Opera House.

Sources: Cantor, *Historic Landmarks of Black America,* pp. 297–98; Pelz, *Black Heroes of the Wild West,* pp. 25–28

1871 ◆ **George Washington** (1817–1905) was the first black American to found a large integrated city in the United States. Born in Virginia to a white mother, Washington was then adopted by a white family who moved to the frontier. In 1850 he moved to the Oregon Territory and homesteaded in present-day Washington. He established Centralia in 1872, when the Northern Pacific Railroad crossed his land. A city park bears his name.

Sources: Cantor, *Historic Landmarks of Black America,* p. 336; *Dictionary of American Negro Biography,* p. 638; Katz, *The Black West,* pp. 72–73.

1887 ◆ Eatonville, Florida, was the first incorporated town in the United States established by blacks. The town is also celebrated as the birthplace of black author Zora Neale Hurston, for whom Eatonville's annual Festival of the Arts is named.

Sources: Garrett, *Famous First Facts About Negroes,* p. 191; Pederson, ed., *African American Almanac,* U·X·L ed., p. 160.

1889 ◆ **"Nigger Add"** (Old Add, Old Negro Ad) was the first known range boss in the Southwest in the early part of the twentieth century. He was also a rider and roper. He worked most of his active life with cattleman George W. Littlefield or his outfits in the Texas Panhandle and Eastern Mexico.

Source: Dictionary of American Negro Biography, pp. 5–6.

1900 ◆ One of the few black pioneers of Alaska, **Mattie Crosby** first came to the territory in 1900 with a Maine family who adopted her. Some blacks came into the territory during the era of the Gold Rush, and others were occasionally seen aboard ships that brought in supplies. Still, for nearly 17 years Crosby lived in Fairbanks without meeting another black.

Source: Estell, ed., *The African-American Almanac,* 6th ed., p. 215.

1905 ◆ **George McJunkin** (1851–1922), cowboy, bronc buster, Indian arrowhead collector, and explorer, was the first person to recognize bones of extinct bison near Folsom, New Mexico, and try to call them to the attention of other people. The bones themselves were less significant than the spear points found with them. He had discovered the first site that proved people lived in North America over 10,000 years ago.

Sources: Dictionary of American Negro Biography, pp. 417-18; Durham, *The Negro Cowboys,* pp. 159–60; *Negro Almanac,* p. 215.

Matthew Henson

1909 ◆ **Matthew Alexander Henson** (1866–1955) was the first black man to reach the North Pole, of which he was co-discoverer with Robert E. Peary. There is some debate whether Peary was accurate in his claim to have reached the pole, but Henson went ahead to blaze the trail while Peary, whose toes were frozen, was pulled on the sledge. Henson planted the flag at the location Peary determined to be the pole, since Peary was unable to stand. In 1961 Maryland erected a monument on the grounds of the state capital to honor Henson. He recounted his experiences in *A Negro Explorer at the North Pole* (1912).

Sources: Cantor, *Historic Landmarks of Black America,* pp. 62–64; *Dictionary of American Negro Biography,* p. 308; Garrett, *Famous First Facts About Negroes,* p. 68.

Film and Television

Film

1905 ◆ *The Wooing and Wedding of a Coon* became the earliest known American-made film with an all-black cast. The one-reel, white-produced film presented undisguised mockery of a black couple.

Sources: Bergman, *The Chronological History of the American Negro in America*, p. 347; Klotman, *Frame by Frame*, p. 585; *Negro Almanac*, p. 1234.

c. 1912 ◆ Around 1912 **William Foster** (1884–?) produced the first short black film, *The Railroad Porter*. A show business veteran, Foster worked as a press agent for such stars as the dance-comedy duo Williams & Walker. His other films include *The Fall Guy* and *The Barber*.

Sources: Bennett, *Before the Mayflower*, p. 631; Bogle, *Toms, Coons, Mulattoes, Mammies, & Bucks*, p. 102.

1914 ◆ **Sam Lucas** (Samuel Milady, 1840–1916) was the first African American to play the title role in *Uncle Tom's Cabin*. He had been the first black man to play Uncle Tom on stage in 1878. Born in Washington, Ohio, Lucas performed with major minstrel troupes, wrote one of the most popular minstrel songs of the 1870s ("Carve dat 'Possum"), appeared in vaudeville, and starred in musical comedies, including *A Trip to Coontown* (1898). He is also known as the first black composer of popular ballads.

Sources: Emery, *Black Dance*, pp. 205, 209; Johnson, *Black Manhattan*, pp. 90–92, 102, 113; Southern, *The Music of Black Americans*, p. 237.

1915 ◆ **Madame Sul-Te-Wan** (1873–1959) was the first black American to be hired by a major movie producer on a continuing basis. D. W. Griffith hired her after she worked on *Birth of a Nation*.

Sources: Beasley, *The Negro Trail Blazers of California*, p. 237; *Black Women in America*, pp. 1129–32; *Notable Black American Women*, pp. 1093–94; *Our World* 9 (February 1954), 80–82.

1919 ◆ In 1919 **Oscar Deveraux Micheaux** (1884–1951) produced and directed *The Homesteader*, the first full-length film by an African American. A year earlier the Lincoln Picture Company, an independent black film pro-

Hattie McDaniel

duction company, tried to buy the film rights to Micheaux's novel of the same title. When Micheaux insisted that he direct the planned movie, the deal fell through. Micheaux then went to New York, where he formed the Oscar Micheaux Corporation and completed the film himself. Between 1919 and 1937 Micheaux made about 30 films, including *Body and Soul* (1924), in which Paul Robeson made his screen debut. In 1931 Micheaux released the first all-talking film by a black company, *The Exile*.

Sources: Bogle, *Toms, Coons, Mulattoes, Mammies, & Bucks,* pp. 109–16; *Encyclopedia of Black America,* pp. 574–75; Estell, ed., *African American Almanac,* 6th ed., pp. 985–86.

1926 ◆ **Stepin Fetchit** (Lincoln Theodore Monroe Andrew Perry, 1902–1985) and **Carolynne Snowden** played in the first on-screen black romance in the film *In Old Kentucky.* Fetchit, an actor and comedian, was the first black actor to receive feature billing in movies, and the first African American to appear in films with such stars as Will Rogers and Shirley Temple. He appeared in films in the 1920s and 1930s. The Key West, Florida, native took his stage name from a race horse on which he had bet in Oklahoma, before he left for Hollywood in the 1920s.

Sources: Encyclopedia of Black America, p. 38; Hornsby, Jr., *Milestones in Twentieth-Century African-American History,* pp. 345–46; *Split Image,* p. 138.

1928 ◆ The first black sound film was *Melancholy Dame,* a comedy two-reeler starring Evelyn Preer, Roberta Hyson, Edward Thompson, and Spencer Williamson.

Source: Klotman, *Frame by Frame,* p. 347.

1929 ◆ The first two full-length films with all-black casts were *Hearts in Dixie,* starring Daniel Haynes, Nina Mae McKinney, and Victoria Spivey, and *Hallelujah,* starring Clarence Muse, Stepin Fetchit, and Mildred Washington. *Hearts in Dixie* was also the first black-oriented full sound film from a major company.

Sources: Bergman, *The Chronological History of the Negro in America,* p. 447; Kane, *Famous First Facts,* p. 401; Klotman, *Frame by Frame,* pp. 217–18, 227; Southern, *The Music of Black Americans,* pp. 436–437.

1940 ◆ **Hattie McDaniel** (1895–1952) was the first African American to win an Oscar. She was named best supporting actress for her portrayal of Mammy in *Gone with the Wind*. (In 1990 Whoopi Goldberg became the second black actress so honored, for her supporting role in *Ghost*.) McDaniel made her radio debut in 1915 and is said to be the first black American woman to sing on radio. Often called "Hi-Hat Hattie," she was born in Wichita, Kansas, and moved to Hollywood in 1931. She made her movie debut in *The Golden West* in 1932 and appeared in more than 300 films during the next two decades. Her career was built on the "Mammy" image, a role she played with dignity. In 1947 she continued the role in "Beulah" on the radio.

Dorothy Dandridge and Harry Belafonte in *Carmen Jones*

Sources: Dictionary of American Negro Biography, pp. 414–15; Hornsby, Jr., *Milestones in Twentieth-Century African-American History,* p. 35; *Negro Almanac,* p. 1426; *Notable Black American Women,* pp. 703–5.

Sidney Poitier

1955 ♦ **Dorothy Dandridge** (1922–1965) was the first black woman nominated for an Oscar in a leading role for her portrayal of Carmen in *Carmen Jones*. From 1937 to 1964 Dandridge appeared in a number of films, often typecast in the stereotypical roles commonly given to black actresses. In 1951 she was the first African American to perform in the Empire Room of New York's Waldorf Astoria. *Island in the Sun*, a 1957 film in which she appeared opposite white actor John Justin, marked the first time the theme of interracial love was explored in the movies. Harry Belafonte and Joan Fontaine were also paired in this film. Dandridge returned to nightclub performances when her film career ended.

Sources: Dictionary of American Negro Biography, pp. 157–58; Lee, Interesting People, p. 129; Notable Black American Women, pp. 248–49.

1958 ♦ The first black male nominated for an Academy Award for best actor was **Sidney Poitier** (1924–), for his performance in *The Defiant Ones*. He made his Hollywood debut in 1950 and won an Oscar for best actor in the film *Lilies of the Field* in 1963, becoming the first African American to win an Oscar for a starring role. In 1967 Poitier became the first African American to have the prints of his hands and feet installed in front of Grauman's Chinese Theater.

Sources: Encyclopedia of Black America, p. 697; Kane, Famous First Facts, p. 405; Negro Almanac, pp. 191, 1153.

1969 ♦ A gifted film director, **Gordon Parks** (1912–) was the first African American to direct movies for a major studio. His first was *The Learning Tree*, released in 1969. Two years later he ushered in a new era in black film with the huge box office hit *Shaft*, which was quickly followed by *Shaft's Big Score!* (1972). (*See* **1971**; *See also* **Media: Photojournalism, 1949**.)

Sources: Bogle, Toms, Coons, Mulattoes, Mammies, & Bucks, pp. 226–27, 239; Estell, ed., African American Almanac, 6th ed., pp. 1190–91.

1970 ♦ **Maya Angelou** (Marguerite Johnson, 1928–) was the first black woman to have an original screenplay produced, *Georgia, Georgia,* which she directed. Angelou was also the first black woman to have a nonfiction work on the best-seller list. Her autobiographical *I Know Why the Caged Bird Sings* (1969) evoked images of a black girl's childhood in the South. It was nominated for a 1974 National Book Award and aired as a television movie in 1979. An artist of wide-ranging talents, she was nominated for a Tony award for acting and a Pulitzer Prize for poetry. She became the first black inaugural poet, at the swearing in of President Bill Clinton. (*See also* **Literature: Poetry, 1993**.)

Sources: Current Biography, 1974, pp. 12–15; *Jet* (8 February 1993), pp. 4–10; Lanker, *I Dream a World,* p. 162; *Notable Black American Women,* pp. 23–27.

1971 ◆ **Richard Roundtree** (1942–) became the first black private detective and super-hero character in the trend-setting movie *Shaft.* Born in New Rochelle, New York, he attended Southern Illinois University on a football scholarship and became interested in acting in campus theater. In 1967 he was a model for the Ebony Fashion Fair and later advertised hair care products for black men in *Ebony* magazine. After Bill Cosby advised him to study dramatic arts in New York, Roundtree joined the Negro Ensemble Company and appeared in three of their productions.

Source: Ebony Success Library, vol. 2, pp. 224–27.

1982 ◆ **Louis Gossett, Jr.** (1936–) became the first African American to win an Oscar for best supporting actor for his role as a drill instructor in *An Officer and a Gentleman.* (Denzel Washington became the second African American so honored, for his role in the 1989 film *Glory*.) Gossett began acting at 17 when a leg injury prevented him from pursuing his first love, basketball. In 1953 he won out over 445 contenders for the role of a black youngster in *Take a Giant Step,* for which he received a Donaldson Award as Best Newcomer of the Year. Gossett has appeared in more than 60 stage productions and has also played numerous characters on television. In 1977 he won an Emmy for his performance in *Roots.* He has also starred in such films as *Skin Game* (1971), *The Deep* (1977), *Iron Eagle* (1986), and *Iron Eagle II* (1988).

Source: Estell, ed., *African American Almanac,* 6th ed., pp. 973–74.

1985 ◆ *The Color Purple* became the first black-oriented film to capture 11 Oscar nominations. Adapted from Alice Walker's Pulitzer Prize-winning novel and directed by Steven Spielberg, the controversial film unfortunately never received a single award, despite several fine performances, including those by Whoopi Goldberg and Oprah Winfrey, both in debut roles. (*See also* **Literature: Novels, 1983**.)

Source: Bogle, *Toms, Coons, Mulattoes, Mammies, & Bucks,* pp. 292–93.

1986 ◆ **Spike Lee** (1957–) released his first major picture, *She's Gotta Have It,* which also ranks as the first artistically and financially successful black film made independently of Hollywood. Although completed on a shoe-string budget of $175,000, the film grossed over $7 million and firmly launched Lee's filmmaking career. While at New York University he wrote and directed *Joe's Bed-Sty Barbershop: We Cut Heads,* for which he won the 1982 Student Academy award given by the Academy of Motion Picture Arts and Sciences. The film that solidified Lee's reputation (and prompted every Hollywood studio to seek its own maverick black director) was *Do the Right Thing* (1989). Movie critic Roger Ebert called it "the most honest, complex and unblinking film I have ever seen about the subject of racism." The film that clinched Lee's hold upon the title "America's first black movie mogul" (a title given him in Alex Patterson's unauthorized biography) was *Malcolm X* (1992), which also ranks as his most controversial film to date. In 1994 Lee released *Crooklyn,* his seventh feature film.

Sources: Estell, ed., *African American Almanac,* 6th ed., pp. 982–83; Pederson, ed., *African American Almanac,* U·X·L ed., pp. 459–61.

1989 ◆ **Euzhan Palcy** was the first black woman director of a full-length film, *A Dry White Season,* for a major U.S. studio. Starring Donald Sutherland and Susan Sarandon, the film deals with apartheid in South Africa. Palcy was born in Martinique.

Sources: Jet 81 (18 November 1991), p.62; *Movies on TV and Videocassette, 1993–1994,* p. 295.

1992 ◆ **Julie Dash** (1952–) became the first black woman writer and director to have a feature-length film in national distribution. The film *Daughters of the Dust* is the story of one day in the lives of a black family living on Ibo Island, South Carolina.

Sources: Black Women in America, pp. 301–2; *Essence* 22 (February 1992), pp. 38.

John Singleton (1968–) was the first black director nominated for an Academy Award for the box office hit *Boys N the Hood,* starring rap artist Ice Cube, Cuba Gooding, Jr., Larry Fishburne, and Morris Chesnut. Although the film presents an anti-drug and anti-violence message, it sparked violence when it opened in several cities in the United States on July 12, 1991.

Sources: Hornsby, Jr., *Milestones in Twentieth Century African-American History,* p. 479; *Time* 139 (23 March 1992).

1993 ◆ **Woody Strode** (1914–), known for his groundbreaking roles in films, was the first African American inducted into the Walk of Western stars at a ceremony held at the California Institute of the Arts in Valencia, California. Strode acted in such films as *Sergeant Rutledge* and *Posse.*

Source: *Jet* 84 (3 May 1993), p. 34.

John Singleton

Television

1948 ◆ **Timmie Rogers,** entertainer, comedian, dancer, singer, composer, and musician, launched the first all-black show, *Sugar Hill Times,* on CBS television. Known for his famous "Oh, Yeah!" trademark, he is sometimes called the "dean of black comedians" and has inspired such black entertainers as Red Foxx, Dick Gregory, Nipsey Russell, and Slappy White. He also wrote song hits for Nat King Cole and Sarah Vaughan.

Source: *Ebony Success Library,* vol. 1, p. 268.

Hazel Dorothy Scott (1920–1981) was the first black performer to have her own network television program, from 1948 to 1950. The musician, singer, actress, social activist, and child prodigy was born in Port-of-Spain, Trinidad, and moved to the United States at about age four. She studied at Juilliard School of Music.

Sources: Feather, *Encyclopedia of Jazz,* p. 412; *Notable Black American Women,* pp. 997–98.

1949 ◆ *Happy Pappy* was the first black variety talent show series with an all-black cast. First televised on April 1, 1949, on WENR-TV in Chicago, the show featured the Four Vagabonds and the Modern Modes. Ray Grant was master of ceremonies.

Source: Kane, *Famous First Facts,* p. 657.

1952 ◆ The first black variety show on network television was *The Billy Daniels Show,* shown on CBS. A 15-minute musical variety series, this was the first network television show with a black host. It lasted 13 weeks. The second black variety show, *The Nat King Cole Show,* appeared in 1956–57 on NBC.

Source: *Split Image,* pp. 257, 285.

Cicely Tyson

1956 ♦ **Sammy Davis, Jr.** (1926–1990) became the first African American to star in a dramatic role for mainstream TV in an episode of *GE Theater.* Known as America's "Ambassador of Goodwill" and "the world's greatest entertainer," he began his career at age three, performing in vaudeville with his father, Sam, Sr., and his uncle, Will Mastin. This singer, dancer, and actor appeared on almost every variety show and comedy series on network television between 1956 and 1980. In 1969 Davis became the first black entertainer to sleep in the White House. He made his last film appearance in 1989 with Gregory Hines in *Tap.*

Sources: Davis and Boyar, *Why Me?* pp. 77–8, 89–91; Estell, ed., *African American Almanac,* 6th ed., p. 966–67; Hornsby, Jr., *Milestones in Twentieth Century African-American History,* p. 447; *Jet* 78 (June 4, 1990), pp. 32, 34; Southern, *Biographical Dictionary of Afro-American and African Musicians,* p. 96.

1957 ♦ The first black producer of network television programs at NBC was **George E. Norford** (1918–). He was the only black correspondent on the staff of the army weekly magazine *Yank* during World War II.

Source: Ebony Success Library, vol. 1, p. 237.

1959 ♦ **Harry (Harold George) Belafonte, Jr.** (1927–) singer, actor, and civil rights crusader, was the first African American to have an hour-long special on television. Born in New York City, he lived in Jamaica from 1935 to 1940. He received a Tony Award in 1954 for a supporting role in *John Murray Anderson's Almanac.* In 1966 Belafonte was the first African American to produce a major show for television. During President John F. Kennedy's administration, he became the first cultural adviser to the Peace Corps. In 1990 he was the first person to receive the Nelson Mandela Courage Award of TransAfrica Forum.

Sources: Current Biography, 1956, pp. 45–47; *Ebony Success Library,* vol. 2, pp. 6–9; *Encyclopedia of Black America,* p. 170; Garrett, *Famous First Facts About Negroes,* p. 189; *Jet* 78 (23 April 1990), p. 6, 81 (18 November 1991), pp. 6, 8.

1963 ♦ **Cicely Tyson** (1942–) became the first African American to appear in a key part on a television series when she won a regular feature role in *East Side, West Side.* She studied acting at the Actors Playhouse and made

her Broadway debut with a hit role in *The Dark of the Moon*. Tyson had successful roles in a number of films, including black films, and was universally hailed by critics for her portrayal of a sharecropper's wife in *Sounder*. She is regarded as one of the most gifted actresses in Hollywood.

Bill Cosby with cast of *The Cosby Show*

Sources: *Current Biography, 1975*, pp. 422–25; *Ebony Success Library*, vol. 2, pp. 264–67; *Notable Black American Women*, pp. 1160–64.

1965 ◆ **Bill Cosby** (1937–) broke the color barrier in television and became the first black to star in a mainstream TV series, NBC's *I Spy*. By the end of the season, the show was a hit and Cosby was honored with an Emmy—the first of three and the first by a black—for best actor in a dramatic series. Cosby was also the first black star in a television series that excluded racial themes. Born in Germantown, Pennsylvania, he began comedy routines when he was in the fifth grade. Cosby entered Temple University on a track and football scholarship, dropped out in his sophomore year to perform in Philadelphia coffee houses, and later returned to Temple to complet his doctorate degree. In 1972 Cosby launched the Saturday morning cartoon series *Fat Albert and the Cosby Kids,* the first show of its kind to feature blacks as its main characters. In 1984 *The Cosby Show*—the first black show to break with all the stereotypes about black families—debuted and quickly soared to the number one position in the TV ratings. Until the final episode in 1992, it remained consistently among the ten most popular shows on television. Cosby, an outspoken critic of black images in television, became the first and only black to make a bid to purchase NBC on October 28, 1992. (*See also* **Education: College Fund-Raising, 1988.**)

Sources: *Ebony Success Library,* vol. 1, p, 80; *Encyclopedia of Black America,* pp. 289, 724; Estell, ed., *African American Almanac,* 6th ed., pp. 963-64; Herbert and Hill, *Bill Cosby,* pp. ; Lee, *Interesting People,* p. 154; Pederson, ed., *African American Almanac,* U·X·L ed., pp. 464-66; Rosenberg, *Bill Cosby: The Changing Black Image; Tennessean Showcase* (26 April 1992).

1968 ◆ **Diahann Carroll** (1935–) was the first black woman to have her own television series in a nonstereotypical role in the weekly NBC series *Julia.* Born Carol Diahann Johnson in the Bronx, New York City, she graduated from the High School of Music and Art. She began singing at age six in Adam Clayton Powell's Abyssinian Baptist Church in Harlem.

Sources: *Current Biography, 1962,* pp. 74–76; *Ebony Success Library,* vol. 1, p. 59; *Notable Black American Women,* pp. 160–63.

Charles Hobson wrote what may have been the nation's first black-produced community program on television, *Inside Bedford-Stuyvesant,* while he was with WNEW-TV in New York City. He has also served as writer-producer for the National Educational Television series *Black Journal.*

Source: *Ebony Success Library,* vol. 1, p. 153.

1969 ◆ The first black actress to receive an Emmy award was **Gail Fisher** (1935–). She was also the first African American to have a speaking part in a nationally televised commercial in 1961 and is the only black woman to receive the Duse Award from the Lee Strasberg Actors Studio.

Sources: *Ebony* (November 1974), p. 77 (November 1975), p. 158 (October 1978), p. 40; *Negro Almanac,* pp. 1137–38; *Who's Who among Black Americans, 1992-1993,* p. 458.

Della Reese (1932–) was the first black woman to host a television variety show, *The Della Reese Show.* The show was broadcast five days a week in the 1969–70 season. Reese also appeared in the television shows *Chico and the Man* (1976–78) and *The Royal Family* (1991–92). Reese sang with Mahalia Jackson's chorus and also appeared with Erskine Hawkins's band.

Sources: Black Women in America, p. 967; *Current Biography, 1971,* pp. 338–40; *Encyclopedia of Black America,* p. 729; Southern, *Biographical Dictionary of African-American and African Musicians,* p. 319.

1970 ◆ **Flip (Clerow) Wilson** (1933–) was the first black man to have a weekly prime time comedy television show in his own name. Through such characters as Geraldine and the Reverend Leroy he quickly gained national fame. Wilson served in the U.S. Air Force and was a regular at the Apollo Theater in Harlem.

Sources: Current Biography, 1969, pp. 454–56; *Ebony* 25 (December 1970), pp. 176–82, 27 (December 1971), p. 67; *Encyclopedia of Black America,* p. 860.

1972 ◆ The first black television show sponsored by a black business was *Soul Train.* Johnson Products, Inc., supported the show, which began locally in Chicago and then spread nationwide.

Source: Alford, *Famous First Blacks,* p. 76.

1975 ◆ *The Jeffersons,* the first and only black show to run 11 seasons, made its debut. Starring Isabel Sanford, Sherman Hemsley, and Marla Gibbs, the show not only became the longest-running black series in TV history but also was the first to feature an interracial couple (the Jeffersons' neighbors) and the first to portray wealthy African Americans.

Source: Jet 81 (18 November 1991), p. 45.

1977 ◆ *Roots,* the television miniseries inspired by Alex Haley's novel, was the first show of its kind in network history to deal forthrightly with the African American experience. It aired for eight consecutive days in January 1977 and scored the highest ratings of any TV program ever. In all some 130 million viewers saw *Roots,* which became the most talked about black program of the decade. Prominent among the large cast were LeVar Burton (better known to younger viewers as Lieutenant Geordi LaForge in *Star Trek: The Next Generation,* 1987–94), John Amos, Ben Vereen, Leslie Uggams, Louis Gossett, Jr., Cicely Tyson, and Richard Roundtree. A sequel, *Roots: The Next Generation,* appeared in 1979 over the course of seven nights. Although not quite as popular as the original miniseries, the sequel won all of its time slots and attracted an overall audience of 110 million. (*See also* **Literature: Novels, 1977.**)

Sources: Estell, ed., *African American Almanac,* 6th ed., pp. 829–31; Pederson, ed., *African American Almanac,* U˙X˙L ed., pp. 469-70.

1980 ◆ **Robert L. Johnson** (1946–) was the first African American to found and own a black-oriented cable television network, Black Entertainment Television (BET). BET premiered on January 25, 1980, and marked the first time that viewers had access to quality programming that reflected the needs, interests, and lifestyles of black Americans.

Sources: Hornsby, Jr., *Milestones in Twentieth-Century African-American History,* p. 494; *Jet* 77 (16 October 1989), p. 40.

1989 ◆ **Arsenio Hall** (1960–) was the first African American to host a nationally broadcast weekly television talk show. He was born in Cleveland and began his career as a standup comic. Hall starred with Eddie Murphy in the film *Coming to America.*

Sources: Negro Almanac, p. 1142; *Who's Who Among Black Americans, 1992–1993,* p. 581.

Jennifer Karen Lawson (1946–) became executive vice-president of programming for the Public Broadcasting Service (PBS) in Washington, D.C. The highest-ranking black woman to serve in public television, she oversees the creation, promotion, and scheduling of national programming for 330 stations. For the first time, her appointment centralizes national program decision-making in one executive. *The Civil War,* which was aired under her administration, drew over 50 million viewers and became the most-watched show in PBS history.

Sources: Contemporary Black Biography, vol. 1, pp. 137–38; *Essence* 21 (August 1966), p. 37.

Fine and Applied Arts

Architecture • Cartoons • Painting • Photography • Sculpture

Architecture

1806 ◆ The African Meeting House was the first major building in Boston to be constructed entirely by African Americans. (*See also* **Religion: Baptists, 1806.**)

Sources: Cantor, *Historic Landmarks of Black America,* pp. 70–71; *Dictionary of American Negro Biography,* p. 483; *Negro Almanac,* p. 208.

1908 ◆ **Vertner W. Tandy, Sr.** (1885–1949) was the first black American architect registered in New York State. He designed Villa Lewaro, the mansion of hair care millionaire Madame C.J. Walker, on the Hudson River. Tandy is also known for founding Alpha Phi Alpha fraternity at Cornell University.

Sources: Garrett, *Famous First Facts About Negroes,* p. 72; *Who's Who in Colored America, 1929,* p. 352.

1953 ◆ **Paul Revere Williams** (1894–1980) was the first black architect to become a fellow of the American Institute of Architects. Certified in California in 1915, he designed homes and buildings for Hollywood celebrities. In addition to designing more than 3,000 homes, Williams served as associate architect for the $50 million Los Angeles International Airport.

Sources: Cederholm, *Afro-American Artists,* p. 307; *Negro Almanac,* p. 1092; Robinson, *Historical Negro Biographies,* pp. 262–63.

1954 ◆ **Norma Merrick Sklarek** (1928–) was the first black woman registered architect. Certified in New York and later in California (1962), she was also the first black woman fellow of the American Institute of Architects in 1980.

Sources: Black Women in America, pp. 1042–43; Lanker, *I Dream a World,* p. 41; *Notable Black American Women,* p. 1027.

Cartoons

1910 ◆ **George Herriman** (1880–1944) was the first African American to achieve fame as a syndicated cartoonist. Early versions of Herriman's Ignatz Mouse and Krazy Kat appeared on July 26, 1910. The strip *Krazy Kat* was extremely popular, especially with intellectuals, in the 1920s, and continued with somewhat less success until July 25, 1944. Herriman was born in New Orleans in a family classified as black, and the family moved to Los Angeles to escape racial labeling. Some of his friends called him "The Greek," but he never revealed his background.

Source: McDonnell, O'Connell, de Havenon, *Krazy Kat,* p. 30–31, 55.

1933 ◆ **E(lmer) Simms Campbell** (1906–1971) was the first black cartoonist to work for national publications. The St. Louis–born artist contributed cartoons and other art work to *Esquire* (he was in nearly every issue from 1933 to 1958), *Cosmopolitan, Red Book, New Yorker, Opportunity,* and syndicated features in 145 newspapers. Campbell created the character "Esky," the pop-eyed mascot who appeared on the cover of *Esquire.*

Sources: Dictionary of Black Culture, p. 81; *Encyclopedia of Black America,* 214; *Who's Who in Colored America, 1950,* p. 592.

1964 ◆ **Morrie (Morris) Turner** (1923–) created "Wee Pals," the first integrated comic strip in the world. Influenced by Charles Schulz's "Peanuts" and inspired by comedian and civil rights activist Dick Gregory, "Wee Pals" became nationally syndicated and appeared in all of the large daily and Sunday comics. Nippie, the main character in "Wee Pals," is named for the comedian Nipsey Russell.

Sources: Contemporary Authors, vol. 29–32, p. 646; *Ebony Success Library,* vol. 1, p. 311; *Essence* 5 (July 1974), pp. 58–59, 64, 67.

1991 ◆ **Barbara Brandon** (1958–) became the first black woman cartoonist nationally syndicated in the white press. Her comic strip, "Where I'm Coming From," appeared first in the *Detroit Free Press* and was acquired by Universal Press Syndicate in 1991. Brandon's father, Brumsic Brandon, Jr., was creator of the "Luther" comic strip, which first appeared in the late 1960s.

Sources: Black Women in America, pp. 161–62; *Contemporary Black Biography,* vol. 3, pp. 16–17.

Painting

1798 ♦ **Joshua Johnston** (1765–1830) was the first black portrait painter to win recognition in America. Born a slave, he lived and worked in the Baltimore, Maryland, area. A highly accomplished craftsman, Johnston was probably the first African American in America to become a professional artist. An advertisement in the *Baltimore Intelligencer* on December 19, 1798, stated that Johnston was a "self-taught genius." He painted many prominent citizens and his works are in many museum collections.

Sources: Dictionary of American Negro Biography, p. 362; *Encyclopedia of Black America,* p. 118; Garrett, *Famous First Facts About Negroes,* p. 17.

1842 ♦ **Robert Scott Duncanson** (1817–1872) was the first black American painter to win acclaim at home and abroad as a serious landscape artist and muralist.

Sources: Cederholm, *Afro-American Artists,* pp. 83–85; *Dictionary of American Negro Biography,* p. 203; Dwight, *Negro History Bulletin* 18 (December 1954), p. 53.

Henry Ossawa Tanner

1876 ♦ **Edward Mitchell Bannister** (1828–1901) was the first African American to achieve full recognition in America as a painter. The most renowned black artist of the nineteenth century, he specialized in landscapes. Bannister received the gold medal in the Philadelphia Centennial Exhibition of 1876 for his huge landscape *Under the Oaks.* He was one of the founders of the Providence Art Club, which developed into the Rhode Island School of Design.

Sources: Cederholm, *Afro-American Artists,* pp. 15–16; *Dictionary of American Negro Biography,* p. 25–26; Garrett, *Famous First Facts About Negroes,* p. 18.

1927 ♦ **Henry Ossawa Tanner** (1859–1937) was the first black artist elected to full membership in the National Academy. Tanner studied at the Pennsylvania Academy of the Fine Arts and in France, where he settled. He developed a fine reputation, based principally on his biblical paintings, on both sides of the Atlantic.

Sources: Cederholm, *Afro-American Artists,* pp. 272–75; *Dictionary of American Negro Biography,* p. 577; Garrett, *Famous First Facts About Negroes,* p.18.

Edmonia Lewis

Laura Wheeler Waring (1887–1948) was the first black woman to receive the Harmon Award for her painting. She painted prominent persons in the struggle for black culture and taught for more than 30 years at Cheyney Training School for Teachers in Philadelphia.

Sources: Black Women in America, pp. 1124–25; *Dictionary of American Negro Biography,* p. 632; *Jet* 65 (6 February 1984), p. 67; *Notable Black American Women,* pp. 1205–06.

1970 ◆ **Jacob Lawrence, Jr.** (1917–) was the first black artist to receive the NAACP's Spingarn Award. Considered one of America's premier artists, he is represented in many museum collections. Lawrence depicted Toussaint L'Ouverture, John Brown, Harriet Tubman, the struggles of the Revolutionary heroes, and Harlem settings in his paintings.

Sources: Encyclopedia of Black America, p. 498; *Negro Almanac,* pp. 1050–51; Robinson, *Historic Negro Biographies,* p. 222.

Photography

1884 ◆ **James Conway Farley** (1854–1910) of Richmond, Virginia, was the first black American to gain recognition as a photographer. He won first prize at the Colored Industrial Fair in Richmond in 1884 and a premium at the New Orleans World Exposition in 1885, where he exhibited with white photographers. Of the many photographs he made, only one remains that is attributed to him with certainty.

Sources: Dictionary of American Negro Biography, p. 219; Richings, *Evidences of Progress Among Colored People,* p. 495; Simmons, *Men of Mark,* pp. 801–04.

Sculpture

1870 ◆ **Mary Edmonia Lewis** (1845–c. 1890) was the first black American sculptor to study abroad and in 1871 was the first black artist to exhibit in Rome. After studying at Oberlin College, Ohio, she opened a studio in Boston and earned enough money to move to Europe. Lewis received many commissions for her neoclassical sculptures from eminent and wealthy persons in the United States. She received national recognition at Philadelphia's Centennial Exhibition in 1876.

Sources: Cederholm, *Afro-American Artists*, pp. 176–78; *Dictionary of American Negro Biography*, pp. 393–95; *Notable Black American Women*, pp. 663–66.

1934 ◆ **Augusta Fells Savage** (1892–1962) was the first black member of the National Association of Women Painters and Sculptors. One of her major commissions was the sculpture *Lift Every Voice and Sing* for the 1939–40 New York World's Fair. This work, which became Savage's best known and most widely recognized, symbolizes African American contributions to music. Another of her better-known works is *The Negro Urchin.*

Sources: Black Women in America, pp. 1010–13; *Encyclopedia of Black Culture*, p. 741; *Notable Black American Women*, pp. 979–83.

Augusta Savage

1943 ◆ **Selma (Hortense) Burke** (1900–) was the first black sculptor to design a U.S. coin. She won a competition to design the portrait of President Franklin D. Roosevelt that appeared on the dime.

Sources: Black Women in America, pp. 190–95; Cederholm, *Afro-American Artists*, p. 41; *Notable Black American Women*, pp. 128–30; *Who's Who in Colored America, 1950*, p. 77.

1945 ◆ **Richmond Barthé** (1901–1989) was the first black sculptor elected to the National Academy of Arts and Letters. In 1946 he was commissioned to sculpt the bust of Booker T. Washington, to be placed in the American Hall of Fame of New York University. He is noted for his sensitive small bronzes and monumental statues.

Sources: Cederholm, *Afro-American Artists*, pp. 17–18; *Encyclopedia Americana*, 1988, vol. 3, p.278; Garrett, *Famous First Facts About Negroes*, p. 175.

Justice, Law Enforcement, and Public Safety

Lawyers and Judges

1845 ◆ **Macon B. Allen** (1816–1894) of Worcester, Massachusetts, was the first African American formally admitted to the bar in any state on May 3, 1845. He had been allowed to practice in Maine two years earlier. Born in Indiana, Allen was a businessman in Portland, Maine. He moved to Massachusetts to practice law. By 1870 he moved to South Carolina, where he entered politics and, in 1872, became one of the first black judges, as a judge of the Inferior Court. (Mifflin W. Gibbs was the first black judge that year in the municipal court of Little Rock.) Little is known of his life after the 1870s; in 1894 he died in Washington, D.C.

Sources: Bennett, *Before the Mayflower,* p. 639; *Dictionary of American Negro Biography,* pp. 11–12; Garrett, *Famous First Facts about Negroes,* p. 93; *Negro Almanac,* p. 13.

1865 ◆ **John Sweat Rock** (1825–1866) was the first black man admitted to practice before the U.S. Supreme Court, but not the first to argue a case. Following his admission to the court, he may have been the first black lawyer received on the floor of the House of Representatives. A native of Salem, New Jersey, Rock practiced both dentistry and medicine before his health forced him to give up his practice and study law.

Sources: Dictionary of American Negro Biography, pp. 529–31; Garrett, *Famous First Facts About Negroes,* p. 23, 93; *Journal of Negro History* 52 (July 1967), pp. 169–75; Kane, *Famous First Facts,* p. 345.

1869 ◆ **George Lewis Ruffin** (1834–1886) was the first African American to graduate from Harvard University Law School and perhaps the first black American to graduate from any university law school in the United States. Also in 1869 he became one of the first African Americans to practice law in Boston. He became the first black Massachusetts judge when he was named to the District Court of Charlestown, Massachusetts, on November 19,

ANTISLAVERY LAWS

August 6, 1861	The Congressional confiscation bill frees slaves forced to fight against the U.S. government or work in support of the rebellion.
July 22, 1862	The District of Columbia passes a law abolishing slavery.
January 1, 1863	Emancipation Proclamation.
June 19, 1863	West Virginia admitted as a state with a constitution forbidding slavery.
January 11, 1864	Missouri amends constitution, forbidding slavery.
March 14, 1864	Arkansas amends constitution, forbidding slavery.
May 11, 1864	Louisiana amends constitution, forbidding slavery.
June 28, 1864	Fugitive Slave Acts of 1793 and 1850 are repealed.
July 6, 1864	Maryland amends constitution, forbidding slavery.
June 19, 1865	Texas slaves are informed by proclamation that they are free.
July 13, 1865	The provisional governor of Georgia abolishes slavery by proclamation.
July 20, 1865	The provisional governor of Arkansas abolishes slavery by proclamation.
July 21, 1865	Mississippi amends constitution, forbidding slavery.
August 3, 1865	The provisional governor of Florida abolishes slavery by proclamation.
September 28, 1865	South Carolina amends constitution, forbidding slavery.
October 2, 1865	North Carolina amends constitution, forbidding slavery.
December 18, 1865	The Thirteenth Amendment, which abolishes slavery in the United States, is adopted.

Sources: Bennett, *Before the Mayflower*, p. 463; Hornsby, Jr., *Chronology of African-American History*, p. 39; *Negro Almanac*, p. 16; *Negro Year Book, 1921–1922*, pp. 134–35.

1883. He married Josephine St. Pierre Ruffin (1842–1924), a leader in the black women's club movement.

Sources: Dictionary of American Negro Biography, p. 535; Simmons, Men of Mark, pp. 740–43.

1870 ◆ **Jonathan Jasper Wright** (1840–1885) was the first black state supreme court justice in the United States. Born in Pennsylvania, Wright studied law in that state, where he was the first African American to be admitted to the bar in 1866. He was elected to the Supreme Court on February 1, 1870, to fill an unexpired term and re-elected to a full term in November. After the overthrow of the Reconstruction government, Wright resigned December 1, 1877, and died in obscurity of tuberculosis.

Sources: Bennett, *Before the Mayflower,* pp. 233, 487, 639; *Dictionary of American Negro Biography,* pp. 669–70; Hornsby, Jr., *Chronology of African-American History,* p. 43; *Negro Almanac,* p. 1425.

1872 ◆ The first black woman lawyer in the United States and the third woman admitted to law practice in this country was **Charlotte E. Ray** (1850–1911). As a graduate of Howard Law School (Washington, D.C.), she was automatically admitted to practice in the lower courts of the District of Columbia, and on April 23, 1872, she became the first black woman admitted to practice before the district Supreme Court. She was born in New York City. Hampered by her gender in trying to establish a practice, she eventually became a teacher in the Brooklyn schools. Her father, Charles Bennett Ray (1807–1886), was a notable abolitionist, minister, and editor. Her sister, Florence T. Ray (1849–1916), was an accomplished poet.

Sources: *Black Women in America,* pp. 965–66; *Encyclopedia of Black America,* p. 500; *Notable Black American Women,* pp. 922–24.

1880 ◆ **Samuel R. Lowery** (1832–c. 1900) on February 2, 1880, was the first black lawyer to argue a case before the Supreme Court. This first is distinct from John Sweat Rock's first in 1865—Rock was admitted to practice before the court, a recognition of standing as a lawyer obtained by many more lawyers than ever actually appear before the court to argue a case.

Sources: *Encyclopedia of Black America,* p. 499; *Leaders of Afro-American Nashville;* Simmons, *Men of Mark,* pp. 144–48.

1891 ◆ The first African American appointed to Chicago's law department was **Franklin A. Denison** (1862–19?), who served for six years under two mayors as assistant city prosecuting attorney. Neither Denison nor his law partner, S.A.T. Watkins, received appointments to the city government until 1911. In 1915 Denison became commander of the 8th Illinois Infantry, which he led in a Mexican expedition in 1916 and in France during the American intervention in World War I.

Sources: Barbeau, *Unknown Soldiers of World War I,* pp. 75–77; Gosnell, *Negro Politicians,* pp. 112, 198–99.

1902 ◆ **Robert H. Terrell** (1857–1925) was the first black justice of the peace in Washington, D.C., which made him the first black federal judge at any level. He held this position until his death. An 1884 magna cum laude graduate of Harvard (the first African American ever to receive this honor),

Terrell took his law degree at Howard University Law School in Washington, D.C., in 1889.

Sources: Dictionary of American Negro Biography, pp. 585–86; Encyclopedia of Black America, p. 815; Negro Almanac, p. 338.

1919 ◆ **Scipio Africanus Jones** (c. 1863–1943) was the first black lawyer in charge of an important case for the NAACP in a Southern state. Until then African Americans only assisted white lawyers. Jones handled the appeal process of 12 African Americans sentenced to death for the Elaine, Arkansas, riot of October 1919 and helped take the case to the Supreme Court. An attempt to organize share-croppers in Phillips County had resulted in violence. Twelve of the 79 African Americans tried for murder and insurrection as a result were sentenced to death; 56 of the others received long prison terms after a mere semblance of a trial. Black witnesses were beaten to compel testimony, a mob surrounded the courthouse calling for convictions, court-appointed counsel called no defense witnesses, and the jury deliberated five minutes. In the U.S. Supreme Court, *Moore v. Dempsey* resulted in overturning the verdicts in 1923.

William Henry Hastie

Sources: Dictionary of American Negro Biography, pp. 368–69; Encyclopedia of Black America, pp. 500, 618; Negro Almanac, pp. 314–15; Negro Year Book, 1921–1922, pp. 78–79.

1926 ◆ **Violette N. Anderson** (1882–19?) was the first black woman lawyer admitted to practice before the U.S. Supreme Court on January 29, 1926. She was also the first black woman admitted to the Illinois bar (1920) and the first woman assistant prosecutor in Chicago (1922).

Sources: Garrett, Famous First Facts About Negroes, p. 94; Opportunity 4 (March 1926), p. 107; Who's Who in Colored America, pp. 13–14.

1937 ◆ **William Henry Hastie** (1904–1976) was the first African American appointed to the federal bench. He was appointed U.S. district judge in the Virgin Islands. He was also the first black governor of the Virgin Islands in 1944, and became judge of the circuit court of appeals in 1949. Hastie served as civilian aide to the Secretary of War (1941–43)—he resigned to protest the lack of a positive commitment to recruit black pilots. In 1939 he resigned his judgeship to teach at Howard University's School of Law (Washington, D.C.), where he later also served as dean.

Sources: Garrett, *Famous First Facts About Negroes,* p. 86; *Negro Almanac, 1976,* p. 281; Robinson, *Historical Negro Biographies,* p. 199.

1939 ◆ **Jane M. Bolin** (1908–) became the first black woman judge in the United States when she was appointed to the Domestic Relations Court of New York City. Bolin was born in Poughkeepsie, New York. Her father, Gaius C. Bolin, was the first black graduate of Williams College in 1889. Jane Bolin retired on January 1, 1979, after 40 years of service on the bench.

Source: Encyclopedia of Black America, p. 185; *Negro Almanac,* p. 1426; *Notable Black American Women,* pp. 94–95.

1945 ◆ **Irving Charles Mollison** (1899-1962) was the first black judge of a U.S. Customs Court. This was the first time that an African American served as a federal judge in the United States. He served in New York City.

Sources: Garrett, *Famous First Facts About Negroes,* p. 87; *Negro Almanac, 1976,* p. 1045; *Negro Year Book, 1941-1946,* p. 285.

1948 ◆ **William Thaddeus Coleman, Jr.** (1920–) was the first black clerk in the Supreme Court. He was selected to serve as law secretary to Justice Felix Frankfurter.

Sources: Kane, *Famous First Facts,* p. 625; *Who's Who in Colored America, 1950,* p. 116.

1954 ◆ **Charles Vernon Bush** (1939–) was the first black Supreme Court page.

Sources: Alford, *Famous First Blacks,* p. 56; Kane, *Famous First Facts,* p. 626; *Who's Who Among Black Americans, 1992–1993,* p. 207.

1961 ◆ **Cecil Francis Poole** (1907–) was the first black U.S. attorney in the continental United States. He was appointed to the San Francisco office. In 1976 he became a U.S. district judge.

Sources: Dictionary of Black Culture, p.354; Kane, *Famous First Facts,* p. 49; *Who's Who Among Black Americans, 1992–1993,* p. 1135.

James Benton Parsons (1911–1993) was the first African American appointed judge of a U.S. district court in the continental United States. Parsons, a Chicago attorney, was appointed judge of the U.S. District Court of Northern Illinois on August 9, 1961. The second black federal judge, Wade H. McCree, Jr., was sworn in on October 9, 1961, in the District of Eastern

Michigan. In 1975 Parsons became the first African American to serve as chief of a U.S. district court.

Sources: Bennett, *Before the Mayflower,* p. 639; Hornsby, Jr., *Chronology of African-American History,* p. 112; Kane, *Famous First Facts,* p. 333; *Negro Almanac, 1976,* p. 284.

In 1961 **Otis M. Smith** (1922–) was named a Michigan State Supreme Court justice. He was the first African American to serve in this capacity in any state since Reconstruction. A year earlier he became the first African American to win a statewide election since Reconstruction when he was elected auditor general of Michigan. In 1967 Smith joined General Motors as a lawyer and was elevated to head of the firm's legal staff in 1977. He held this post until his retirement in 1983.

Sources: Ebony 16 (March 1961), pp. 75–80, 33 (December 1977), pp. 33–42, 37 (March 1982), p. 130; *Ebony Success Library,* vol. 1, p. 286; *Encyclopedia of Black America,* p. 798; *Who's Who Among Black Americans, 1992–1993,* p. 1309.

Constance Baker Motley

1962 ◆ **Edith Spurlock Sampson** (1901–1979) was the first black woman elected judge to a municipal court, in Chicago. In 1927 Sampson was the first woman to receive a law degree from Loyola University. She was also the first African American appointed to serve on the U.S. delegation to the United Nations in 1950.

Sources: Black Women in America, pp. 1002–3; *Encyclopedia of Black America,* p. 740; *Notable Black American Women,* pp. 969–72.

1964 ◆ On February 23, 1964, **Austin T. Walden** (1885–1965) became the first black judge in Georgia since Reconstruction, when he became a municipal judge in Atlanta.

Source: Hornsby, Jr., *Chronology of African-American History,* p. 117.

1966 ◆ **Constance Baker Motley** (1921–) was the first black woman federal judge. She was elected to the New York state senate in 1964, and in 1965 she became president of the Borough of Manhattan. Her appointment as a judge of the U.S. Circuit Court of the Southern District of New York made her the highest-paid black woman in government. Motley worked with the NAACP as legal assistant and associate counsel and won many difficult civil

Thurgood Marshall

rights cases. Her most famous victory was the case of James Meredith against the University of Mississippi. The case broke the barriers of segregation in Southern universities.

Sources: *Black Women in America,* vol. 2, pp. 822–24; *Notable Black American Women,* pp. 779–82; Robinson, *Historical Negro Biographies,* p. 230.

1967 ◆ In 1967 President Lyndon B. Johnson named **Thurgood Marshall** (1908–1993) the first black associate justice of the Supreme Court. By this time Marshall was known as the nation's foremost civil rights lawyer. From 1936 until 1961 he served as counsel for the NAACP. In 1946 he received the coveted NAACP Spingarn Medal. In 1950 he became director of the organization's legal arm, the NAACP Legal Defense and Education Fund. In this position Marshall brilliantly argued the case of *Brown v. Board of Education* before the Supreme Court, which ruled in 1954 that racial segregation in the public schools was unconstitutional. President John F. Kennedy appointed Marshall judge of the Second Circuit Court of Appeals in 1962. And in 1965 President Lyndon B. Johnson appointed him U.S. Solicitor General—the highest law enforcement position ever held by an African American. Marshall retired from the Supreme Court on June 27, 1991, and was replaced by Clarence Thomas, who became the second African American to sit on the highest court in the country.

Sources: Kane, *Famous First Facts,* p. 624; Hornsby, Jr., *Chronology of African-American History,* pp. 101, 112, 125; Robinson, *Historical Negro Biographies,* p. 226.

1970 ◆ **Milton B. Allen** (1917–) was the first African American elected state's attorney for the city of Baltimore. He was the first African American to be public prosecutor in any major American city. Allen had tried more than 7,000 cases and built a very prosperous law practice before he ran for elected office. He became a judge of the Supreme Bench of Baltimore in 1976.

Sources: *Ebony Success Library,* vol. 2, pp. 2–5; *Negro Almanac,* p. 1397; *Who's Who Among Black Americans, 1992–1993,* p. 23.

1975 ◆ As the first black woman appointed judge of the District of Columbia Appellate Court, **Julia P. Cooper** (1921–) became the highest ranking woman in the federal courts.

Sources: *Ebony* 12 (February 1957), p. 5; *Negro Almanac,* p. 71.

1976 ♦ **Theodore Roosevelt Newman, Jr.** (1934–) was named the chief judge of the Washington Court of Appeals; he was the first African American in the United States to head a court at this level. At the time of his appointment, there were fewer than a dozen black judges on appeals courts in the various states.

Sources: Jet 51 (9 December 1976), p. 20; Who's Who Among Black Americans, 1992–1993, p. 1055.

1978 ♦ **Robert Frederick Collins** (1931–) was the first black federal judge in the Deep South in modern times. Active in legal services in Louisiana, Collins was appointed a U.S. District Court judge in 1978. In 1991 he was also the first federal judge to be found guilty of taking a bribe.

Sources: Negro Almanac, p. 341; Who's Who Among Black Americans, 1992–1993, p. 293.

1979 ♦ **Joyce London Alexander** is the first black American U.S. judge in the District of Massachusetts.

Source: Who's Who Among Black Americans, 1992–1993, p. 16.

Amalya Lyle Kearse (1937–) is the first black woman judge on the U.S. Court of Appeals, Second District of New York. She is active in legal circles, the National Urban League, and the NAACP Legal Defense Fund.

Sources: Kane, Famous First Facts, p. 333; Who's Who Among Black Americans, 1992–1993, p. 809.

1980 ♦ **Odell Horton** (1929–) is the first black federal judge in the state of Tennessee. He was president of Le Moyne-Owen College (1970–74) before his appointment to the U.S. District Court in Tennessee.

Source: Who's Who Among Black Americans, 1992–1993, p. 685.

1982 ♦ **Reginald Walker Gibson** (1927–) is the first African American to sit on the bench of the U.S. Claims Court.

Source: Who's Who Among Black Americans, 1992–1993, p. 518.

1984 ♦ **Ann Claire Williams** (1949–) is the first black woman nominated to the federal bench in Chicago. Prior to her appointment to the U.S. District Court, Williams was a U.S. attorney and an adjunct professor at Northwestern University.

Source: Who's Who Among Black Americans, 1992–1993, p. 1511.

Joan B. Armstrong became the first black woman state judge when she was appointed to the Louisiana state court of appeal.

Sources: Jet 67 (24 September 1984), p. 32; Who's Who Among Black Americans, 1992–1993, p. 42.

Juanita Kidd Stout

Robert N. C. Nix, Jr. (1928–), son of Robert Nelson C. Nix (see **Politics: State Offices, 1958**) was the first African American to sit on a state supreme court bench since Reconstruction. He was inaugurated as chief justice of the Pennsylvania Supreme Court in 1984.

Sources: Dictionary of Black Culture, p. 331; Garrett, Famous First Facts About Negroes, p. 40; Hornsby, Jr., Chronology of African-American History, p. 327.

1988 ◆ In January 1988, **Juanita Kidd Stout** (1919–) became the first black woman to serve on any state supreme court. Thirty years earlier she had become the first woman judge in the history of Pennsylvania when she was appointed to the Philadelphia Municipal Court. After 10 years on the municipal court, she spent 20 years on the court of common pleas.

Sources: Encyclopedia of Black America, p. 811; Negro Almanac, p. 1392; Notable Black American Women, pp. 1087–89.

1990 ◆ **Thelton Eugene Henderson** (1933–) is the first black chief judge of the Northern California U.S. District Court.

Source: Who's Who Among Black Americans, 1992–1993, p. 639.

Leander J. Shaw, Jr. (1930–) is the first black Florida supreme court chief justice, and the first African American to head any branch of government in the state. Shaw was appointed to the court in 1983.

Sources: Jet 77 (2 April 1990), p. 8, 78 (23 July 1990), p. 33; Who's Who Among Black Americans, 1992–1993, p. 1265.

Fire Prevention, Law Enforcement, and Corrections

1944 ◆ **Doris E. Spears** was the first black woman deputy sheriff in the United States.

Source: Lee, Interesting People, p. 19.

1947 ◆ In April 1947 **John White** was the first black police officer in the state of Georgia. He retired from the Savannah force on November 1, 1984, with the rank of sergeant.

Source: Jet 67 (8 October 1984), p. 5.

1966 ◆ On January 1, 1966, **Robert O. Lowery** (1916–) became the first black fire commissioner of a major city, New York. Lowery had joined the department as a fireman in 1941.

Sources: Ebony Success Library, vol. 2, pp. 154–57; *Negro Almanac,* p. 1412; *Who's Who Among Black Americans, 1992–1993,* p. 893.

1967 ◆ On January 16, 1967, **Lucius D. Amerson** (1933–) became the first black sheriff in the South since Reconstruction. Amerson became sheriff of Macon County.

Sources: Alford, *Famous First Blacks,* p. 48; Bennett, *Before the Mayflower,* p. 578; Hornsby, Jr., *Chronology of African-American History,* pp. 131, 164, 172; *Negro Almanac,* p. 44.

1972 ◆ **Benjamin J. Malcolm** (1920–) was the first African American appointed commissioner of corrections for New York City.

Source: Encyclopedia of Black America, p. 544.

1976 ◆ **Johnnie Mae M. Gibson** (1949–) became the first black woman agent with the FBI.

Source: Who's Who Among Black Americans, 1992–1993, p. 518.

1978 ◆ **Burtell Jefferson** became the first black chief of police in the District of Columbia. He was named second-in-command of the department in 1974 by Mayor Walter Washington.

Source: Jet 53 (19 January 1978), p. 5.

1982 ◆ **JoAnn M. Jacobs** became the first black woman firefighter in New York City.

Source: Jet 63 (13 December 1982), p. 44.

Reuben M. Greenberg (1943–) became the first black chief of police in Charleston on March 17, 1982; this also made him the first black police chief in South Carolina in modern times.

Sources: Hornsby, Jr., *Chronology of African-American History,* p. 310; *Who's Who Among Black Americans, 1992–1993,* p. 558.

Lee P. Brown (1937–) became Houston's first black chief of police on March 23, 1982. In 1990 he became police commissioner of New York City but soon resigned due to illness in the family. On April 28, 1993, President Clinton announced Brown's nomination as director of the Office of National Drug Policy, a position to which Clinton gave cabinet rank.

Sources: Hornsby, Jr., *Chronology of African-American History,* p. 311; *Jet* 84 (19 July 1993), p. 10; (Nashville) *Tennessean,* 29 April 1993; *U.S. News and World Report* 109 (31 December 1990), p.73; *Who's Who Among Black Americans, 1992–1993,* p. 175.

1983 ♦ **Fred Rice** (1926–) became the first black police superintendent. His career with the Chicago Police Department began in 1955.

Sources: Jet 65 (12 September 1983), p. 8; *Who's Who Among Black Americans, 1992–1993,* p. 1185.

1984 ♦ **Benjamin Ward** (1926–) was the first black police commissioner of New York City. He served until 1989, when he resigned for health reasons. He had joined the department in 1951.

Sources: Jet 77 (16 October 1989), p. 38; *Who's Who Among Black Americans, 1992–1993,* p. 1455.

1988 ♦ **Jacqueline Murray** became the first black woman commander on the Chicago police force. She had served on the force for 21 years.

Source: Jet 75 (10 October 1988), p. 20.

Willie L. Williams was the first black commissioner of police in Philadelphia. In 1992 Williams became the first black chief of police in Los Angeles, California.

Sources: Ebony 48 (December 1992), pp. 71–74, 132; *Jet* 74 (20 June 1988), p. 8; (Nashville) *Tennessean,* 1 July 1992.

1989 ♦ **Janice White** became the first woman warden of the Manhattan House of Corrections, often called the Tombs, and at the time the only woman warden in the New York prison system.

Source: Jet 76 (17 April 1989), pp. 28–31.

Literature

Autobiography • Drama • Essay • History • Nonfiction • Novels
Poetry • Short Stories

Autobiography

1760 ◆ **Briton Hammon** was the first black American writer of prose. In 1760 he published *A Narrative of the Uncommon Sufferings and Surprising Deliverance of BRITON HAMMON, A Negro Man Servant to General Winslow, of Marshfield in New England; Who Returned to Boston, After Having Been Absent Almost Thirteen Years.* The 14-page account tells of his escape from Indians.

Sources: Dictionary of American Negro Biography, p. 281; Jackson, A History of Afro-American Literature, vol. 1, pp. 47–48.

1798 ◆ *A Narrative of the Life and Adventure of Venture, a Native of Africa But Resident Above Sixty Years in the United States of America* was the first slave narrative written by a black American. Slave narratives before this were either dictated to or written by whites (e.g., *Some Memoirs of the Life of Job,* 1734, by Thomas Bluett), difficult to credit fully (e.g., *A Narrative of the Lord's Dealings with John Marrant,* 1789), or complete fictions.

Sources: Dictionary of American Negro Autobiography, pp. 617–18; Jackson, A History of Afro-American Literature, vol. 1, pp. 61–62.

Drama

1916 ◆ *Rachel,* a play by poet **Angelina Grimké** (1880–1958), was the first known play written by a black American and presented on stage by black actors in this century. It portrays a respectable black family destroyed by prejudice. The play was first produced by the Drama Committee of the NAACP at Myrtilla Miner Normal School in Washington, D.C.

Sources: Encyclopedia of Black America, p. 532; Notable Black American Women, pp. 416–21.

1923 ◆ The first nonmusical play by a serious black writer to reach Broadway was *Chip Woman's Fortune,* a one-act play presented by the Ethiopian Art Players on May 7, 1923, along with Oscar Wilde's *Salome* and an interpretation of Shakespeare's *The Comedy of Errors.* Written by Willis Richardson (1889–1977), it was presented at the Frazee Theater and was the only play on the bill to be fully approved by the critics. The North Carolina native wrote and published several other plays, but he had little commercial success.

Sources: Brawley, Negro Genius, pp. 282–84; Johnson, Black Manhattan, pp. 190–91; Kellner, The Harlem Renaissance, p. 302; Rush, Black American Writers, vol. 2, pp. 629–30; Who's Who in Colored America, 1927, pp. 167–68.

1935 ◆ *Mulatto,* by **Langston Hughes** (1902–1967), was the first play by a black author to be a long-run Broadway hit. It opened at the Vanderbilt Theatre on October 24, 1935, and played continuously until December 9, 1937. The poet and author was born James Mercer Langston Hughes in Joplin, Missouri, and graduated from Lincoln University, Pennsylvania. A major figure of the Harlem Renaissance, he published 10 volumes of poetry; more than 60 short stories; a number of dramas, operas, and anthologies; and two autobiographies, *The Big Sea* (1940) and *I Wonder as I Wander* (1956). Hughes created the black folk character Jesse B. Simple and wrote about him in *Simple Speaks His Mind* (1950) and *Simple Stakes a Claim* (1957).

Sources: Bontemps, Harlem Renaissance Remembered, pp. 90–102; Dictionary of American Negro Biography, pp. 331–34; Encyclopedia of Black America, p. 456.

1959 ◆ **Lorraine Hansberry** (1930–1965) was the first African American to win the New York Drama Critics Award for her play *A Raisin in the Sun* in May 1959. The play was the first on Broadway written by a black woman and the first serious black drama to influence mainstream culture. In 1973 the musical *Raisin,* a revival of her play, won the Tony Award for best musical.

Sources: Abramson, Negro Playwrights in the American Theatre, pp. 239–54; Black Women in America, pp. 524–29; Encyclopedia of Black America, p. 425; Notable Black American Women, pp. 452–57.

1970 ◆ **Charles Gordone** (1925–) was the first black dramatist to win the Pulitzer Prize for drama. The play was *No Place to be Somebody.*

Sources: Black Writers, pp. 224–26; Dictionary of Black Culture, p. 187.

Essay

1829 ♦ **David Walker** (1785–1830) published the first pamphlet by a black American calling for a slave revolt, *David Walker's Appeal.* Walker was a free black who had wandered across the South before settling in Boston as the proprietor of a clothing shop. Despite efforts to suppress the *Appeal,* it became one of the most widely circulated pamphlets of the time. Distribution of the work became a crime in the South, and a bounty was placed on Walker's life. In 1848 the *Appeal* was published with Henry Highland Garnet's *Address* (1843), another call to revolt, in a volume financially supported by John Brown, a white champion of black freedom.

Sources: Dictionary of American Negro Biography, pp. 622–23; Hornsby, Jr., *Chronology of African-American History,* p. 16; Jackson, *A History of Afro-American Literature,* vol. 1, pp. 100–2.

1852 ♦ **Martin Robinson Delany** (1812–1885) wrote the first major appeal for emigration: *The Condition, Elevation, Emigration, and Destiny of the Colored People of the United States, Politically Considered.* In 1859 Delany wrote *Blake,* the first black nationalist novel, which today exists only in an incomplete form. (*See also* **Explorers, Pioneers, and Wild West Heroes, 1859** and **Media: Periodicals, 1841**.)

Sources: Dictionary of American Negro Biography, pp. 169–72; Jackson, *A History of Afro-American Literature,* vol. 1, pp. 364–69; Robinson, *Historical Negro Biographies,* p. 72; Simmons, *Men of Mark,* pp. 1007–15; Smythe, *Black American Reference Book,* pp. 660–61.

History

1836 ♦ **Robert Benjamin Lewis** was the first African American to publish a history, *Light and Truth.* Practically nothing is known about Lewis except that he was a native of Boston and had both black and Indian ancestors. Characterized by a remarkable disregard for any standard of evidence, the book tries among other things to create a black presence in history and to establish Native Americans as the descendants of the lost tribes of Israel.

Source: Jackson, *A History of Afro-American Literature,* vol. 1, pp. 200–1.

1841 ♦ **James William Charles Pennington** (1807–1870) was the author of the first history of black people written by an African American for children, *The Origin and History of the Colored People.* A slave blacksmith in Maryland, Pennington escaped and then learned to read and write. He became a teacher, a Congregational minister, and a Presbyterian minister. An active and prominent abolitionist, he officiated at Frederick Douglass's wedding.

Sources: *Dictionary of American Negro Biography,* pp. 488–90; Garrett, *Famous First Facts About Negroes,* p. 77; Jackson, *A History of Afro-American Literature,* vol. 1, p. 201.

1855 ◆ The first black history founded on written documentation is *The Colored Patriots of the American Revolution* by **William Cooper Nell** (1816–1874). Although flawed by modern standards, it nonetheless contains materials of lasting value. Nell's work began as a 23-page pamphlet in 1851. A native of Boston, Nell was a major leader in the ultimately successful fight to desegregate the Massachusetts public schools. He was also an associate of William Lloyd Garrison and Frederick Douglass in the abolition movement.

Sources: *Dictionary of American Negro Biography,* pp. 472–73; Garrett, *Famous First Facts About Negroes,* p. 156; Jackson, *A History of Afro-American Literature,* vol. 1, pp. 201–2.

1882 ◆ **George Washington Williams** (1849–1891) was the author of the first major history of African Americans in America. His *History of the Negro Race in America from 1619 to 1880,* in two volumes, was a major event and earned him respect for meeting the standards of professional historians. Born in Bedford Springs, Pennsylvania, he served as an underage soldier in the Union Army. In 1875 he became an ordained Baptist minister, then turned to law and politics, serving a term in the Ohio legislature. His other writings include the valuable *History of the Negro Troops in the War of the Rebellion* (1877). His last efforts were attacks on the inhumane government of the Congo Free State in Africa, following an 1890 visit there.

Sources: *Dictionary of American Negro Biography,* pp. 657–59; Garrett, *Famous First Facts About Negroes,* p. 77; Jackson, *A History of Afro-American Literature,* vol. 1, pp. 211–18.

1896 ◆ **William Edward Burghardt (W.E.B.) Du Bois** (1868–1963) wrote the first academic history by a black American, *The Suppression of the African Slave Trade, 1638–1870.* The book was published as the first volume in the Harvard University Historical Studies. *The Souls of Black Folk* (1903) established Du Bois as a peerless essayist. His 1935 account of the Reconstruction era, *Black Reconstruction in America,* was the first account of the era from a black viewpoint. A founding member of the National Association for the Advancement of Colored People (NAACP), Du Bois edited *The Crisis,* the magazine of the NAACP, taught at Atlanta University for a number of years, and was an ardent supporter of African liberation movements. He was the leading African American intellectual of the first half of the twentieth century. (*See also* **Civil Rights and Political Organizations, 1905,**

1909; Education: College Degrees, 1895; Organizations: Academic and Intellectual Societies, 1943.)

Sources: Dictionary of American Negro Biography, pp. 193–99; Garrett, *Famous First Facts About Negroes,* pp. 77, 79-80.

1916 ◆ The *Journal of Negro History* was the first American black historical research journal. **Carter Goodwin Woodson** (1875–1950) was its founder and first editor. His early education was limited due to his need to work in the West Virginia coal fields for his family's support. However, he completed his high school program in 18 months and began a college career that led to a Ph.D. from Harvard in 1912. He was a co-founder and the first executive director of the Association for the Study of Negro Life and History, established on September 9, 1915. In 1926 Woodson launched the first Negro History Week (now Black History Month). In 1937 he began publishing *The Negro History Bulletin.* Throughout his life he was devoted to the establishment of black history as a serious discipline and to African Americans' understanding of their heritage. (*See also* **Miscellaneous: Organizations, 1915.**)

Sources: Dictionary of American Negro Biography, pp. 665-67; Garrett, *Famous First Facts About Negroes,* p. 77.

Nonfiction

1918 ◆ **Benjamin Griffith Brawley** (1882–1939) edited the first book devoted exclusively to black art and literature, *The Negro in Literature and Art.* The book was reprinted in 1937 as *The Negro Genius.* He was a poet and a prolific scholar who had a distinguished teaching career at Atlanta Baptist Seminary (now Clark Atlanta University) and Shaw and Howard universities.

Sources: Brown, Davis, and Lee, *The Negro Caravan,* p. 757; *Dictionary of American Negro Biography,* pp. 60–61; Hughes and Bontemps, *The Poetry of the Negro 1746–1949,* p. 390.

Novels

1853 ◆ **William Wells Brown** (1814–1884) was the first black novelist. His only novel, *Clotel; or, The President's Daughter: A Narrative of Slave Life in the United States,* was published in England. The son of a slave mother and plantation owner in Kentucky, he escaped in 1834. In 1843 he became an agent of abolitionist societies. He spent five years in Europe championing emancipation and also wrote the first travel book, *Three Years in Europe*

(1852), and the first drama by a black American, *Experience; or, How to Give a Northern Man a Backbone* (1856). His second play, *Escape; or, A Leap for Freedom,* also written in 1856, was the first drama published by a black American. Before the end of the Civil War he became a physician and maintained a practice until his death; his interest also turned to writing the history of black achievement. Brown wrote more than a dozen books and pamphlets.

Sources: Abramson, *Negro Playwrights,* pp. 8–14; *Dictionary of American Negro Biography,* pp. 71–73; *Encyclopedia of Black America,* p. 532; Garrett, *Famous First Facts About Negroes,* p. 100; Jackson, *A History of Afro-American Literature,* vol. 1, pp. 322–42.

1857 ♦ **Frank J. Webb** published (in England) the first novel to deal with the problems of Northern free blacks, *The Garies and Their Friends.* The novel also includes the first in-depth treatment of a mixed marriage, the first presentation of a lynch mob, and the first use of passing for white as a major theme.

Source: Jackson, *A History of Afro-American Literature,* vol. 1, pp. 343–50.

1859 ♦ **Harriet E. Adams Wilson** (c. 1827–1870) was the first black woman to publish a novel. *Our Nig; or, Sketches from the Life of a Free Black, in A Two-Story White House North, Showing That Slavery's Shadows Fall Even There* was published in Boston, where she was living alone after her husband had abandoned her and her son. She hoped to make enough money from the book to reunite with her son, but he died before this was accomplished. The book was also the first novel published in the United States by a black man or woman. William Wells Brown's *Clotel* and Frank J. Webb's *The Garies and Their Friends* were both published in England. *Our Nig* presents social, racial, and economic brutality suffered by a free mulatto woman in the pre–Civil War North.

Sources: Jackson, *A History of Afro-American Literature,* vol. 1, p. 351–63; *Notable Black American Women,* p. 1266–68; Shockley, *Afro-American Women Writers 1746–1933,* p. 84.

1930 ♦ **Nella Marian Larsen** (1893–1964) was the first black woman to receive a Guggenheim Fellowship in creative writing. Her novels, *Quicksand* (1928) and *Passing* (1929), were highly acclaimed. Both deal with the tragic mulatto theme. She treated black women characters in urban settings and was the foremother to many African American novelists. Larsen was also one of the first black women novelists to deal with female sexuality and sexual politics.

Sources: Black Women in America, pp. 695–97; *Notable Black American Women,* pp. 652–57; Shockley, *Afro-American Women Writers 1746–1933,* p. 432.

1932 ♦ **Rudolph Fisher** (1897–1934) was the first black writer to write a detective novel, *The Conjure Man Dies.* Fisher earned an M.D. at Howard University Medical School in 1924, became a radiologist, and died of cancer.

In addition to his detective thriller, he wrote a number of very good short stories and two novels. He was considered one of the wittiest of the Harlem Renaissance group.

Sources: Brown, Davis, and Lee, *The Negro Caravan,* p. 54; *Dictionary of American Negro Biography,* pp. 222–23; Garrett, *Famous First Facts About Negroes,* p. 102.

1940 ◆ *Native Son* by **Richard Wright** (1908–1960) was the first Book-of-the-Month Club selection by an African American. The shocking novel was an outstanding critical and popular success and became a significant milepost in African American literature. Born in poverty in Mississippi, Wright sought to escape with a move to Chicago. He became a member of the Federal Writers Project (1935), moved with the project to New York (1937), and won a Guggenheim Fellowship (1939). His works include *Uncle Tom's Children* (1938), which established his reputation, and the autobiographical *Black Boy* (1945), another Book-of-the-Month Club selection.

Sources: Dictionary of American Negro Biography, pp. 674–75; Hughes and Bontemps, *The Poetry of the Negro 1746–1949,* p. 408; *Negro Almanac,* pp. 1021–22.

Ralph Ellison

1949 ◆ **Frank Garvin Yerby** (1916–1991) was the first African American to write a series of best-selling novels. Beginning with *The Foxes of Harrow* in 1949, he concentrated on costume novels, producing an annual best-seller. The general reading public was unaware of his racial identity, and there is little in the novels to suggest it.

Sources: Hornsby, Jr., *Milestones in Twentieth-Century African-American History,* p. 484; *Negro Almanac,* p. 1022; Wilson and Ferris, *Encyclopedia of Southern Culture,* p. 1143.

1953 ◆ **Ralph Waldo Ellison** (1914–) was the first African American to win a National Book Award, which recognized his first and only novel, *Invisible Man.* Written in 1952, the book, which many consider an American masterpiece, deals with a black man's "place" in a white man's world. He has published two collections of essays, *Shadow and Act* (1964) and *Going to the Territory* (1986). Portions of a novel-in-progress have been published in several literary journals. Elected to the National Institute of Arts and Letters and the

Alice Walker

American Academy of Arts and Letters, Ellison also received the Medal of Freedom from President Richard M. Nixon in 1969.

Sources: *Black Writers,* pp. 176–83; *Encyclopedia Americana,* vol. 10, p. 255; *Negro Almanac,* pp. 989–90.

1977 ◆ **Alex Haley** (Alexander Murray Palmer Haley, 1921–1992) became the first African American to win a Pulitzer Prize for his novel *Roots.* When he was six weeks old Haley and his mother moved to Henning, Tennessee, where they lived at her family home. In 1939, after two years of college, he volunteered in the U.S. Coast Guard. Haley devoted much of his free time to reading, composing letters, and writing adventure stories. The Coast Guard created the position of chief journalist for him in 1949, and he retired 10 years later to become a full-time writer. In 1962 *Playboy* magazine retained Haley to write a series of interviews, including an interview with Malcolm X. In 1964 this interview led him to write *The Autobiography of Malcolm X,* a bestseller that outsold *Roots.* Haley then launched upon a 12-year venture to track the ancestry of his mother's family. His search eventually took him to Gambia in West Africa, where his fourth great-grandfather, Kunte Kinte, had been born. Blending fiction with fact, Haley wrote *Roots: The Saga of an American Family.* Published in fall 1976, the work brought him prompt renown. Haley received a Pulitzer Prize, a National Book Award, and numerous other honors. The book was translated into 30 languages. The ABC television network telecast of *Roots* in 1977 in an eight-episode miniseries was one of the most watched television events ever. (*See also* **Film and Television: Television, 1977.**)

Sources: *Current Biography, 1977,* pp. 184–87; *Ebony Success Library,* vol. 1, p. 136; *Encyclopedia of Black America,* pp. 411–12; Hornsby, Jr., *Milestones in Twentieth-Century African-American History,* pp. 283, 488; *Jet* 81 (18 November 1991), p. 46.

1983 ◆ **Alice Walker** (1944–) was the first black woman to win a Pulitzer Prize for a work of fiction. The novel, *The Color Purple,* was popular but controversial. It also won the American Book Award and was made into an Oscar-nominated movie that intensified discussion among black men and women over her presentation of black men. Walker is also a poet, essayist, and short fiction writer. An ardent feminist, Walker uses the term "womanist" to describe her work. (*See also* **Film and Television: Film, 1985.**)

Sources: *Black Writers*, pp. 571–73; Lanker, *I Dream a World*, p. 24; *Notable Black American Women*, pp. 1178–82; Wilson and Ferris, *Encyclopedia of Southern Culture*, p. 898.

1993 ◆ Novelist **Toni Morrison** (1931–) was the first black American to win the Nobel Prize in literature, which was awarded on October 7. The Swedish Academy called her "a literary artist of first rank" and one who "gives life to an essential aspect of American reality." Informed of the honor, Morrison said that her work was inspired by "huge silences in literature, things that had never been articulated, printed or imagined and they were the silences about black girls, black women." Her novel *Song of Solomon,* published in 1977, won the National Book Critics Circle Award for fiction. And in 1988 she won the Pulitzer Prize for fiction for *Beloved.* Her other novels are *The Bluest Eye*

Toni Morrison

(1970), *Sula* (1974), *Tar Baby* (1981), and *Jazz* (1992). In 1965 Morrison became a textbook editor for a branch of Random House Publishing in Syracuse, New York, and three years later she moved to New York City as a senior editor in the trade department at Random House. She mixed her editorial work with a teaching career and taught at a number of colleges. She left the publishing field in 1984 and in 1989 became the Robert F. Goheen Professor of the Council of the Humanities at Princeton University.

Sources: *Black Women in America*, pp 815-19; *Contemporary Biography,* vol. 2, pp. 167-72; (Nashville) *Tennessean,* 8 October 1993, 9 October 1993; *Notable Black American Women*, pp. 770-75; *Washington Post,* 8 October 1993.

Poetry

1746 ◆ **Lucy Terry** (Prince) (c. 1730–1821), a slave, was the first black American poet. "Bars Fight," written this year (her only known poem), was inspired by an Indian ambush of haymakers in the Bars, a small plateau near Deerfield, Massachusetts. It was not published until 1855 in Josiah Gilbert Holland's *History of Western Massachusetts.* Terry was kidnapped as an infant in Africa and brought to Rhode Island. In 1756 Terry married Abijah Prince and obtained her freedom. She is also noted for her determined, if unsuccessful, attempt to persuade Williams College (Massachusetts) to accept her son as a student—she is reported to have argued before the board of trustees for three hours.

Sources: Jackson, A History of Afro-American Literature, *vol. 1, pp. 29–33;* Notable Black American Women, *pp. 881–82; Shockley,* Afro-American Women Writers 1746-1933, *p. 13.*

1760 ◆ **Jupiter Hammon** (1711–c. 1806) was the first African American to publish a poem as a separate work in America. This poem was the 88-line "An Evening Thought: Salvation by Christ, with Penitential Cries; Composed by Jupiter Hammon, a Negro belonging to Mr.[Henry] Lloyd of Queen's Village on Long Island, the 25th of December, 1760." Born a slave on Long Island, Hammon revealed an intensely religious conviction in this and his other publications.

Sources: Dictionary of American Negro Biography, pp. 281–82; Garrett, Famous First Facts About Negroes, *p. 98; Jackson,* A History of Afro-American Literature, *vol. 1, pp. 33–37.*

1773 ◆ **Phillis Wheatley** (c. 1753–1784), born on the West Coast of Africa, published the first book of poetry by a black person in America (and the second published by a woman). *Poems on Various Subjects, Religious and Moral* was published in London, England. A Boston merchant, John Wheatley, had bought Phillis as a child of about seven or eight, and had allowed her to learn to read and write. Wheatley's first published poem, "On the Death of the Reverend George Whitefield," appeared in 1770. In 1773 she traveled abroad with the Wheatleys' son, partially in the hope of restoring her health with exposure to sea air, and she attracted considerable attention in England as a poet. It was at about this time that she was freed.

Sources: Dictionary of American Negro Biography, pp. 640–43; Jackson, *A History of Afro-American Literature, vol. 1, pp. 38–46;* Notable Black American Women, *p. 1243–48.*

1829 ◆ **George Moses Horton** (1797–c. 1883) was the first black Southerner to publish a collection of poetry. *The Hope of Liberty,* containing 21 poems, was published in Raleigh, North Carolina. He anticipated proceeds from this volume would pay his way to Liberia. As with all his attempts at gaining freedom before Emancipation, this did not succeed.

Sources: Dictionary of American Negro Autobiography, pp. 327–28; Jackson, A History of Afro-American Literature, *vol. 1, pp. 83–100.*

1845 ◆ **Armand Lanusse** (1812–1867) compiled the first collection of American black poets, *Les Cenelles,* devoted to poetry in French. Lanusse was a free man of color and the leader of a New Orleans group of young poets. From

1852 to 1866 he was principal of the Bernard Couvent Institute for Indigent Catholic Orphans.

Sources: Dictionary of American Negro Biography, pp. 384–85; Hughes and Bontemps, Poetry of the Negro 1746–1949, p. 400; Jackson, A History of Afro-American Literature, vol. 1, pp. 225–34.

1877 ◆ **Albery Allson Whitman** (1851–1902) was the first black American poet to publish a poem more than 5,000 lines long, *Not a Man and Yet a Man.* Born a slave near Munfordville, Kentucky, Whitman began life as a laborer and had only a few months' formal education. He nevertheless became a very effective African Methodist Episcopal preacher and, by many accounts, the finest black poet of the Reconstruction era. (Whitman's poem was surpassed in length by some 3,500 lines with the publication of Robert E. Ford's *Brown Chapel: A Story in Verse* in 1903.)

Sources: Brown, Davis, and Lee, The Negro Caravan, p. 297; Dictionary of American Negro Biography, pp. 650–51; Jackson, A History of Afro-American Literature, vol. 1, pp. 272–92.

Paul Laurence Dunbar

1893 ◆ **Paul Laurence Dunbar** (1872–1906) was the first black poet to gain national fame. The Ohio-born writer was accepted wholeheartedly and widely recognized in the late nineteenth century. He used dialect and standard English in his work. His first book, *Oak and Ivy,* appeared in 1893, and two years later his second book, *Majors and Minors,* attracted the attention of the celebrated critic William Dean Howells. His third book, *Lyrics of Lowly Life* (1896), gained him his national reputation.

Sources: Brown, Davis, and Lee, The Negro Caravan, p. 303; Dictionary of American Negro Biography, pp. 200–3; Hughes and Bontemps, The Poetry of the Negro 1746–1949, p. 395.

1917 ◆ The birth of the Harlem Renaissance—a major black literary and artistic movement spanning the era from World War I through the early 1930s—is difficult to pinpoint. However, several starting dates for the movement have been suggested. The earliest is 1917, the year in which Claude McKay's poem "The Harlem Dancer" first appeared. Other possible dates include 1919, when McKay published the poem "If We Must Die," and 1921, when Langston Hughes published the poem "The Negro Speaks of Rivers." (*See* **Drama, 1935.**)

Source: Benét's Reader's Encyclopedia of American Literature, p. 12.

Gwendolyn Brooks

1950 ◆ **Gwendolyn Brooks** (1917–) was the first African American to win a Pulitzer Prize for poetry for *Annie Allen.* She became established as a major American poet, and in 1976 she was the first black woman inducted into the National Institute of Arts and Letters. A sensitive interpreter of Northern ghetto life, she began to write poetry at age seven; her first poems were published in the *Chicago Defender.* From 1969 on she has promoted the idea that African Americans must develop their own culture. She changed her writing style in an effort to appeal to the ordinary black reader. She was poet laureate of Illinois for 16 years and is poetry consultant to the Library of Congress.

Sources: Garrett, *Famous First Facts About Negroes,* p. 103; Hughes and Bontemps, *The Poetry of the Negro 1746–1949,* p. 390; *Notable Black American Women,* pp. 105–9.

1993 ◆ **Maya Angelou** (1928–) became the first black inaugural poet at the swearing in of President Bill Clinton. Robert Frost was the first inaugural poet at the inauguration of President John F. Kennedy. (*See also* **Film and Television: Film, 1970.**)

Sources: Jet (8 February 1993), pp. 4–10; (Nashville) *Tennessean,* 20 January 1993; *USA Today,* 21 January 1993.

Short Stories

1853 ◆ **Frederick Douglass** (1817–1895) wrote the first short story published by an African American, "The Heroic Slave." It appeared in four installments in his newspaper, *The North Star.* This long short story is based on the real-life exploit of Madison Washington, who took the lead in seizing the ship on which he was bound from Virginia to Louisiana, and regained his freedom by sailing the vessel to Nassau in the Bahamas. Although known mainly as a brilliant abolitionist speaker, journalist, and statesman, Douglass is also recognized as the author of the most popular slave account in American history, the *Narrative of the Life of Frederick Douglass, an American Slave, Written by Himself,* published in 1845. An extraordinary work (which many at the time believed could not have been written by a former slave), the *Narrative* also ranks with some of the best of all American auto-biographies. Later in his career, Douglass also became the first African American to own a publishing house. (*See also* **Civil Rights and Protest** and **Politics: National, 1872.**)

Sources: *Benét's Reader's Encyclopedia of American Literature*, p. 985; Jackson, *A History of Afro-American Literature*, vol. 1, pp. 118–20.

1859 ♦ **Frances Ellen Watkins Harper** (1825–1911) wrote "The Two Offers," the first short story published by a black woman in the United States. It appeared in the *Anglo-African* magazine in 1859. Harper was born in Baltimore, Maryland, of free parents. She became a noted speaker in the abolition movement and after the Civil War supported the suffrage and temperance movements. She was also an extremely successful poet; her *Poems on Miscellaneous Subjects* is reported to have sold 50,000 copies by 1878. Her novel *Iola Leroy* (1892) was the first widely distributed novel—and the second ever—by an African American woman.

Frederick Douglass

Sources: Brown, Davis, and Lee, *The Negro Caravan*, p. 293; *Dictionary of American Negro Biography*, pp. 289–90; *Dictionary of Literary Biography: Afro-American Writers Before the Harlem Renaissance*, Vol. 50, p. 170; Hughes and Bontemps, *The Poetry of the Negro 1746–1949*, p. 397; Jackson, *A History of Afro-American Literature*, vol. 1, pp. 265–72; 392–97; *Notable Black American Women*, pp. 457–62; Shockley, *Afro-American Women Writers 1746–1933*, p. 56.

1899 ♦ **Charles Waddell Chesnutt** (1858–1932) published the story collection *The Conjure Woman,* the first literary work on African Americans by a mainstream publisher (Houghton Mifflin) to carry a serious social message. Consequently Chesnutt is often called the first major African American fiction writer. His other writings include *The Wife of His Youth, and Other Stories of the Color Line* (1899); the novels *The House Behind the Cedars* (1900), *The Marrow of Tradition* (1901), and *The Colonel's Dream* (1905); and a biography of Frederick Douglass. In 1928 Chesnutt received the NAACP's Spingarn Medal for his dedication to black advancement.

Sources: *Benét's Reader's Encyclopedia of American Literature*, p. 11; *Black Writers*, pp. 98–100; *Dictionary of Literary Biography,* vol. 50: *Afro-American Writers Before the Harlem Renaissance*, pp. 36–51.

Media

Newspapers • Periodicals • Photojournalism • Press Secretary
Radio • Television

Newspapers

1817 ◆ The first abolitionist newspaper was the *Philanthropist,* published and edited by Charles Osborn on August 29, 1817, in Mount Pleasant, Ohio.

Source: Kane, *Famous First Facts*, p. 426.

1827 ◆ *Freedom's Journal* began publication on March 16, 1827, in New York. The first black newspaper, it championed the rights of African Americans and spoke out against slavery. The *Journal* was owned and edited by Presbyterian minister Samuel E. Cornish (1795–1858) and black nationalist John B. Russwurm (1799–1851).

Sources: Bennett, *Before the Mayflower*, p. 174; Estell, ed., *African American Almanac*, 6th ed., p. 855.

1855 ◆ **Mifflin Wistar Gibbs** (1823–1915) was owner and editor of the *Mirror of the Times,* California's first black newspaper.

Sources: Dictionary of American Negro Biography, pp. 258–59; *Encyclopedia of Black America*, p. 403; Penn, *The Afro-American Press*, p. 77.

1864 ◆ **Thomas Morris Chester** (1834–1892) was the first and only black correspondent for a major daily, the *Philadelphia Press,* during the Civil War. He read law under a Liberian lawyer, then spent three years at Middle Temple in London. In April 1870 he became the first black American lawyer admitted to practice before English courts.

Sources: Blackett, *Thomas Morris Chester;* Simmons, *Men of Mark*, pp. 671–76; Spradling, *In Black and White*, vol. 1, p. 182.

BLACK ANTI-SLAVERY NEWSPAPERS

Title	Location	Established
Freedom's Journal	New York City	March 16, 1827
Rights of All	New York City	March 28, 1828
The Weekly Advocate	New York City	January 1837
Colored American (formerly *The Weekly Advocate*)	New York City	March 4, 1837
The Elevator	Albany, NY	1842
The National Watchman	Troy, NY	1842
The Clarion	—	1842
The People's Press	New York City	1843
The Mystery	Pittsburgh, PA	1843
The Genius of Freedom	—	1845
The Ram's Horn	New York City	January 1, 1847
The North Star	Rochester, NY	November 1, 1847
The Moral Reform Magazine	Philadelphia, PA	1847
The Impartial Citizen	Syracuse, NY	1848
The Christian Herald	Philadelphia, PA	1848
The Colored Man's Journal	New York City	1851
The Alienated American	Cleveland, OH	1852
The Christian Recorder (formerly *The Christian Herald*)	Philadelphia, PA	1852
The Mirror of the Times	San Francisco, CA	1855
The Herald of Freedom	Ohio	1855
The Anglo African	New York City	July 23, 1859

Sources: *Dictionary of American Negro Biography,* pp. 134–35, 538–39; *Negro Yearbook, 1913,* p. 75; Penn, *The Afro-American Press.*

La Tribune de la Nouvelle Orléans was the first black daily published in the United States. It began on October 4, 1864.

Source: *Dictionary of American Negro Biography,* p. 534.

1885 ◆ The *Philadelphia Tribune,* the oldest continually published non-church black newspaper, was first published in 1885.

1888 ◆ **Edward Elder Cooper** (1859–?) established *The Freeman* at Indianapolis, Indiana. This was the first black newspaper to make a feature of

THE OLDEST CONTINUALLY PUBLISHED BLACK NEWSPAPERS

Name	Established
Christian Recorder (African Methodist Episcopal)	1846
Star of Zion (AME Zion)	1867
American Baptist	1880
Philadelphia Tribune	1885
Houston Informer	1892
Baltimore Afro-American	1892
Des Moines, Iowa, Bystander	1894
Indianapolis Recorder	1895

Sources: Encyclopedia of Black America, p. 642; Gale Directory of Publication and Broadcast Media, 1993.

portraits and cartoons. First published July 14, 1888, the newspaper reached national prominence and made a fortune for its owner.

Sources: Alexander's Magazine 6 (August 15, 1908), editorial; Penn, The Afro-American Press, pp. 334–39.

1905 ◆ **Robert Abbott Sengstacke** (Robert Sengstake Abbott, 1870–1940) first published the *Chicago Defender* on May 6, 1905, eventually calling it "The World's Greatest Weekly." The *Defender* reached national prominence during the great black migration from the South during World War I and, by Sengstacke's death, was the most widely circulated black weekly.

Sources: Dictionary of American Negro Biography, pp. 1–2; Hornsby, Jr., Milestones in Twentieth-Century African-American History, pp. 5–6.

1909 ◆ The New York *Amsterdam News* was first published by James H. Anderson on December 4, 1909. The four-page newspaper sold for a penny a copy. At the peak of its popularity around World War II, the paper claimed a circulation of more than 100,000; the paper began to decline in 1971.

Sources: Encyclopedia of Black America, p. 647; Jet 67 (10 December 1984), p. 37; Split Image, p. 362.

1912 ◆ **Charlotta Bass** (1880–1969) is thought to be the first woman to own and publish a newspaper in this country. She bought the *California Eagle* in 1912, and ran it for some 40 years. Bass was the Progressive party vice-presidential candidate in 1952, another first for a black woman.

Sources: Black Women in America, vol. 1, pp. 93, 664; Notable Black American Women, pp. 61–64.

1932 ♦ The first black daily newspaper in modern times was the *Atlanta Daily World,* which was published daily beginning March 13, 1932. It was founded on August 3, 1928, by William A. Scott III (1903–1934). In 1930 it became a biweekly.

Sources: Alford, *Famous First Blacks,* p. 75; *Going Against the Wind,* pp. 79, 101; *Jet* (3 March 1992), p. 29; *Negro Yearbook,* 1947, p. 386.

1935 ♦ Joel Augustus Rogers (1883–1966) became the first black foreign correspondent when he was sent to Addis Ababa, Ethiopia. From October 1935 through April 21, 1936, he covered the Italian-Ethiopian War for the *Pittsburgh Courier.*

Sources: *Dictionary of American Negro Biography,* pp. 531–32; *Encyclopedia of Black America,* p. 735; Kane, *Famous First Facts,* p. 425.

Mifflin Wistar Gibbs

1944 ♦ **Harry S. McAlpin** (?–1985) became White House Correspondent for the National Negro Press Association and the *Atlanta Daily World* and was the first African American admitted to White House press conferences. He first attended a White House press conference on February 8, 1944.

Sources: *Jet* 53 (9 February 1978), p. 58; Kane, *Famous First Facts,* p. 425; *Negro Almanac,* p. 1427; *Negro Year Book, 1952,* pp. 46–48.

Elizabeth B. Murphy Moss (Phillips) (1917–) was the first black woman certified as a war correspondent during World War II. She became ill and had to return without filing reports. Later Moss became vice-president and treasurer of the Afro-American Company and publisher of the largest black chain of weekly newspapers in the United States, the *Baltimore Afro-American* group.

Sources: *Black Women in America,* vol. 1, p. 664; *Encyclopedia of Black America,* p. 570; *Negro Yearbook, 1947,* p. 387.

1947 ♦ On March 18, 1947, the Senate Rules Committee ordered that **Louis Lautier** (1896–) be granted access to the congressional press galleries, making him the first black newspaperman to have such a privilege since 1871. Lautier was Bureau Chief of the Negro Newspapers Publishers Association and had been denied access on the grounds that he did not represent a daily newspaper. He based his appeal of the original decision that barred him in 1946 on the grounds that he did indeed represent a daily, *The Atlanta Daily*

Alice Dunnigan

World. Shortly before, Percival L. Prattis (1895–1980) had gained access to the Periodical Gallery of both the House and Senate as part owner of *Our World* magazine. Prattis was also an executive editor of the *Pittsburgh Courier* and was the first African American admitted to the National Press Club, on February 5, 1956.

Source: *Negro Year Book, 1952,* pp. 46–47.

Alice Dunnigan (1906–1983) of the Associated Negro Press was the first black woman to gain access to the White House, the State Department, and the House and Senate press galleries. At the State Department she joined James L. Hicks, assistant chief of the Negro Newspapers Publishers Association, who had been the first African American accredited to the department shortly before. Dunnigan was also the first black American elected to the Women's National Press Club. In 1948 she became the first black news correspondent to cover a presidential campaign when she followed Harry S Truman's whistlestop trip.

Sources: *Black Women in America,* vol. 1, pp. 368–70; *Jet* 64 (30 May 1983), p. 42; *Notable Black American Women,* pp. 301–3; *Negro Year Book, 1952,* p. 47.

1949 ◆ The first black full-time reporter for the *Mirror-News,* owned by the *Los Angeles Times,* was **Chester Lloyd Washington** (1902–). He specialized in superior court cases. Originally a reporter for the *Los Angeles Sentinel,* he became its editor in 1961 and its editor-in-chief in 1965. Through purchases and mergers of existing weekly newspapers and the creation of others in the L.A. area, he established Central News-Wave Publications, which became the largest black-owned newspaper operation in any single metropolitan area.

Sources: *Encyclopedia of Black America,* pp. 845–46; *Negro Almanac, 1989,* pp. 1256, 1263–64; *Who's Who Among Black Americans, 1988,* p. 721.

1950 ◆ **Marvel Jackson Cooke** was the first full-time black woman reporter on a mainstream newspaper, the *Daily Compass.* She began her career as an editorial assistant to W.E.B. Du Bois in 1926 at the *Crisis* and became assistant manager of Adam Clayton Powell's *People's Voice* in 1935.

Source: *Black Women in America,* vol. 1, p. 664.

Albert L. Hinton, representing the Negro Newspaper Association, and **James L. Hicks,** representing the *Afro-American* group, were the first black war correspondents of the Korean War. Hinton died when his plane went down between Japan and Korea, but Hicks carried out his assignment.

Sources: *Jet* 70 (29 June 1970), p. 9; *Negro Year Book, 1952,* p. 46.

1952 ◆ **Simeon S. Booker** (1918–) was the first full-time black reporter for the *Washington Post,* from 1952 to 1954. In 1982 he was the first African American to win the Fourth Estate Award of the National Press Club, Washington, D.C. The Baltimore native later became Washington Bureau Chief of Johnson Publishing Company.

Sources: *Ebony Success Library,* vol. 1, p. 34; Rush, *Black American Writers,* vol. 1, p. 84; *Who's Who Among Black Americans, 1992–1993,* pp. 129–30.

1964 ◆ **Stanley S. Scott** (1933–) became the first black full-time general assignment reporter for United Press International (UPI). In 1965 he was nominated for a Pulitzer Prize for his eyewitness account of the assassination of Malcolm X. In 1967 he became the first full-time black news announcer for WINS, an all-news radio station in New York City. Scott won the Russwurm Award for Excellence in Radio News Reporting, as well as the New York Silurians Award.

Sources: *Ebony Success Library,* vol. 1, p. 277; *Who's Who Among Black Americans, 1992–1993,* p. 1254.

1971 ◆ **William A. Hilliard** was the first black city editor on a mainstream paper, the *Portland Oregonian.* He joined the newspaper in 1952 as a copy aide, and on April 5, 1982, he became the first black executive editor of the news department. In 1993 the American Society of Newspaper Editors elected Hilliard its first black president.

Sources: *Jet* 62 (5 April 1982), p. 29; *Negro Almanac,* p. 1258.

1974 ◆ **Hazel Garland** (?–1988), editor-in-chief of the *Pittsburgh Courier,* was the first woman head of a nationally circulated black newspaper in the United States.

Sources: *Black Women in America,* vol. 1, p. 664; *Jet* 74 (25 April 1988), p. 59.

1979 ◆ **Robert C. Maynard** (1937–1993) was the first African American to direct the editorial operations of a major American daily, the *Oakland Tribune* in California. In 1983 he became owner and publisher of the *Oakland Tribune* and the first black American to become a majority shareholder in a major metropolitan daily newspaper. Maynard worked for 10 years at the *Washington Post* as its first black national correspondent and later as ombudsman and editorial writer. On October 15, 1992, the name and certain assets of the *Oakland Tribune*, then the nation's only black-owned major daily newspaper, were sold to the Alameda Newspaper Group.

Sources: Atlanta Journal and Constitution (19 August 1993); Hornsby, Jr., *Milestones in Twentieth-Century African-American History,* pp. 495, 503; *Split Image,* p. 366; *State of Black America, 1993,* p. 302; *Who's Who Among Black Americans, 1992–1993,* p. 935.

1982 ◆ **Pamela McAllister Johnson** (1945–) became the first black woman publisher of a mainstream paper, the *Ithaca Journal,* in New York state on December 10, 1982. In 1987 Johnson received the Candace Award from the National Coalition of 100 Black Women.

Sources: Black Women in America, vol. 2, p. 1450; *Negro Almanac,* p. 1432; *Split Image,* p. 367; *Who's Who Among Black Americans, 1989,* pp. 766–67.

1987 ◆ **Roger Wood Wilkins** (1932–) was the first black chair of the National Pulitzer Prize Board (1987–88) on which he served from 1980 to 1989. In 1973 he shared a Pulitzer Prize with the *Washington Post* for his reports on the Republican break-in of Democratic National Committee head-quarters at the Watergate office and apartment building in Washington, D.C. His autobiography, *A Man's Life,* was published in 1982. The Kansas City, Missouri, native is the nephew of former NAACP director Roy Wilkins.

Sources: Contemporary Black Biography, vol. 2, pp. 250–53; *Jet* 72 (18 May 1987), p. 10; *Who's Who Among Black Americans, 1992–1993,* p. 1509.

1989 ◆ **Clarence Page** (1947–) was the first black columnist to be awarded a Pulitzer Prize. He joined the *Chicago Tribune* staff in 1969 and later became a syndicated columnist and editorial writer for the newspaper.

Sources: Contemporary Black Biography, vol. 4, pp. 187–90; *Jet* 76 (17 April 1989), p. 23.

Cynthia Tucker was the first black woman to edit a major daily newspaper with a circulation of over 300,000, the *Atlanta Constitution.* She joined the newspaper in 1976, serving as reporter, columnist, and editorial writer.

Source: Jet 81 (27 January 1992), p. 9.

Keith Woods (1958–) was named the first black city editor of the *Times Picayune.* The New Orleans native began his career in the sports department of the newspaper in 1978, became a full-time sports writer for the paper in 1988, and was named assistant city editor in 1989. He graduated from Dillard and Tulane universities.

Sources: Hornsby, Jr., Milestones in Twentieth-Century African-American History, p. 465; *Jet* 79 (7 January 1991), p. 37.

1992 ◆ On December 1, 1992, **Pearl Stewart** (1951–) became the first black woman editor of a major U.S. daily with a circulation of over 100,000, the *Oakland Tribune.*

Source: *Jet* 82 (5 October 1992), p. 36.

Periodicals

1820 ◆ *The Emancipator,* the first antislavery magazine, was issued monthly from April 30 to October 31, 1820. It was edited and published by Elihu Embree.

Source: Kane, *Famous First Facts,* p. 456.

1838 ◆ The first black periodical, the *Mirror of Liberty,* began publication in June 1838 under David Ruggles (1810–49). Until it folded in 1841, *The Mirror* strongly protested colonization, segregation, disfranchisement, and slavery. (*See also* **Business: Retailing, 1834** and **Science, Medicine, and Invention: Medicine, 1846**.)

Sources: *Dictionary of American Negro Biography,* pp. 536–38; Kane, *Famous First Facts,* p. 456.

1841 ◆ The first issue of the oldest continuously published periodical, now known as the *Christian Recorder,* was published by the African Methodist Episcopal church. Issued first as the *A.M.E. Church Magazine* and intended as a weekly, it became a quarterly in its first year. Renamed the *Christian Herald* in 1848, it became a weekly again and was published by Martin Robinson Delany, an author, physician, abolitionist, black nationalist, and army officer. In 1852 it was renamed the *Christian Recorder.* (*See also* **Explorers, Pioneers, and Wild West Heroes, 1859** and **Literature: Essay, 1852.**)

Sources: *Encyclopedia of Black America,* p. 33; Penn, *The Afro-American Press,* pp. 78–81.

1853 ◆ **Mary Ann Shadd** (Cary) (1823–1893) became the first black woman journalist, editor, and publisher, for the *Provincial Freeman.* In 1855 she was also the first woman admitted as a corresponding member of the black convention movement.

Sources: *Dictionary of American Negro Biography,* pp. 552–53; *Negro Almanac,* p. 195; *Notable Black American Women,* pp. 998–1003.

Gordon A. Parks, Sr.

1910 ◆ The first issue of *Crisis* magazine, the official organ of the NAACP, was published in April 1910 under the editorship of W.E.B. Du Bois.

Sources: Hornsby, Jr., *Milestones in Twentieth-Century African-American History*, p. 9; Joyce, *Gatekeepers of Black Culture*, pp. 37, 84; *Negro Almanac*, pp. 21, 260.

1918 ◆ **Ralph Waldo Tyler** (1860–1921), reporter and government official, was the first (and only) black official war correspondent during World War I.

Sources: Dictionary of American Negro Biography, pp. 613–14.; *Jet* 78 (2 July 1990), p. 23; Scott, *The American Negro in the World War*, pp. 284–99.

1942 ◆ **John H. Johnson** (1918–) published the *Negro Digest,* the first magazine devoted to summarizing and excerpting articles and news about African Americans published in mainstream publications. Immediately successful, the magazine laid the foundation for Johnson Publishing Company's success, which was only increased by magazines like *Ebony* and *Jet. Negro Digest,* published from 1942 through 1976, became *Black World* in 1970. In 1945 *Ebony* became the first advertising medium owned by African Americans to attract advertising from white-owned companies. In 1972 Johnson purchased Chicago radio station WGRT and became the first African American in the city to own a broadcasting outlet. (*See also* **Business: Publishing, 1938.**)

Sources: Contemporary Black Biography, vol. 3, pp. 102–4; *Ebony Success Library*, vol. 2, pp. 132–37; *Encyclopedia of Black America,* p. 331; Joyce, *Gatekeepers of Black Culture,* p. 63; *Split Image,* pp. 372–74.

1963 ◆ *Time* magazine's first black national correspondent was **Wallace Houston Terry II** (1938–), whose many assignments included coverage of the Vietnam War. He was named 1993 holder of the John Seigenthaler Chair of Excellence in First Amendment Studies at Middle Tennessee State University.

Sources: Tennessean, 15 October 1992; *Who's Who Among Black Americans, 1992–1993,* p. 1237.

Photojournalism

1949 ◆ **Gordon A. Parks, Sr.** (1912–) became the first black photojournalist on the staff of *Life* magazine. He began his photography in 1937 with a camera purchased in a pawn shop. In 1941 he was the first African

American to receive a Rosenwald Fellowship for photography; in 1942 he was the first black American to work for the U.S. Farm Security Administration (as a photographer); and in 1943, he was the first to work for the U.S. Office of War Information (as a photojournalist and a war correspondent). Parks was named the Magazine Photographer of the Year in 1961. (*See also* **Film and Television: Film, 1969**.)

Sources: *Contemporary Black Biography,* vol. 1, pp. 184-88; Lee, *Interesting People,* p. 88; *Split Image,* pp. 161, 163, 376.

1969 ◆ The first black journalist to win a Pulitzer Prize for a feature photograph was **Moneta J. Sleet, Jr.** (1926–). He won the award for his photograph of Coretta Scott King and her daughter at the funeral of Martin Luther King, Jr.

Sources: *Ebony Success Library,* vol. 1, p. 283; *Encyclopedia of Black America,* p. 796.

Press Secretary

1990 ◆ **Lynette Moten** (1954–) became the first black woman press secretary for a U.S. senator, Thad Cochran of Mississippi.

Source: *Jet* 78 (13 August 1990), p. 4.

Radio

1927 ◆ **Jack L. Cooper** (1889–) originated a community news broadcast about black Americans, *The Negro Hour,* a pioneering achievement in black radio history. Cooper, the only broadcaster who played popular black music on race labels, built up a loyal black audience and gathered news from black publications to develop the first regular black newscast. He created a missing persons bureau to help black migrants locate relatives who had moved to Chicago. By 1949 Cooper owned his own broadcast studio and advertising agency and had become a millionaire.

Sources: *Ebony* 3 (December 1947), p. 47, 7 (July 1952), p. 14, 12 (July 1957), p. 5; Garrett, *Famous First Facts About Negroes,* p. 166; *Negro Digest* 3 (February 1945), pp. 11–12; *Split Image,* pp. 182, 185–86.

Floyd Joseph Calvin (1902–1939) had the first radio talk show, which focused on black journalism. Broadcast on WGBS, it was the first show of its kind sponsored by a black newspaper, the *Pittsburgh Courier.*

Sources: *Encyclopedia of Black America,* p. 213; *Split Image,* p. 184.

1949 ◆ The first black-owned radio station, which was located in Atlanta, Georgia, was WERD, purchased on October 4, 1949, by J. B. Blayton. Broadcast began on October 7. Jack Gibson was the first black program director and oriented programming to black Atlantans. In 1955 he was an organizer of the National Association of Radio Announcers. The station signed off the air, was sold, and relocated in 1957.

Sources: Alford, *Famous First Blacks*, p. 76; Bergman, *The Chronological History of the Negro in America*, p. 521; *Going Against the Wind*, pp. 123, 161; *Split Image*, p. 213.

1960 ◆ **Edmund Stanley Dorsey** (1930–) became the first African American White House broadcast correspondent, with radio station WWDC. Three years later, while he was news director with radio-television station WOOK, he became the first black television news reporter in Washington, D.C. In 1964 he joined station WIND and was sent to Saigon, South Vietnam, in 1966, where he became the first black bureau chief for the Washington Broadcasting Network. While serving with the U.S. Army in Tokyo, Japan, in 1949, he had become the first black managing editor of the military publication *Stars and Stripes*.

Source: Ebony Success Library, vol. 1, p. 98.

1972 ◆ The first black-controlled station of the National Federation of Community Broadcasters was KPOO-FM, in San Francisco. Called "Poor People's Radio," it was founded by Lorenzo Milam to serve the inner-city poor and predominantly black people.

Source: Split Image, p. 233.

1987 ◆ **Adam Clayton Powell III** (1946–), son of the legendary congressman Adam Clayton Powell, Jr., was the first African American to direct a major national radio news network, National Public Radio. He is now a New York City councilman.

Sources: Jet 73 (26 October 1987), p. 22; *Split Image*, p. 214; *Who's Who Among Black Americans, 1992–1993*, p. 1141.

Television

1958 ◆ The first black newscaster, for WNTA-TV in New York City, was **Louis Emanuel Lomax** (1922–1970). Lomax was also an author and educator.

Sources: Dictionary of Black Culture, p. 275; *Encyclopedia of Black America,* pp. 539–40.

The first major black television news correspondent, for CBS-TV, was **Joan Murray** (1941–). In 1969 she co-founded Zebra Associates, the first integrated, black-owned advertising agency.

Sources: Ebony 21 (October 1966), p. 50; Encyclopedia of Black America, 584; Notable Black American Women, pp. 782–83.

1962 ♦ **Malvin (Mal) Russell Goode** (1908–), hired by ABC, became the first black network news correspondent. He became the first black member of the National Association of Radio and Television News Directors in 1971.

Sources: Ebony Success Library, vol. 1, p. 127; Negro Almanac, p. 1280; Split Image, p. 389; Who's Who Among Black Americans, 1992–1993, p. 534.

1968 ♦ **Xernona Clayton** (1930–) was the first black woman to host a television show in the South, in Atlanta, in August 1968. In 1988 she became the first black assistant corporate vice-president of urban affairs at Turner Broadcasting System.

Sources: Clayton, I've Been Marching All the Time; Contemporary Black Biography, vol. 3, pp. 34–36; Encyclopedia of Black America, p. 274; Who's Who Among Black Americans, 1992–1993, p. 274.

1969 ♦ **Mal Johnson** (1924–) was the first black woman television reporter to cover the White House. In 1970 she became the first national correspondent for WKBS-TV.

Sources: Jet 80 (10 June 1991), p. 10; Klever, Women in Television, pp. 134–38; Who's Who Among Black Americans, 1992–1993, p. 764.

1975 ♦ WGPR-TV (Detroit) was the first television station owned and operated by African Americans.

Source: Encyclopedia of Black America, p. 725.

1978 ♦ **Charlayne Hunter-Gault** (1942–) was the first black woman to anchor a national newscast, *The MacNeil/Lehrer Report*. In January 1961 she and Hamilton Holmes were the first two black students to attend the University of Georgia. The university awarded her the prestigious George Foster Peabody Award in 1986. (*See also* **Education: College Integration, 1961.**)

Sources: Black Women in America, vol. 1, pp. 595–96; Current Biography, 1987, pp. 261–64; Jet 7 (26 March 1990), p. 33; Notable Black American Women, pp. 535–36.

Max Robinson (1939–1988) was the first black network news anchor, with ABC-TV, broadcasting from Chicago, Illinois. He had been the first co-anchor on the midday newscast with WTOP, Washington, D.C., in 1969. Robinson left

Ed Bradley

ABC in 1983 to become the first black anchor for WMAQ-TV in Chicago and won an Emmy Award in 1980 for coverage of the national election.

Sources: Contemporary Black Biography, vol. 3, pp. 209–12; Hornsby, Jr., *Milestones in Twentieth-Century African-American History,* p. 390; *Jet* 76 (1 May 1989), p. 25.

1980 ◆ **Bernard Shaw** (1940–) was appointed chief Washington correspondent and became was the first black anchor at Cable News Network (CNN). In 1987 Shaw joined the major television networks in a nationally televised interview with President Ronald Reagan. The next year he moderated the second presidential debate in Los Angeles.

Sources: Contemporary Black Biography, vol. 2, pp. 217–21; *Essence* 21 (November 1990), p. 42; *Negro Almanac,* p. 1285–86; *Split Image,* p. 389.

1981 ◆ **Edward R. Bradley** (1941–) became the first black co-editor of *Sixty Minutes,* a weekly news magazine on CBS-TV. His previous assignments included principal correspondent for *CBS Reports,* CBS News White House correspondent, anchor of the *CBS Sunday Night News,* and reports broadcast on *CBS Evening News with Walter Cronkite.*

Sources: Contemporary Black Biography, vol. 2, pp. 28–32; *Negro Almanac,* pp. 1278–79; *Who's Who Among Black Americans,* 1992–1993, p. 143.

1982 ◆ The first black co-host of the *Today* show was **Bryant Charles Gumbel** (1948–). Since 1975 he had been co-host for NBC's Rose Bowl Parade. Gumbel worked as chief anchor of NBC's football games and in 1977 was co-host for Super Bowl XI. In 1988 he was NBC's host for the Olympics in Seoul, South Korea.

Sources: Jet 61 (12 November 1981), p. 15; *Split Image,* p. 389; *Who's Who Among Black Americans, 1992–1993,* p. 573.

1986 ◆ **Valerie Coleman,** veteran television reporter in Los Angeles, was named weekday anchor for KCBS-TV in Los Angeles, becoming the first African American in that time slot.

Source: Jet 70 (8 September 1986), p. 20.

WLBT-TV, in Jackson, Mississippi, was the first black-owned network affiliate; the owner was the Civic Communications Corporation.

Source: Jet 71 (13 October 1986), p. 17.

Oprah Winfrey (1954–) became the first black woman to host a nationally syndicated weekday talk show, *The Oprah Winfrey Show.* She moved from WTVF, a CBS local affiliate in Nashville, Tennessee (where in 1971 she was the first woman co-anchor), to Baltimore, Maryland, and subsequently to Chicago. In 1984 Winfrey took over *A.M. Chicago,* which aired opposite Phil Donahue, and later expanded to the one-hour television show. She formed Harpo Productions, which enabled her to develop her own projects, and in 1989 bought her own television and movie production studio.

Sources: Black Women in America, vol. 2, pp. 1274–76; *Contemporary Black Biography,* vol. 2, pp. 262–66; *Notable Black American Women,* pp. 1273–76; *Who's Who Among Black Americans, 1992–1993,* p. 1556.

Oprah Winfrey

1990 ◆ **Dana Tyler** and **Reggie Harris**

formed the first black anchor team in a major metropolitan city for WCBS-TV, in New York City. Tyler is the great-granddaughter of Ralph Waldo Tyler, the first black war correspondent during World War I. (*See* also **Periodicals, 1918.**)

Source: Jet 78 (2 July 1990), p. 23.

Military

The Revolutionary War • The Civil War • The Post–Civil War Era
The Indian Campaigns • The Spanish-American War and the Early 1900s
World War I • World War II • The Post–World War II Era
The Korean War • The Vietnam War • The Post-Vietnam Era
The Persian Gulf War • Women in the Military

The Revolutionary War

1775 ◆ On April 19, 1775, **Lemuel Haynes** (1753–1833), Peter Salem, Pomp Blackman, Caesar Ferrit, John Ferrit, Prince Estabrook, and Samuel Craft were among the African Americans who participated in the first armed encounter of the Revolutionary War, the defense of Concord Bridge. (For Haynes, *see also* **Education: Honorary Degrees, 1804** and **Religion: Congregationalists, 1795.**)

Source: *Negro Almanac*, p. 803.

Salem Poor (c.1758–?) was the first black soldier to be recognized for heroism in battle. On June 17, 1775, he fought boldly at the battle known as Bunker Hill (which was actually fought on Breed's Hill) and wounded a British officer. Several officers asked the Continental Congress to recognize his bravery. There is no record that he received such notice though. Other African Americans at the battle were Barzillai Lew, Cuff Whittemore, Titus Coburn, Charlestown Eads, Peter Salem, Sampson Taylor, and Caesar Brown.

Sources: *Dictionary of American Negro Biography*, p. 500; *Encyclopedia of Black America*, p. 684; *Negro Almanac*, p. 804.

1778 ◆ The First Rhode Island Regiment was the first and only all-black unit to fight in the Revolutionary War. On February 2, 1778, Rhode Island passed the first slave enlistment act. In August, at the Battle of Rhode Island, the regiment of 125 African Americans successfully faced three attacks by the British, allowing the rest of the American army to make a safe retreat.

Sources: Cantor, *Historic Landmarks of Black America*, p. xvii; *Negro Almanac*, pp. 806–7.

The Civil War

1861 ◆ **Nicholas Biddle** was the first African American wounded in the Civil War. The 65-year-old former slave was injured while he accompanied the first Pennsylvania troops through Baltimore on April 18, 1861.

Sources: Encyclopedia of Black America, p. 62; Garrett, Famous First Facts About Negroes, p. 9.

James Stone (?–1862) was the first African American to fight with the Union forces during the Civil War. A very light-skinned runaway slave, he joined the 1st Fight Artillery of Ohio on August 23, 1861, and fought with the unit in Kentucky, the state in which he had been a slave. His racial identity was revealed after his death.

Source: Hornsby, Jr., Chronology of African-American History, p. 33.

1862 ◆ The 1st South Carolina Volunteers was the first regiment of black soldiers formed in the Civil War. They were quickly followed by the 1st and 2nd Kansas Colored Volunteers, a group who fought the first battle by black troops in the Civil War, in Clay County, Missouri.

Sources: Encyclopedia of Black America, p. 63; Negro Almanac, p. 833.

1863 ◆ The 54th Massachusetts Regiment was the first Northern black unit formed during the Civil War. Black leaders helped to recruit African Americans from free states, slave states, and Canada. The regiment fought bravely in July at Fort Wagner, the first major engagement seen by black troops. The regiment objected to the unequal pay of black and white enlisted men and served a year without pay rather than accept lesser wages.

Sources: Cantor, Historic Landmarks in Black America, pp. 73–74; Hornsby, Jr., Chronology of African-American History, p. 35; Hughes and Meltzer, Pictorial History of Black Americans, 1972, p. 180.

William Harvey Carney (1840–1908), of the 54th Massachusetts Colored Infantry, was the first African American in the Civil War to earn the Medal of Honor. Carney enlisted on February 17, 1863, and earned his medal of honor five months later at Fort Wagner, South Carolina. When the colors-bearer was wounded in the battle, Carney, also seriously hurt, sprang forward and seized the flag before it slipped from the bearer's grasp. The medal of honor was not issued until May 23, 1900. Upon Carney's death, the flag on the Massachusetts state house was flown at half mast—an honor formerly restricted to presidents, senators, and governors.

Sources: Alexander's Magazine 7 (15 January 1909), p. 109; Dictionary of American Negro Biography, p. 90–91; Encyclopedia of Black America, p. 835; Lee, Negro Medal of Honor Men, pp. 24–26.

Robert Smalls (1839–1915) was the first and only African American to attain the rank of captain in the navy during the Civil War. He was also one of the war's first black heroes. A member of a crew in the Confederate Navy, Smalls sailed a steamer named the *Planter* out of Charleston and turned it over to the Union on May 13, 1862 (the steamer was eventually refitted as a gunboat). He was then made a captain of the Union Navy. Smalls also distinguished himself following the war as a five-term U.S. Congressman.

Sources: *Dictionary of American Negro Biography*, pp. 560–61; Hornsby, Jr., *Chronology of African-American History*, p. 34; *Negro Almanac*, p. 833.

1864 ◆ **Robert Blake,** a powder boy aboard the U.S.S. *Marblehead,* was the first African American awarded the Naval Medal of Honor. Blake displayed unusual heroism during a victorious battle off the coast of South Carolina on December 23, 1863.

Sources: Bergman, *The Chronological History of the Negro in America*, p. 233; *Black Americans in Defense of Our Nation*, p. 54; Lee, *Negro Medal of Honor Men*, p. 35; *Negro Almanac*, p. 875.

The Post–Civil War Era

1869 ◆ **Robert Brown Elliott** (1842–1884) was the first black commanding general of the South Carolina National Guard. He was elected to the South Carolina legislature in 1868 and later served as a U.S. Congressman (1871 and 1874). In March 1869 Elliott was appointed assistant adjutant-general of the state and was given responsibility for forming and maintaining a state militia—often called the Black Militia—to protect white and black citizens from the Ku Klux Klan.

Sources: *Dictionary of American Negro Biography*, pp. 210–11; *Encyclopedia of Black America*, p. 354; *Negro Almanac*, p. 405.

1870 ◆ **James Webster Smith** was the first African American admitted to the military academy at West Point. He left the academy after being repeatedly harrassed and excluded by his classmates.

Sources: *Black Americans in Defense of Our Nation*, p. 131; Garrett, *Famous First Facts About Negroes*, p. 12; Kane, *Famous First Facts*, p. 36.

1877 ◆ **Henry Ossian Flipper** (1856–1940) was the first African American to graduate from the U.S. Military Academy at West Point, New York. Flipper graduated 50th out of a class of 76 after suffering four years of exclusion by white cadets. He joined the 10th Calvary in 1878, serving in Oklahoma and Texas. The only black officer in the army, Flipper was cleared of a theft charge in 1882 but was convicted of conduct unbecoming an officer and then discharged. He remained in the West and, for the next 50 years, engaged in engineering, mining, and survey work. Nearly a century later, in 1976, Flipper was finally found innocent by the army (his fellow officers had framed him in the theft), and on May 3, 1977—the centennial of his graduation—a bust was unveiled in his honor at West Point. His *Colored Cadet at West Point* (1878) gives a penetrating insight into his early life.

Sources: *Black Americans in Defense of Our Nation*, p. 27; *Dictionary of American Negro Biography*, pp. 227–28; Garrett, *Famous First Facts About Negroes*, p. 12.

The Indian Campaigns

1867 ◆ Congress approved the first all-black units in the regular army. These soldiers, known as "Buffalo Soldiers," served in the West and included the 9th and 10th Calvary Regiments as well as the 24th and 25th Infantry Regiments—U.S. Colored Troops. Their nickname came from the Indians, who believed their short curly hair was similar to that on the buffalo's neck and that their brave and fierce fighting matched the buffalo. Eleven black soldiers earned the Congressional Medal of Honor in combat against Utes, Apaches, and Comanches. Soldiers served in black regiments until the integration of U.S. forces in 1952. A monument honoring the Buffalo Soldiers was unveiled at Fort Leavenworth in 1992.

Sources: *Black Americans in Defense of Our Nation*, pp. 25–27; *Jet* 82 (7 September 1992), p. 34; Katz, *Black Indians*, p. 174.

1870 ◆ **Emanuel Stance** (c.1848–1887), a Buffalo Soldier of the 9th United Calvary, was the first African American in the Indian Campaigns to earn the Medal of Honor. He and a small group of comrades defeated a band of marauding Indians. It is believed that Stance was murdered by one of his own men.

Sources: *Black Americans in Defense of Our Nation*, pp. 26–27; *Dictionary of American Negro Biography*, pp. 568–69; Lee, *Negro Medal of Honor Men*, p. 59.

The Spanish-American War and the Early 1900s

1898 ◆ **Dennis Bell, George H. Tomkins, Fitz Lee, William H. Thompkins,** and **George H. Wanton**, privates in the 10th Calvary, were the first black soldiers honored with Medals of Honor in the Spanish-American

War. They selflessly rescued a stranded group of soldiers, despite three other failed attempts.

Sources: Black Americans in Defense of Our Nation, pp. 60–61; Lee, Negro Medal of Honor Men, p. 90.

Robert Penn (1872–?) was the only black seaman during the Spanish-American War to receive the Naval Medal of Honor. On July 20, 1898, the U.S.S. *Iowa* was anchored off Santiago, Cuba, when an explosion occurred in the boiler room. Penn saved a coal handler, single-handedly preventing an explosion that could have destroyed the *Iowa* and taken the lives of many crewmen. The medal was issued to Penn on December 14, 1898.

Sources: Lee, Negro Medal of Honor Men, p. 53; Negro Almanac, p. 876.

1906 ◆ **Allen Allensworth** (1842–1914) was the first black American to hold the rank of lieutenant colonel. Born a slave, he taught under the auspices of the Freedmen's Bureau, operated a number of businesses, and served as a chaplain during the Spanish-American War. At the time of his retirement, he was the senior chaplain in the army. He founded an all-black town named Allensworth in Tulare County, California, in 1908. A town resident named Oscar Over became California's first black justice of the peace in 1914.

Sources: Cantor, Historic Landmarks of Black America, p. 290; Dictionary of American Negro Biography, pp. 13–14; Foner, Blacks and the Military in American History, p. 65, 70.

World War I

1916 ◆ **Charles Young** (1864–1922) was the first and only African American to rise to the rank of lieutenant colonel during World War I. In 1904 Young (the third African American to graduate from the U.S. Military Academy) became the first black military attaché, or diplomat, in the history of the United States. He was assigned first to Haiti but also served in the Philippines and Mexico.

The same year he attained the rank of lieutenant colonel, Young was honored as the first military person to receive the NAACP's Spingarn Medal. In 1917 he was forced to retire for reasons of "physical unfitness for duty." (He was suffering from extremely high blood pressure and Bright's disease, which affects the kidneys.) In response Young mounted his favorite horse at Wilberforce, Ohio, and rode 500 miles to Washington, D.C., to prove that he was indeed fit for service. The army reinstated him in 1918, and he was assigned to train black troops at Fort Grant, Illinois. In 1919 Colonel Young was sent as military attaché to Liberia on a second tour of duty. He died in Lagos, Nigeria, during an inspection tour.

Sources: Dictionary of American Negro Biography, pp. 679–80; Foner, Blacks and the Military, pp. 64, 113; Jet 80 (29 July 1991), p. 4; Robinson, Historical Negro Biographies, p. 268.

1917 ◆ Fort Dodge near Des Moines, Iowa, was the first army camp for training black officers in World War I. About half (639) of the black officers commissioned during the war were trained there.

Sources: Dictionary of Black Culture, p. 166; Kane, Famous First Facts, p. 31.

In December 1917 the 369th Infantry Regiment became the first group of black combat soldiers to arrive in Europe. Cited 11 times for bravery, the regiment was awarded the Croix de Guerre (Cross of War) by the French government. In 1918 the 369th became the first Allied regiment to reach the Rhine in an offensive against Germany. The regimental band, conducted by James Reese Europe and Noble Sissle, is credited with the introduction of American jazz abroad.

Sources: Dictionary of Black Culture, p. 432; Encyclopedia of Black America, p. 836.

1918 ◆ **Henry Johnson** (1897–1929) and **Needham Roberts** were the first black soldiers to be awarded the French Croix de Guerre as individuals. Both men were privates with the 369th and were injured in an assault by German soldiers but succeeded in routing their attackers.

Sources: Dictionary of American Negro Biography, p. 351; Dictionary of Black Culture, p. 240; Kane, Famous First Facts, p. 367.

1991 ◆ Corporal **Freddie Stowers** (?-1918) was the first African American to earn the Medal of Honor in World War I. A heroic squad leader, Stowers had been recommended for the medal during World War I, but it was awarded 72 years later, following an army investigation of prejudice during the awards selection process. On September 28, 1918, Stowers's company was trying to capture a hill in the Champagne-Marne section in France. The Germans faked surrender to lure the Americans into a trap that killed more than half of the company, including those in command. Stowers took charge, leading a squad that destroyed the German guns. He was mortally wounded, but the company pressed on and captured the hill.

Sources: Atlanta Constitution, 8 April 1993; Jet 80 (13 May 91), p. 9.

World War II

1940 ♦ **Benjamin Oliver Davis, Sr.** (1877–1970) was the first black American general in the U.S. Army. Davis served in the 8th U.S. Volunteers Infantry from 1898 to 1899, then in the 9th Calvary from 1899 to 1917, and in the U.S. Army from 1918 to 1948. He was made a brigadier general in 1940 and retired in 1948, having served in the U.S. armed forces for a half century.

Sources: Black Americans in Defense of Our Nation, pp. 106–7; Encyclopedia of Black America, pp. 303–4; Hornsby, Jr., Milestones in Twentieth-Century African-American History, p. 36; Who's Who in Colored American, 1950, p. 139.

1941 ♦ **Dorie Miller** (1919–1943) was the first national black hero during World War II and was honored with the Navy Cross. A messman on the battleship U.S.S. *Arizona* during the Japanese attack on Pearl Harbor, Miller downed four enemy planes with a machine gun after ensuring the safety of his injured captain. As a messman Miller had not been trained in the use of a weapon. Miller was among the crew of the U.S. carrier *Liscome Bay* when it sank at sea after a torpedo struck her on November 24, 1943.

Sources: Dictionary of American Negro Autobiography, pp. 434–35; Encyclopedia of Black America, p. 837; Lee, Negro Medal of Honor Men, p. 107.

1942 ♦ Tuskegee Institute, Alabama, was the first and only training facility for black airmen in World War II. The U.S. Army established a school for black pilots, in spite of black opposition to the establishment of segregated Air Force facilities. While pilots began their training at Tuskegee, ground crews were prepared at Chanute Field in Illinois. By the end of the year the 99th Pursuit Squadron, the first black air unit in the history of the United States, was ready for action. In April 1943 the unit was in French Morocco for training under experienced combat pilots. The following month the leader of the squadron, Captain Benjamin Oliver Davis, Jr., was promoted to major, then lieutenant colonel—all in one day. About 600 black pilots received their wings during World War II.

Sources: Black Americans in Defense of Our Nation, p. 35; Cantor, Historic Landmarks of Black America, p. 352; Hornsby, Jr., Chronology of African-American History, p. 90; Negro Almanac, pp. 847–48.

1943 ♦ The U.S.S. *Mason* was the first naval destroyer with a primarily black crew and at least one black officer.

Source: Black Americans in Defense of Our Nation, p. 35.

1944 ♦ The U.S.S. *Harmon* was the first navy fighting ship named after an African American, Leonard Roy Harmon. Harmon (1916–1942) was a World War II naval hero who "deliberately exposed himself to hostile gunfire in order to protect a shipmate and as a result ... was killed in action." He was awarded the Navy Cross.

Sources: Black Americans in Defense of Our Nation, p. 37; Dictionary of Black Culture, p. 201.

Samuel Lee Gravely, Jr. (1922–) was the first black commissioned officer of the navy during World War II. He was released from active service after the war but was recalled in 1949. In January 1962 Gravely was given command of the destroyer U.S.S. *Falgout.* This was the first time a black officer had been given command of a ship in the modern navy. In 1963 Gravely and George I. Thompson were the first two African Americans chosen to attend the Naval College. A veteran of three wars, Gravely was the first black admiral in U.S. history. His promotion was confirmed by the U.S. Senate on May 15, 1971.

Sources: Encyclopedia of Black America, p. 408; Garrett, Famous First Facts About Negroes, pp. 15–17; Kane, Famous First Facts, p. 421; Lee, Negro Medal of Honor Men, p. 118.

Benjamin Oliver Davis, Sr.

The Post–World War II Era

1948 ◆ **John Earl Rudder** became the first black commissioned officer in the U.S. Marine Corps.

Source: Estell, ed., African American Almanac, 6th ed, p. 113.

1949 ◆ **Wesley A. Brown** was the first black graduate of the U.S. Naval Academy at Annapolis.

Sources: Black Americans in Defense of Our Nation, p. 142; Dictionary of Black Culture, p. 70.

The Korean War

1950 ◆ In 1949 **Jesse Leroy Brown** (?–1950) became the first black pilot in the Naval Reserve. A year later he became the first black flier killed in Korea. In 1971 a frigate was named for him, the first ever named for a black naval officer.

Sources: Black Americans in Defense of Our Nation, pp. 48–49; Kane, Famous First Facts, pp. 90, 561; Lee, Negro Medal of Honor Men, p. 14.

Daniel H. "Chappie"
James, Jr.

1951 ◆ Private first class **William Henry Thompson** (1928–1950) of the 24th Infantry Regiment became the first African American to earn the Medal of Honor in the Korean War. He was mortally wounded on August 2, 1951, while manning his machine gun during a surprise attack on his platoon. His actions allowed the unit to withdraw to a more defensible position.

Sources: Black Americans in Defense of Our Nation, p. 62; Kane, Famous First Facts, p. 371; Lee, Negro Medal of Honor Men, p. 9–12.

1954 ◆ **Benjamin Oliver Davis, Jr.** (1912–) was the first air force general and the first black man to command an airbase. Davis paralleled his father's career in rising to the rank of general, though in another branch of the armed forces. His *Autobiography: Benjamin O. Davis, Jr., American,* was published in 1991.

Sources: Contemporary Black Biographies, vol. 2, pp. 51–53; Hornsby, Jr., Milestones in Twentieth-Century African-American History, p. 55; Negro Almanac, p. 909.

The Vietnam War

1965 ◆ **Milton L. Olive III** (1946–1965) was the first black Medal of Honor hero in the Vietnam War. Private First Class Olive was a member of the 503rd Infantry. On October 22, 1965, he caught an exploding grenade and died to save his comrades.

Sources: Black Americans in Defense of Our Country, p. 76; Cantor, Historic Landmarks of Black America, p. 8; Lee, Negro Medal of Honor Men, p. 123.

1967 ◆ Private First Class **James Anderson, Jr.** (1947–1967) was the first black Marine to receive the Medal of Honor. On January 22, 1967, he threw himself on a grenade to save his comrades. A military supply ship was named after Anderson in his honor.

Source: Black Americans in Defense of Our Nation, p. 63.

Daniel H. "Chappie" James, Jr. (1920–78) became the first black four-star general in the U.S. Air Force. He was promoted to the rank of brigadier general in 1970 and received many awards and citations.

Sources: Encyclopedia of Black America, pp. 468–69; Negro Almanac, p. 911; Who's Who Among Black Americans, 1977, p. 466.

The Post-Vietnam Era

1982 ♦ Roscoe Robinson, Jr. (1928–1993) was the first black four-star general in the U.S. Army.

Sources: Jet 84 (9 August 1993), p. 15; (Nashville) Tennessean, 23 July 1993; Negro Almanac, 1976, p. 656; Who's Who Among Black Americans, 1992–1993, p. 1214.

The Persian Gulf War

1991 ♦ **Colin L. Powell** (1937–) was the first African American to serve, in the capacity of chairman of the Joint Chiefs of Staff, as one of the key planners of an American-led war. In 1991, working directly with Secretary of Defense Dick Cheney and President George Bush, he launched the Gulf War, which began with the biggest single air offensive in U.S. history. In

Colin L. Powell

1989 he became the first African American to be named chairman of the Joint Chiefs, the highest-ranking military position in the country. For the two years prior to that he served as the first black National Security Adviser. Because of his highly visible role in the Gulf War, his gift for leadership and diplomacy, and his widespread appeal, Powell has been mentioned as a good candidate for the presidency, though he himself has yet to express an interest in high-level politics. Powell announced his retirement from his job as chairman in 1993.

Sources: Contemporary Black Biography, vol. 1, pp. 195–98; Hornsby, Jr., Milestones in Twentieth-Century African-American History, pp. 412, 419, 460; Who's Who Among Black Americans, 1992–1993, p. 1142.

Women in the Military

1943 ♦ On August 21 **Harriet M. West** was the first black woman major in the Women's Army Corps (WAC). She was chief of the planning in the Bureau Control Division at WACs headquarters in Washington, D.C.

Sources: Foner, Blacks and the Military in American History, p. 165; Lee, Interesting People, p. 44.

1944 ♦ **Nancy C. Leftenant** was the first black nurse in the regular army. She was a graduate of Lincoln Hospital School for Nurses and joined

Clara Leach Adams-Ender

the army reserve nurse corps in February 1945.

Sources: Alford, *Famous First Blacks,* p. 65; *Black Women in America,* vol. 1, p. 795.

1945 ♦ **Phyllis Mae Dailey** was the first black woman to serve as a nurse in the U.S. Navy.

Sources: Black Women in America, vol. 1, pp. 795–96; *Dictionary of Black Culture,* p. 125.

1976 ♦ **Clara Leach Adams-Ender** (1930–) was the first black woman and nurse to graduate with a master's degree from the U.S. Army Command and General Staff College. In 1987, with the rank of brigadier general, Adams-Ender became head of the U.S. Army Nurse Corps.

Sources: Black Women in America, vol. 1, pp. 10–11; *Jet* 63 (15 November 1982), p. 16; *Notable Black American Women,* pp. 1–2.

1979 ♦ **Hazel Johnson** (1927–) became the first black woman general and the first African American to be placed in command of the Army Nurse Corps. In 1983 Johnson retired from the service and began working for the American Nursing Association as director of government affairs.

Source: Estell, ed., *African American Almanac,* 6th ed, p. 1330–1332.

1980 ♦ **Janie L. Mines** was the first black woman student at the U.S. Naval Academy, and in 1980, she became the first black woman to graduate from the academy.

Sources: Black Americans in Defense of Our Nation, p. 142; *Jet* 50 (27 June 1976), p. 16.

1985 ♦ **Sherian Grace Cadoria** (1940–) was the first black woman to obtain the rank of brigadier general in the regular army. She served as one of the four women army generals. Cadoria's tours of duty included Vietnam and key assignments with the Joint Chiefs of Staff, the Law Enforcement Division, and the Criminal Investigation Command. She retired in 1990.

Sources: Black Women in America, vol. 1, p. 214; Lanker, *I Dream a World,* p. 150.

1990 ♦ **Marcelite J. Harris** (1943–) became the first black woman brigadier general in the air force. Born in Houston, Texas, Harris was educated at Spelman College, Central Michigan University, Chapman College, the University of Maryland, and Harvard University. She entered the air force in

1965, and in 1971 she became the first black woman to become an aircraft maintenance officer. In 1978, as commander of a cadet squadron at the U.S. Air Force Academy, Harris became one of the first two female commanding air officers.

Sources: Black Women in America, vol. 1, pp. 538–39; *Notable Black American Women,* pp. 467–68; *Who's Who Among Black Americans, 1992–1993,* p. 610.

Marcelite J. Harris

Miscellaneous: A Variety of Milestones

Aviation • Beauty Industry • Commemoratives and Monuments
Festivals • Honors and Awards • Organizations • Various

Aviation

1921 ◆ **Bessie Coleman** (1893–1926) was the first black woman to earn a pilot's license. Coleman was also the first African American woman stunt pilot, and on the Labor Day weekend of 1922 she appeared for the first time as a stunt flyer. Four years later Coleman died in an air crash.

Sources: Alford, *Famous First Blacks*, p. 71; *Black Women in America*, pp. 262–63; *Notable Black American Women*, pp. 202–3.

1933 ◆ **Albert Ernest Forsythe** and **Charles Alfred Anderson** were the first black pilots to make a round-trip transcontinental flight. They left Atlantic City on July 17, 1933, in their plane *The Pride of Atlantic City*, arrived in Los Angeles, and completed their route on July 28.

Source: Powell, *Black Wings*, pp. 181–88.

1934 ◆ **Willa Brown-Chappell** (1906–1992) was the first black woman in the United States to hold a commercial pilot's license and the first black woman to gain officer rank (lieutenant) in the Civil Air Patrol Squadron. She also formed the National Airmen's Association of America, the first black aviators' group. In 1938, with her husband Cornelius R. Coffey, she established the first black-owned flying school, the Coffey School of Aeronautics. This school was also the first black-owned school certified by the Civil Aviation Authority. In 1972 Brown-Chappell was the first black member of the Federal Aviation Agency's Women's Advisory Commission.

Sources: *Atlanta Constitution*, 22 July 1992; *Black Women in America*, vol. 1, pp. 184–86; *Nashville Banner*, 21 July 1992.

1957 ◆ **Perry H. Young** (1919–) was the first black pilot of a scheduled passenger commercial airline. He flew for New York Airways.

Sources: Alford, *Famous First Blacks*, p. 70; *Who's Who Among Black Americans, 1992–1993*, p. 1587.

1958 ◆ **Ruth Carol Taylor** (1933–) was the first black commercial airline stewardess. Taylor was hired by Mohawk Airlines.

Source: Garrett, *Famous First Facts About Negroes*, p. 6.

1970 ◆ **Otis B. Young, Jr.,** was the first black pilot of a 747 jumbo jet.

Sources: Alford, *Famous First Blacks*, p. 70; Lee, *Interesting People*, p. 202.

1978 ◆ **Jill Brown** was the first black woman pilot on a major airline. Brown was a former naval pilot.

Sources: *Encyclopedia of Black America*, p. 146; Lee, *Interesting People*, p. 202.

Willa Brown-Chappell

Beauty Industry

1970 ◆ The first black contestant in a Miss America pageant was **Cheryl Adrenne Brown,** Miss Iowa.

Source: Alford, *Famous First Facts*, p. 68.

1974 ◆ The first black woman to appear on the cover of a major fashion magazine was **Beverly Johnson** (1952–). The model, actress, and singer appeared on the August issue of *Vogue* in 1974. In the early 1970s she also became the first black woman to appear on the cover of the French magazine *Elle,* and by 1992 she would appear on the covers of some 500 magazines.

Sources: *Contemporary Black Biography*, vol. 2, pp. 123–24; *Ebony* 47 (September 1992), p. 32; Hornsby, Jr., *Milestones in Twentieth-Century African-American History*, pp. 222–23; *Notable Black American Women*, pp. 575-76.

1983 ◆ **Vanessa Lynn Williams** (1963–) of New York became the first black Miss America. She also was the first to resign the title, in 1984. Suzette Charles, the first black Miss New Jersey, and the first black runner-up in the

Vanessa Williams

Miss America contest, took Williams's place. Williams later became an actress and singer.

Sources: Black Women in America, pp. 409; 1266–68; Jet 71 (2 February 1987), p. 56, 76 (18 September 1989), p. 27; The Negro Almanac, p. 1432; Who's Who Among Black Americans, 1992–1993, p. 1537.

1990 ◆ The first black Miss USA was **Carole Gist** (c. 1970–), who was crowned in Wichita, Kansas, on March 3, 1990. Gist was also first runner-up in the Miss Universe Pageant later that year.

Sources: Contemporary Black Biography, vol. 1, pp. 84–85; Hornsby, Jr., Milestones in Twentieth-Century African-American History, p. 441; Jet 77 (19 March 1990), p. 59, (26 March 1990), p. 58-60.

Commemoratives and Monuments

1876 ◆ A monument to Richard Allen, dedicated June 12, 1876, in Philadelphia's Freemont Park, may have been the first erected to a black American by African Americans.

Source: Dictionary of American Negro Biography, p. 13.

1940 ◆ The first black American depicted on a U.S. postage stamp was **Booker Taliaferro Washington** (1856–1915). His photograph was reproduced on the 10-cent brown stamp, which became available on April 7, 1940, at Tuskegee Institute in Alabama. The stamp was part of the Famous American Commemorative series issued in 1940. He was honored again on a stamp in 1956, marking the centennial (100th) anniversary of his birth. Perhaps the two most important black-related stamps are the 13th Amendment issue of 1940, which celebrated the 75th anniversary of the Constitutional abolition of slavery in the United States, and the Emancipation Proclamation stamp of 1963, which honored the 100th anniversary of the freeing of slaves in federally controlled areas during the Civil War. (*See also* **Education: Honorary Degree, 1896**.)

1946 ◆ The first coin honoring an African American and designed by an African American was issued. The 50-cent piece, which became available on

AFRICAN AMERICANS COMMEMORATED ON POSTAGE STAMPS

Date	Honoree	Area of Citation
April 7, 1940	Booker T. Washington	Educator
January 5, 1948	George Washington Carver	First black scientist
February 14, 1967	Frederick Augustus Douglass	First black civil rights leader
May 17, 1969	W. C. Handy	First African American blues musician
April 29, 1986	Duke Ellington	First jazz musician
September 10, 1973	Henry O. Tanner	First black painter
May 1, 1975	Paul Laurence Dunbar	First black poet
February 1, 1978	Harriet Tubman	Abolitionist and author; first black woman honored on a stamp
March 5, 1985	Mary McLeod Bethune	First black female educator
May 28, 1986	Matthew Henson	First black explorer
February 20, 1987	Jean Baptiste Pointe Du Sable	First black frontiers man
February 1, 1990	Ida B. Wells (Barnett)	First black woman journalist
September 15, 1991	Jan E. Matzeliger	First black inventor
June 22, 1993	Joe Louis	First black boxer
February 1, 1994	Dr. Allison Davis	First educator to become a fellow in the American Academy of Arts and Sciences
April 22, 1994	Buffalo Soldiers	First all-black units in the regular army

Sources: Jet 84 (28 June 1993), pp. 48–51; Kane, *Famous First Facts,* p. 482.

December 16, 1946, contained the bust of **Booker T. Washington,** the founder of Tuskegee Institute in Alabama. It was designed by Isaac S. Hathaway, who later designed the George Washington Carver half dollar.

Sources: Alford, *Famous First Blacks,* p. 68; *Jet* 81 (March 30, 1992), p. 32; *Negro Year Book,* 1947, p. 33.

George Washington
Carver

1960 ◆ George Washington Carver (1864–1943) who produced more than 400 different products from the peanut, potato, and pecan, became the first black scientist memorialized by a federal monument in the United States. In 1953 the U.S. Congress authorized the establishment of the George Washington Carver National Monument. It was erected on his birth site near Diamond, Missouri, and dedicated July 17, 1960. His scientific work improved the quality of life for millions of people and enhanced agriculture in the South. He took his mule-drawn "movable school" on weekend visits to impoverished farmlands to teach poor farmers to raise, improve, and preserve foods. Carver was born a slave. In 1894 he became the first African American to graduate from Iowa State College. He joined the faculty of Tuskegee Institute (now University) in 1896, where he developed a program of research in soil conservation and crop diversification.

Sources: Current Biography, 1940, pp. 148–50; Dictionary of American Negro Biography, pp. 92–95; Encyclopedia of Black America, p. 744; Hornsby, Jr., Milestones in Twentieth-Century African-American History, pp. 21, 202.

1963 ◆ Georg (George) Olden (1921–) was the first black artist to design a U.S. postage stamp. The stamp was designed to commemorate the centennial (100th) anniversary of the Emancipation Proclamation. It went on sale August 16, 1963.

Sources: Alford, Famous First Blacks, p. 9; I Have a Dream, p. 60; Jet 32 (17 August 1967), p. 11.

1969 ◆ A nuclear-powered submarine named in honor of George Washington Carver was launched and commissioned.

Sources: Garrett, Famous First Facts About Negroes, p. 122; Kane, Famous First Facts, p. 562.

1974 ◆ A monument honoring the life and work of Mary McLeod Bethune (1875–1955) was built in Washington, D.C., and was the first statue of an African American erected on public land. A noted educator, Bethune was named director of the National Youth Administration's Division of Negro Affairs in 1939; she thus became the highest-ranking black woman in government at the time. (*See also* Education: Honorary Degrees, 1946;

Organizations: Civil Rights and Political Organizations, 1935; Politics: Federal Appointments and Diplomacy, 1936.)

Sources: Cantor, *Historic Landmarks of Black America,* p. 275; *Notable Black American Women,* pp. 86–92; Robinson, *Historical Negro Biographies,* p. 163.

1987 ◆ The first state-owned and operated historic site honoring an African American in North Carolina was the Charlotte Hawkins Brown Memorial State Historic Site, in Sedalia. In 1983 the Charlotte Hawkins Brown Historical Foundation was incorporated to assist the state in establishing the site—the 40-acre former campus and 14 buildings of Palmer Memorial Institute, which Brown founded. (*See also* **Education: Awards and Honors, 1928.**)

Sources: Greensboro News and Record, 3 November 1991; *Jet* 73 (12 October 1987), p. 34; *Notable Black American Women,* p. 113.

1988 ◆ The Black Revolutionary War Patriots Memorial was approved for the Washington, D.C., mall location.

Source: Jet 75 (12 September 1988), p. 12.

Mary McLeod Bethune

Festivals

1949 ◆ **(Daniel) Louis "Satchmo" Armstrong** (1900–1971), was the first African American to preside over the New Orleans Mardi Gras. Born in New Orleans, he learned to play the coronet and read music while in the Negro Waifs Home for Boys. Armstrong moved to Chicago and became one of the most influential jazz artists. A superb showman, he was known for his gravelly, growling vocal style. He acquired the nickname "Satchmo" in 1932 from an editor of *The Melody Maker.*

Sources: Cantor, *Historical Landmarks of Black America,* pp. 165–66; *Encyclopedia of Black America,* p. 118; Southern, *Biographical Directory,* pp. 17–18; Southern, *The Music of Black Americans,* pp. 373–77.

1988 ◆ The first National Black Arts Festival in the United States was held in Atlanta.

Source: Jet 74 (25 April 1988), p. 51.

Ralph Bunche

Honors and Awards

1915 ◆ The first African American to receive the NAACP's Spingarn Medal was **Ernest Everett Just** (1883–1941). The award is given annually for the highest or noblest achievement by an American Negro. A zoologist and educator, Ernest Just was born in Charleston, South Carolina, and graduated from Dartmouth College and the University of Chicago. He began teaching at Howard University in Washington, D.C., before he earned his Ph.D. at the University of Chicago in 1916. His career as a distinguished biologist was hampered by racial prejudice, and he increasingly turned to Europe as a base for his research. In 1940 he was interned in France by the Germans but managed to return to the United States, where he died of pancreatic cancer on October 27, 1941.

Sources: *Contemporary Black Biography,* vol. 3, pp. 123–25; *Dictionary of American Negro Biography,* pp. 372–75; *Encyclopedia of Black America,* pp. 481, 807.

1922 ◆ **Mary Burnett Talbert** (1866–1923) was the first black woman to receive the NAACP's Spingarn Medal, for her efforts to preserve the home of Frederick Douglass in Anacostia, Virginia. In 1922 the home was dedicated as the Frederick Douglass Museum. In 1920 Talbert became the first African American delegate to be seated at the International Council of Women.

Sources: Brown, *Homespun Heroines,* pp. 217–19; Dannett, *Profiles of Negro Womanhood,* vol. 1, pp. 316–17; *Encyclopedia of Black America,* p. 807; Garrett, *Famous First Facts About Negroes,* p. 196; *Negro Yearbook, 1921–1922,* p. 18; *Notable Black American Women,* pp. 1095–1100.

1946 ◆ **Emma Clarissa (Williams) Clement** of Louisville, Kentucky, was the first black woman named "American Mother of the Year." The Golden Rule Foundation gave her the honor on May 1, 1946. At the time Clement's son, Rufus, was president of Atlanta University.

Sources: Alford, *Famous First Blacks,* p. 69; *Chronology of African-American History,* p. 93; *Dictionary of American Negro Biography,* p. 117; Hornsby, Jr., *Milestones in Twentieth-Century African-American History,* p. 44; *Negro Year Book, 1947,* p. 33.

1950 ◆ The first African American awarded the Nobel Peace Prize was **Ralph Bunche** (1904–1971). The award was presented on September 22,

1950, for his peace efforts in the Middle East. Other blacks who have received Nobel Peace Prizes are Martin Luther King, Jr. (1964), Albert J. Luthuli of South Africa (1960), and Desmond Tutu of South Africa (1984). Born in the slums of Detroit, Bunche received his Ph.D. in political science from Harvard University in 1934, becoming the first African American to be awarded the degree. In 1968 he became under-secretary general of the United Nations and was the highest ranking African American in the United Nations at that time. (*See also* **Politics: Federal Appointments and Diplomacy, 1944.**)

Sources: Alford, *Famous First Blacks,* p. 13; *Encyclopedia of Black America,* pp. 198–99; Hornsby, Jr., *Milestones in Twentieth-Century African-American History,* pp. 47, 49, 73, 158.

1963 ♦ **Marian Anderson** (1902–1993) and Ralph Bunche (1904–1971) were the first black winners of the Presidential Medal of Freedom. (*See also* **Music, 1955.**)

Source: Alford, *Famous First Blacks,* pp. 13–14.

William Leo Hansberry (1894–1964) was the first recipient of the Hailie Selassie I prize, which he received for his pioneering work in African history and anthropology.

Source: Dictionary of American Negro Biography, p. 386.

Marian Anderson

1970 ♦ **Charlemae Hill Rollins** (1897–1979) was the first black winner of the Constance Lindsay Skinner Award (now the WNBA Award) of the Women's National Book Association. She worked to dispel negative images of African Americans in books for children and young adults and became an expert on intercultural relations and children's literature.

Sources: Black Writers, p. 494; Garrett, *Famous First Facts About Negroes,* pp. 197–98; Josey, *The Black Librarian in America,* pp. 153–54; *Notable Black American Women,* pp. 949–53.

1979 ♦ The first black recipient of the AMC Cancer Research Center Humanitarian Award was **Kenneth Gamble** (1943–). Born in Philadelphia, Gamble became a businessman and songwriter and co-founded Philadelphia International Records. He and his partner, Leon Huff, wrote and produced chart-topping songs and records for such artists as Lou Rawls, Teddy Pendergrass, and the O'Jays. He received a Grammy Award in 1976.

Sources: Jet 59 (January 15, 1981), p. 29; *Who's Who Among Black Americans, 1992–1993*, p. 501.

Organizations

1775 ◆ The Pennsylvania Society for the Abolition of Slavery was the first antislavery society. It was organized in Philadelphia on April 14, 1775, and its first president was John Baldwin.

Sources: Encyclopedia of Black America, p. 789; Hornsby, Jr., *Chronology of African-American History*, p. 7; Kane, *Famous First Facts*, p. 1; *Negro Almanac*, pp. 5, 812.

1905 ◆ Twenty-nine black intellectuals and activists from 14 states met near Niagara Falls, New York, on July 11–13 to establish the Niagara Movement. Led by W. E. B. Du Bois and William Monroe Trotter, the organization rejected the self-help policies of Booker T. Washington and encouraged African Americans to press for immediate civil rights without compromise. In 1909 the movement merged with the National Association for the Advancement of Colored People (NAACP).

Sources: Alford, Famous First Blacks, p. 24; Bennett, *Before the Mayflower*, p. 512; Hornsby, Jr., *Chronology of African-American History*, p. 61.

1909 ◆ The first meeting of the National Association for the Advancement of Colored People (NAACP) was held in New York City on February 12—Abraham Lincoln's birthday. Among those who signed the original charter were Jane Addams, John Dewey, W. E. B. Du Bois, William Dean Howells, and Oswald Garrison Villard. The permanent organization was created May 12–14, 1910; Moorfield Story, a Boston lawyer, was elected president.

Sources: Bennett, Before the Mayflower, pp. 337–39, 512; Hornsby, Jr., *Chronology of African-American History*, p. 64; *Negro Almanac*, p. 21.

1911 ◆ The National Urban League was formed in October from the merger of the Committee for Improving the Industrial Conditions of Negroes in New York (1906), the National League for the Protection of Colored Women (1906), and the Committee on Urban Conditions Among Negroes (1910). George Edmund Haynes and Eugene Kinckle Jones were among the cofounders. Edwin R. A. Seligman was president and Jones was executive secretary. The National Urban League became an early leader among black organizations in research when Charles S. Johnson organized the research department in 1920. In addition, Johnson became editor of *Opportunity: A Journal of Negro Life*, a black periodical founded in 1923.

Bennett, *Before the Mayflower*, pp. 339, 515; *Encyclopedia of Black America*, p. 635; *Negro Almanac*, pp. 22, 262.

1915 ♦ The Association for the Study of Negro Life and History was organized by **Carter G. Woodson** (1875–1950) as the first learned society devoted solely to the study of black history. For both his own research and his encouragement of the research of others, Woodson is known as the Father of Negro History. The first issue of the *Journal of Negro History* appeared in 1916. This organization first sponsored Negro History Week (now Black History Month) in 1926.

Sources: *Cantor, Historic Landmarks of Black America*, p. xxvi; *Dictionary of American Negro Biography*, pp. 665–67; *Ebony* 48 (February 1993), pp. 23–24, 28; *Encyclopedia of Black America*, pp. 867–68; *Negro Almanac*, pp. 22–24.

Carter G. Woodson

1944 ♦ The United Negro College Fund was first founded on April 24, 1944, to coordinate the fund-raising efforts of 41 private, accredited, four-year schools. It was chartered in New York. It was the first attempt by private black colleges to establish a cooperative fundraising organization. Its efforts still contribute significantly to the survival of black higher education. The fund's founder was Frederick D. Patterson (1901–), a veterinarian, who also founded the first veterinary school at Tuskegee Institute (Alabama). He later served as president of Tuskegee for 25 years. Patterson received the Medal of Freedom on June 23, 1987, when he was 86 years old.

Sources: *Ebony Success Library*, vol. 1, p. 242; *Encyclopedia of Black America*, p. 823; Hornsby, Jr., *Chronology of African-American History*, p. 92; *Jet* 72 (11 May 1987), p. 24, 72 (27 July 1987), p. 22; *Negro Almanac*, p. 1369.

1975 ♦ **Gloria Dean Randle Scott** (1938–) was the first black president of the Girl Scouts of America. Scott held this position until 1978. An educator, she became president of Bennett College in 1987.

Sources: *Black Women in America*, pp. 1018–19; *Notable Black American Women*, pp. 993-97; *Who's Who Among Black Americans, 1992–1993*, p. 1250.

1977 ◆ **Karen Farmer** (1951–) was the first known black member of the Daughters of the American Revolution. She traced her ancestry to William Hood, a soldier in the Revolutionary army.

Sources: American Libraries 39 (February 1978), p. 70; *Negro Almanac,* pp. 73, 1431; *Who's Who Among Black Americans, 1992–1993,* p. 446.

1978 ◆ **Faye Wattleton** (1943–) became the first African American, and the first woman, president of the Planned Parenthood Federation. She held the post of president until she resigned in 1992.

Sources: Black Women in America, pp. 1239–40; *Jet* 62 (5 April 1982), p. 41; *Notable Black American Women,* pp. 1230–32; *Who's Who Among Black Americans, 1992–1993,* p. 1474.

Various

1831 ◆ The first black woman to speak publicly on political themes to audiences of men and women and leave texts of her speeches was **Frances Maria Miller W. Stewart** (1803–1979). She was probably the first black woman to lecture in defense of women's rights. A women's rights activist, journalist, and educator, she was born in Hartford, Connecticut. Her public speaking career began in 1832 and lasted less than two years. She wrote for the *Liberator,* which published the texts of her speeches. Between 1861 and 1863 Stewart moved to Washington, D.C., where she was a teacher and a friend of Elizabeth Keckley, Mary Todd Lincoln's dressmaker. In 1871 she opened a Sunday school for destitute children near the Howard University campus.

Sources: Black Women in Nineteenth Century American Life, pp. 183–200; Lerner, *Black Women in White America,* pp. 83–85; *Notable American Women,* vol. 3, pp. 377–78; *Notable Black American Women,* pp. 1083–87.

c. 1850 ◆ A black chef, possibly Hyram S. Thomas Bennett, was reputed to have introduced potato chips in America. It has also been claimed that an American Indian, George Crum, first made potato chips in 1853; they were called Saratoga Potato Chips. Another claim is made on behalf of a locally famous black cook, Mrs. Catherine A. Wicks (1814–1917). She is said to have introduced them at Moon's Clubhouse in Saratoga Lake, New York.

Sources: Bennett, *Before the Mayflower,* p. 650; Kane, *Famous First Facts,* p. 493; *Negro Year Book, 1921–1922,* p. 6.

1871 ◆ **Daniel Alexander Payne Murray** (1852–1925) was the first African American to hold a professional position at the Library of Congress.

As assistant librarian he was asked to prepare an exhibit on black achievements for the 1900 Paris Exposition, and an accompanying bibliography was a cornerstone for future black bibliographies by him and others.

Sources: Dictionary of American Negro Biography, pp. 463–56; Garrett, *Famous First Facts About Negroes,* p. 97.

1919 ◆ Southside Settlement House, the first for African Americans with an African American staff, was founded by **Ada S. McKinley** (1868–1952), who recognized such a need among those African Americans who migrated to Chicago during World War I in search of work. In 1949, with the help of the community, a new home was founded and renamed McKinley House in her honor.

Source: Lee, *Interesting People,* p. 25.

1942 ◆ **Hugh Mulzac** (1886–1971) was the first black captain of an American merchant marine ship. In 1920 he became the first African American to earn a ship master's license, but he couldn't find a position as captain because of racial prejudice. In 1942 he was granted the right to man the liberty ship *Booker T. Washington.* His ship saw anti-aircraft action on a number of occasions.

Sources: Dictionary of Black Culture, p. 311; Hornsby, Jr., *Chronology of African-American History,* p. 91; *Negro Almanac,* p. 1426.

1977 ◆ **Carmen Elizabeth Turner** (?–1992) was the first black woman to head a major public transportation network. Turner was named as general manager of the Washington, D.C., transit authority, and served until 1983. In mid-December 1990 Turner became the first black undersecretary at the Smithsonian Institution.

Sources: Ebony 39 (March 1984), pp. 93–94, 98; *Jet* 79 (29 October 1990), p. 10; *Washington Post,* 3 October 1990; *Who's Who Among Black Americans, 1992–1993,* p. 1419.

Music

1764 ♦ **Newport Gardner** (Occramer Marycoo, 1746–1826) was the first black American to compose in the European tradition. It is likely that Gardner became one of the first black music teachers in the new nation in 1783. In 1791 he purchased his and his family's freedom and established a singing school in Newport. "Crooked Shanks" (1803), which he may have composed, was probably the first musical composition by a black American to be published. The text of *Promise Anthem,* one of his choral pieces performed in Newport and Boston, still exists.

Sources: Detroit Free Press, 9 February 1992; Hornsby, Jr., *Chronology of African-American History,* p. 10; Southern, *Music of Black Americans,* pp. 69–70; Southern, *Readings in Black American Music,* pp. 36–40.

1818 ♦ **Frank (Francis) Johnson** (1792–1844), in the earliest of a long series of firsts, was the first black American musician to publish sheet music. He was also the first African American to win fame as a musician in the United States and in England, the first to give formal band concerts, and the first to tour widely in the United States. In the 1843–44 season Johnson produced the first racially integrated concerts in U.S. history. He was the first American musician of any race to take a musical group abroad, and he introduced the promenade concert to the United States. Said to have been born in Martinique, he migrated to the United States in 1809 and settled in Philadelphia.

Sources: Black Perspective in Music, 5 (Spring 1977), pp. 3–29; Southern, *Biographical Dictionary of Afro-American and African Musicians,* pp. 205–7; Southern, *The Music of Black Americans,* pp. 107–10, 112–16.

1853 ♦ **Elizabeth Taylor Greenfield** (c. 1819–1876), the nation's first black concert singer, became the first black singer to give a command performance before royalty when she appeared before Queen Victoria on May 10, 1853. She was called "The Black Swan" because of her sweet tones and wide vocal range. Greenfield toured the United States and Canada extensively during her career and became the best-known black concert artist of her time. In the 1860s she organized and directed the Black Swan Opera Troupe.

Sources: Dictionary of American Negro Biography, pp. 268–70; *Notable Black American Women,* pp. 412–16; Southern, *The Music of Black Americans,* pp. 103–4.

1858 ♦ The first black pianist to win national fame was **Thomas Greene Bethune,** or "Blind Tom" (1849–1909). Born a blind slave near Columbus, Georgia, his talent as a composer and a pianist was soon recognized by Colonel Bethune, who bought him in 1850. The child prodigy made his debut in Savannah, Georgia, and for over 40 years amazed his audiences "with his artistry and his gift for total recall" of the more than 700 pieces that he played. Bethune had sporadic formal training and is said to have composed over 100 works. The most celebrated of the early black pianists, he began a tour of Europe in 1866 that netted $100,000.

Sources: Dictionary of American Negro Biography, pp. 43–44; *Encyclopedia of Black America,* p. 174; Garrett, *Famous First Facts About Negroes,* pp. 122–23; Southern, *The Music of Black Americans,* pp. 246–47.

Elizabeth Taylor Greenfield

1873 ♦ The first black opera troupe organized to present complete operas in the United States was the Colored American Opera Company of Washington, D.C. The first lasting black opera company was the Theodore Drury Colored Opera Company, which began in Brooklyn, New York, in 1889.

Sources: Garrett, *Famous First Facts About Negroes,* p. 125; Moses, *Alexander Crummell,* p. 202; Southern, *The Music of Black Americans,* pp. 256, 288.

1878 ♦ **James Bland** (1854–1911) was the first African American to compose what later became an official state song. "Carry Me Back to Old Virginny" was adopted by the state in April 1940, though few knew that it was by a black composer. Bland wrote approximately 700 songs in his career, including "Oh, Dem Golden Slippers" and "In the Evening by the Moonlight."

Sources: Dictionary of American Negro Biography, pp. 46–47; *Encyclopedia of Black America,* p. 184; Southern, *The Music of Black Americans,* pp. 234–37.

James Monroe Trotter (1842–92) wrote the first important book on African Americans in music, *Music and Some Highly Musical People.* The book contains valuable biographical material and an appendix reproducing the scores of 13 black compositions.

Sources: Dictionary of American Negro Biography, pp. 602–3; Garrett, *Famous First Facts About Negroes,* p. 126.

W. C. Handy

1891 ◆ **Charles ("Buddy") Bolden** (1877–1931) was the first African American to form what may have been a real jazz band, in New Orleans. He has been called the father of jazz, and because of his fierce, driving tone, he became "King Bolden." His band incorporated blues and ragtime. Bolden developed a coronet style that influenced such musicians as King Oliver and Dizzy Gillespie.

Sources: Encyclopedia of Black America, p. 603; *Negro Almanac,* p. 1204; Southern, *The Music of Black Americans,* pp. 340–41, 375; Williams, *Jazz Masters of New Orleans,* pp. 2–25.

1897 ◆ In December 1897 the first piano rag by an African American, "Harlem Rag," was published. Its composer, **Thomas Million Turpin** (1873–1922), was a St. Louis bar owner.

Source: Southern, *The Music of Black America,* pp. 291, 316, 323.

1902 ◆ **Ma (Gertrude) Rainey** (1886–1939), of the Rabbit Foot Minstrels, was the first African American to sing the blues in a professional show. She learned a blues song from a local woman in Missouri, and audience response was such that she began to specialize in blues.

Sources: Bergman, *The Chronological History of the Negro in America,* p. 336; *Notable Black American Women,* pp. 913–16; Southern, *The Music of Black Americans,* p. 330.

1903 ◆ **Wilbur Sweatman** (1882–1961) and his band were the first black dance band to record. They played Scott Joplin's "Maple Leaf Rag" in a music store in Minneapolis, Minnesota. Sweatman was noted for playing three clarinets at the same time.

Source: Southern, *The Music of Black Americans,* pp. 305–6.

1909 ◆ "Memphis Blues," by **William Christopher Handy** (1873–1958) was the first written blues composition. It was also the first popular song to use a jazz break. Written in 1909 as a campaign song for "Boss" Edward H. Crump when he ran for mayor of Memphis, it was published in 1912. The song was the third blues song published. Black songwriter Artie Matthews published the first, "Baby Seals Blues" in August 1912; a white composer published the second in September 1912; and Handy's song came three weeks later. Handy led the way in the adaptation of Southern black folk blues into popular music. His "St. Louis Blues" (1914) carried the blues all over the world. In 1918 he established himself in New York City, where he made his first recordings and co-founded a music company. Handy lost his sight after World War I, partially regained it, but became totally blind in 1943. Over the years he continued to write music, arrange spirituals and blues, and compose marches and hymns. One of the most celebrated musicians of his time, Handy is known as the "Father of the Blues."

Sources: Bergman, *The Chronological History of the Negro in America,* pp. 273–74; Cantor, *Historic Landmarks of Black America,* pp. 127–28; *Dictionary of American Negro Biography,* pp. 282–83; *Encyclopedia of Black America,* p. 415; Southern, *Biographical Dictionary of African-American and African Musicians,* pp. 165–66; Southern, *The Music of Black Americans,* pp. 336–38.

1915 ◆ "Jelly Roll Blues," by **Jelly Roll Morton** (Ferdinand Joseph La Menthe, 1885–1941), was the first published jazz arrangement. Morton was the first true jazz composer and the first to notate his jazz arrangements.

Sources: Dictionary of American Negro Biography, pp. 445–56; Southern, *The Music of Black Americans,* pp, 376–77.

1917 ◆ **Roland Hayes** (1887–1976) became the first African American to sing in Symphony Hall in Boston. Hayes studied at Fisk University where he was a member of the Fisk Jubilee Singers. He left Fisk to study voice in Boston, then traveled and studied in Europe. The 1917 concert did not attract much public attention, but another in the same venue on December 2, 1923, was a triumph. It was the beginning of a major career for Hayes. In 1923 he sang with the Boston Symphony and may have been the first African American to sing with a major orchestra. Hayes became the first black American to give a recital at Carnegie Hall in 1924. He was known in the United States for his interpretation of classical lieder (German songs) and Negro spirituals and was the leading black singer of his time.

Sources: Encyclopedia of Black America, p. 424; *Negro Almanac,* p. 1184; Southern, *Biographical Dictionary of Afro-American and African Musicians,* p. 173; Southern, *The Music of Black Americans,* pp. 400–402.

1920 ◆ On February 14, 1920, **Mamie Smith** (1883–1946) was the first black woman to make a record. She recorded "You Can't Keep a Good Man Down" and "This Thing Called Love." These songs were written by her black manager, Perry Bradford, who also wrote the next two songs she recorded, "It's Right Here for You" and "Crazy Blues." The first blues song ever recorded, "Crazy Blues" sold 790,000 copies in the first year. Its success led OKeh Records to establish its series "Original Race Records" under black musical director Clarence Williams (1893–1965).

Sources: Encyclopedia of Black America, p. 599; *Notable Black American Women,* pp. 1048–49; Southern, *Biographical Dictionary of African-American and African Musicians,* p. 347; Southern, *The Music of Black Americans,* p. 365.

1921 ◆ The Pace Phonograph Company, which used the Black Swan label, was the first black-owned record company. It was established in January 1921 by Henry Pace (1897–1943), who owned a music publishing company with W. C. Handy. Two former workers for the Pace-Handy Company joined him: Fletcher Henderson (1897–1952) as a recording manager, and William Grant Still (1895–1978) as an arranger. In the spring of 1921 Ethel Waters (1896–1977) recorded the company's first hit, "Down Home Blues/Oh, Daddy." During its first six months the company reportedly sold over 500,000 records. It went broke in 1923 and was sold to Paramount Records the following year.

Source: Southern, *The Music of Black Americans*, pp. 366–67.

1922 ◆ **Kid (Edward) Ory** (1886–1973), jazz trombonist, and his Sunshine Orchestra made the first instrumental jazz recording for the Nordskog label in Los Angeles in June 1922. King (Joseph) Oliver (1885–1938) and his band, often cited as the first to record, did not actually make their first record until April 6, 1923. George Morrison (1891–1974), who headed big bands operating out of Denver, Colorado, made recordings in March and April 1920, but they were never released.

Sources: Garrett, *Famous First Facts About Negroes*, p. 129; Southern, *Biographical Dictionary*, pp. 295–96; Southern, *The Music of Black Americans*, pp. 373, 379.

1923 ◆ The record "Downhearted Blues/Gulf Coast Blues" was the first record by an African American to sell over 1 million copies. The singer **Bessie Smith** (1894–1937) became one of the most important women in the history of American music, both as a stage performer and recording star. Her "Backwater Blues" and "Do Your Duty," among others, have become American classics. Early on Smith performed with Ma (Gertrude) Rainey, the first professional to sing blues, in the Rabbit Foot Minstrels. Smith's only movie appearance was in the first film short featuring black musicians, *Saint Louis Blues,* later retitled *Best of the Blues,* in 1929.

Sources: Dictionary of American Negro Biography, pp. 561–62; *Encyclopedia of Black America,* p. 797; *Notable Black American Women,* pp. 1041–45; Southern, *Biographical Dictionary,* p. 343; Southern, *The Music of Black Americans,* pp. 368–69, 437.

In October the first male to record the blues guitar, either as solo or accompaniment, was **Sylvester Weaver** (1897-1960). However, the first to achieve success was "Papa" Charlie Jackson (?–1938), who recorded "Lawdy, Lawdy Blues" and "Airy Man Blues" in August 1924. These men represented the down-home blues as opposed to the classic city blues of the great women blues singers.

Source: Southern, *The Music of Black Americans*, p. 369.

1924 ♦ **Sidney Bechet** (c. 1897–1959) became the first African American to achieve recognition on the soprano saxophone. He was also one of the first African Americans honored in classical music circles as a serious musician. Born in New Orleans, he was playing the clarinet by the age of six. In his early teens he played professionally, working with famous bands and orchestras such as King Oliver's and Jack Carey's, and made his first recording in 1924. A statue of Bechet was erected in Antibes in honor of his work in France.

Sources: Dictionary of American Negro Biography, p. 36; Garrett, *Famous First Facts About Negroes,* p. 129; *Negro Almanac,* p. 1203.

DeFord Bailey, Sr. (1899–1982), a harmonica player, became the first black musician to perform on the Grand Ole Opry in Nashville, Tennessee, on December 26, 1924. Originally called "The Barn Dance," the show changed its name to "The Grand Ole Opry" in autumn 1927. Bailey was perhaps the first African American heard on nationwide radio. The next year he was the first African American to have a recording session in Nashville. Bailey recorded eight sides for RCA. Known for his train sounds, he was one of the most influential harmonica players in blues and country music and one of the most popular performers in the first 15 years of the Opry, the longest-running radio show in the country. In 1991 a memorial marker was erected near his birth site in Wilson County, Tennessee.

Sources: Essence 7 (September 1977), pp. 154–55; Morton, *DeFord Bailey; Split Image,* p. 176; (Nashville) *Tennessean,* 18 December 1991.

1926 ♦ **Eva Jessye** (1895–1992) became the first black woman to gain fame as director of a professional choral group. The Eva Jessye Choir performed regularly at the Capital Theater in New York City from 1926 to 1929. Jessye directed the choir in Hollywood's first black musical, *Hallelujah,* in 1929. In 1935 Jessye became choral director of the premier of George Gershwin's *Porgy and Bess.*

Sources: Black Women in America, pp. 635–36; *Notable Black American Women,* pp. 573–75; Southern, *Music of Black Americans,* pp. 429–35.

1927 ♦ **Lillian Evanti** (1890–1967) was the first black American to sing opera with an organized European opera company, singing *Lakmé* in Nice, France. Novelist Jessie Fauset suggested the name Evanti, a contraction of her maiden name and her married name. She was a founder of the Negro Opera Company in Washington, D.C.

Sources: Dictionary of American Negro Biography, pp. 215–16; *Notable Black American Women,* pp. 329–31; Southern, *The Music of Black Americans,* p. 406.

William Grant Still

1929 ◆ The Mills Brothers were the first black group to have commercial sponsorship on a national network, CBS. They first broadcast over WLW in Chicago in 1929. The longest-lived group of modern times, the Mills Brothers performed from about 1922 to 1982. During this period there were two changes in personnel: bassist John, Jr., died in 1936, and was replaced by his father, who retired in 1954. The quartet then became a trio.

Source: Southern, *The Music of Black Americans,* pp. 437, 498.

1930 ◆ The first woman to lead an all-male band was **Blanche Calloway** (1902–1973), one of the most successful bandleaders of the 1930s. For a time she and her brother, Cab, had their own act. While in Miami she also became the first woman disk jockey on American radio. Calloway toured from 1931 to 1944 with "The 12 Clouds of Joy" as singer, dancer, and conductor.

Sources: Black Women in America, p. 216; *Encyclopedia of Black America,* p. 212; *Notable Black American Women,* pp. 152–53.

The National Baptist Convention, U.S.A., was the first major religious group to publicly approve gospel music. From this endorsement followed the first choruses, the first publishing houses, the first professional organizations, and the first paid gospel concerts. Thomas Dorsey (1899–1993), the "Father of Gospel," founded the first gospel choir in the world with Theodore Frye at Chicago's Ebenezer Baptist Church in 1931. He established the first music publishing firm dedicated only to gospel music in 1932. The action of the Baptist convention, which had been carried away by Dorsey's "If You See My Savior," called public attention to a major change that had been taking place in the music of black churches and is often considered the starting point for the history of gospel music.

Sources: The New Grove Dictionary of Music and Musicians, pp. 391–92; Southern, *The Music of Black Americans,* pp. 451–53, 472.

1931 ◆ **William Grant Still** (1895–1978) was the first African American to compose a symphony (his first such work, the *Afro-American Symphony*) performed by a major orchestra, the Rochester Philharmonic. In

1936 he was the first African American to conduct a major symphony orchestra, the Los Angeles Philharmonic, and became the first black American to have an opera performed by a major opera company in 1949, when New York City Opera put on *Troubled Island.*

Sources: Abdul, *Blacks in Classical Music,* pp. 29–32; Bergman, *The Chronological History of the Negro in America,* p. 316; *Encyclopedia of Black America,* p. 809; Southern, *Biographical Dictionary of African-American and African Musicians,* pp. 359–61; Southern, *The Music of Black Americans,* pp. 406, 423–27.

1932 ◆ **Don (Donald Matthew) Redman** (1900–1964) was the first orchestra leader to have a sponsored radio series. He was a pioneer jazz arranger-composer and contributed greatly to the development of the big-band sound of the 1920s and 1930s.

Sources: Chilton, *Who's Who of Jazz,* pp. 313–14; *Encyclopedia of Black America,* p. 729; Southern, *Biographical Dictionary of African-American and African Musicians,* p. 318.

1933 ◆ **Caterina Jarboro** (1903–1986) was the first African American to sing with the Chicago Opera Company. She sang the title role in *Aida* with the company in New York City. She began her career in Broadway musicals, including *Shuffle Along* (1921) and *Running Wild* (1923).

Sources: *Encyclopedia of Black America,* p. 469; Southern, *Biographical Dictionary of African-American and African Musicians,* pp. 200–201; Southern, *The Music of Black Americans,* p. 407.

1933 ◆ **Florence Price** (1888–1953) was the first black woman to compose a symphony performed by a major symphony orchestra and the first black woman to achieve distinction as a composer. The Chicago Symphony, under Frederick Stock, first played her Symphony in E Minor at the Chicago World's Fair.

Sources: *Black Women in America,* pp. 940–41; *Notable Black American Women,* pp. 872–74; Southern, *The Music of Black Americans,* pp. 416–19.

1934 ◆ On November 14, 1934, **William Levi Dawson's** (1899–1990) Symphony No. 1, *Negro Folk Symphony,* was the first symphony on black folk themes by a black composer to be performed by a major orchestra. The symphony was substantially revised in 1952 after Dawson visited West Africa. Under his leadership the Tuskegee Choir became internationally renowned.

Sources: *Encyclopedia of Black America,* p. 305; *Famous First Facts,* pp. 72, 630; Southern, *Biographical Directory,* pp. 98–99; Southern, *The Music of Black Americans,* pp. 418–19.

1938 ◆ **"Sister" Rosetta Tharpe** (1921–1973) was the first African American to take gospel music into a popular setting when she sang on a Cab Calloway show from the Cotton Club. When she signed with Decca she became the first gospel singer to record for a major company. Raised in the Holiness Church, Tharpe began touring as a professional when she was six. She took the lead in bringing gospel music to the mainstream. Tharpe was the first to tour extensively in Europe, and in 1943 she was the first to sing gospel at the Apollo Theater in New York City.

Sources: Notable Black American Women, pp. 1120–21; Southern, *The Music of Black Americans,* pp. 456, 472.

1940 ◆ "Surely God is Able," written by Baptist minister W. Herbert Brewster, Sr. (1897–1987) and recorded by the Ward Singers, is said to be the first gospel recording by a black singing group to sell more than 1 million copies. Principal singers in the group were Gertrude Ward (1901–1983) and Clara Mae Ward (1924–73). In 1957 the group was the first to perform at the Newport Jazz Festival. They were also the first to appear in nightclubs in 1961, and the first to sing at Radio City Music Hall in New York City in 1963.

Sources: Ebony, December 1950, p. 95; *Encyclopedia of Black America,* p. 832; Heilbut, *Gospel Sound,* pp. 137-43; *Notable Black American Women,* pp. 1202–5; Southern, *The Music of Black Americans,* pp. 468–69.

1941 ◆ The first black electric guitarist to use single-string solos was **Charlie Christian** (1919–1942). He was also a pioneer in the development of the jazz revolution later named Bop. Christian was one of a group of musicians meeting after hours at Minton's Playhouse, a nightclub in Harlem. The group usually included Thelonius Monk, Kenny Clarke, and Dizzy Gillespie. From 1939 to 1941 he played in Benny Goodman's band.

Sources: Chilton, Who's Who of Jazz, p. 72; *Encyclopedia of Black America,* p. 226; Southern, *The Music of Black Americans,* pp. 474–75.

1941 ◆ **Dean Charles Dixon** (1915–1976) was the first African American to conduct the New York Philharmonic and was possibly the first black American recognized as a symphonic conductor of international stature. He was the first to hold permanent positions for long periods with symphony orchestras and toured worldwide as a guest conductor.

Sources: Ebony Success Library, vol. 1, p. 96; *Encyclopedia of Black America,* 318; Garrett, *Famous First Facts About Negroes,* pp. 131–32; Southern, *Biographical Dictionary of African-American and African Musicians,* pp. 107–8; Southern, *The Music of Black Americans,* p. 510.

1943 ◆ **Muddy Waters** (McKinley Morganfield, 1915–) was the first person to combine blues and amplified guitar to create urban blues. A guitarist and singer, he was born in Rolling Fork, Mississippi, and grew up in Clarksdale, Mississippi. Waters was discovered by folklorist Alan Lomax. In 1943 Waters moved to Chicago, where he adopted the electric guitar. He signed with a recording company in 1948 and became known as the "King of the Delta (or Country) Blues."

Sources: Encyclopedia of Black America, p. 847; Lee, *Interesting People*, p. 95; Southern, *The Music of Black Americans*, pp. 493–94.

"King Biscuit Time" was the first live black country blues program. The program was heard on KFFA in Helena, Arkansas, until 1981, although the music was not always live. Harmonica-player Rice (Willie) Miller (1899–1965), also known as "Sonny Boy Williamson, No. 2," and guitarist Junior (Robert) Lockwood (1915–) began the program in November. For the first time black Americans in the South developed their own radio programs.

Sources: Southern, The Music of Black Americans, pp. 492–93; *Split Image*, p. 208.

Nat King Cole

1945 ◆ **Robert Todd Duncan** (1903–) became the first African American to sing with a major American operatic company. He was also the original Porgy in George Gershwin's *Porgy and Bess* and played the role more than 1,800 times.

Sources: Ebony Success Library, vol. 1, p. 100; *Encyclopedia of Black America*, p. 329; Southern, *The Music of Black Americans*, pp. 406–07.

1945 ◆ **Camilla Williams** (1925–) was the first black woman to sing with the New York City Opera when she performed the title role in Puccini's *Madame Butterfly*. In 1954 she was the first black singer to appear on the stage of the Vienna State Opera.

Sources: Current Biography, 1952, pp. 632–34; *Encyclopedia of Black America*, p. 857; Southern, *Biographical Dictionary of African-American and African Musicians*, p. 403; Story, *And So I Sing*, pp. 72–75.

1948 ◆ **Nat King Cole** (Nathaniel Coles, 1919–1965) led the first black jazz group to have its own sponsored program on radio. Cole soon began to concentrate his attention on his singing, and by 1952 he was one of the most successful singers of popular music. In 1956 and 1957 he was the second African American to host a nationwide network television show. He was born in Montgomery, Alabama, then his family moved to Chicago, and by 1936 he was piano player for the touring black revue *Shuffle Along*. He formed the

King Cole Trio, which toured the country and made recordings. "Straighten Up and Fly Right," his first record, sold more than 500,000 copies. "Nature Boy" (1948), "Mona Lisa" (1949), and "Too Young" (1951) are among his most successful hits.

Sources: Dictionary of American Negro Biography, pp. 120–21; Encyclopedia of Black America, p. 277; Southern, Biographical Dictionary of African-American and African Musicians, p. 76; Southern, The Music of Black Americans, pp. 497–98.

1950 ◆ **Joe Bostic,** the "Dean of Gospel Disc Jockeys," produced the first Negro Gospel and Religious Music Festival at Carnegie Hall in New York. Mahalia Jackson (c. 1911–1972), whose "Move On Up a Little Higher" (1946) was the second gospel recording to sell more than 1 million copies in a year, was the star. Nonetheless, she became the first to bring gospel singing to the general public. Acclaimed as America's greatest gospel singer, Jackson was the first gospel singer to appear on the "Ed Sullivan Show" and became the first gospel artist to sing at the Newport Jazz Festival in 1958.

Sources: Encyclopedia of Black America, p. 467; Notable Black American Women, pp. 557–59; Southern, The Music of Black Americans, pp. 467-68, 472–73.

1953 ◆ **Dorothy Maynor** (1910–) became the first African American to sing at a presidential inauguration when she sang "The Star Spangled Banner" at Dwight D. Eisenhower's inauguration. In 1965 she founded the Harlem School of the Arts.

Sources: Encyclopedia of Black America, p. 548; Notable Black American Women, pp. 739–40; Southern, The Music of Black Americans, p. 405.

1954 ◆ "Sh-Boom" was the first rock 'n' roll record. Recorded by a black male rhythm blues group, it went to the top of that chart and then went to the top of the pop chart. At first most of the records of this kind were covers of black recordings by white groups and soloists. It was some time before non-black consumers began to seek out records cut by African Americans.

Source: Southern, The Music of Black Americans, pp. 504-5.

1955 ◆ **Marian Anderson** (c. 1896–1993), one of the twentieth century's most celebrated singers, was the first African American to sing a principal role with the Metropolitan Opera. In October 1930 Anderson received critical acclaim for a concert in Berlin, Germany, and then embarked on an extensive tour of Europe. She made national news in 1939 when the Daughters of the American Revolution refused to allow her appearance in their Constitution Hall. Anderson continued to tour until her farewell trip in the 1964–65 season. (*See also* **Miscellaneous: Honors and Awards, 1963.**)

Sources: Black Women in America, pp. 29–33; Current Biography Yearbook, 1940, pp. 17–19, 1950, pp. 8–10; Notable Black American Women, pp. 14–20; Story, And So I Sing, pp. 37–58.

Robert McFerrin (1921–) made his debut as the first black man to join the Metropolitan Opera Company and the first black singer to have a permanent position with the Met on January 27. He sang with the National Negro Opera from 1949 to 1952.

Sources: New Grove Dictionary of American Music, p. 147; *New York* (24 February 1992); Southern, *Biographical Directory of African-American and African Musicians*, p. 258; Southern, *Music of Black Americans*, pp. 513–24.

1956 ◆ Jazz trumpeter and bandleader **Dizzy (John Birks) Gillespie** (1917–1993) was the first African American to make an overseas tour sponsored by the U.S. Department of State. He played in Cab Calloway's band from 1939 to 1941 and, along with Oscar Pettiford and Charlie "Bird" Parker, pioneered the formation of the jazz style called Bop.

Sources: Bergman, *The Chronological History of the Negro in America*, pp. 383, 493, 515; *Encyclopedia of Black America*, p. 405; Southern, *The Music of Black Americans*, pp. 475–78.

1958 ◆ **Errol Louis Gardner** (1921–1977) was the first black pianist to give a jazz concert in Carnegie Hall. He had no formal music training but became one of the most important jazz pianists.

Sources: Encyclopedia of Black America, p. 402; Southern, *Biographical Dictionary of African-American and African Musicians*, p. 143; Thorpe, *Black Dance*, pp. 162–65.

1959 ◆ **Count (William) Basie** (1904–1984) was the first black man to win a Grammy. He was also the first African American from the United States to have a band give a command performance before Queen Elizabeth. Born in Red Bank, New Jersey, he began playing the piano while a young teenager and studied with Fats Waller. Basie's own band, formed in 1935 in Kansas City, Missouri, took the flowering of that city's style to Chicago and New York City. The band established itself as one of the leaders in jazz.

Sources: Encyclopedia of Black America, p. 168; *Jet* 81 (18 November 1991), p. 12; Southern, *Biographical Dictionary of African-American and African Musicians*, pp. 29–30; Southern, *The Music of Black Americans*, pp. 384–85.

Ella Fitzgerald (1918–) was the first black woman to win a Grammy. She began her career at age 15 at the Apollo Theater in Harlem and was later hired by Chick Webb's band. Fitzgerald recorded the well-known "A Tisket-A-Tasket" in 1938 and developed her famous skat singing on a tour with Dizzy Gillespie. Known as the "first lady of jazz," she is one of the most celebrated singers of the century.

Sources: Jet 81 (18 November 1991), p. 12; *Notable Black American Women*, pp. 346–49; Southern, *Biographical Dictionary of African-American and African Musicians*, pp. 133–34.

Ella Fitzgerald

1960 ◆ **Chubby Checker** (Ernest Evans, 1941–) became well known for his recording of "The Twist," which remains the first and only record to reach number one on the pop charts twice, in 1960 and 1962. He introduced a dance by the same title and set off the greatest dance craze since the Charleston of the 1920s.

Sources: Ebony 16 (January 1961), pp. 40–44; Southern, *Biographical Directory,* p. 129; *Split Image,* p.85.

1961 ◆ **Quincy (Delight) Jones, Jr.** (1934–) was the first black vice-president of a white record company, Mercury. In 1991 he won six Grammy awards in one year. His career total of 25 awards is second only to conductor Georg Solti, who has 28.

Sources: Negro Almanac, pp. 1147–48; Southern, *Biographical Dictionary of African-American and African Musicians,* p. 219; Southern, *The Music of Black Americans,* pp. 543, 544.

1966 ◆ On September 16, 1966, **Leontyne (Mary Violet Leontine) Price** (1927–) was the first African American to open a Metropolitan Opera Season and to sing the title role at the opening of the new Metropolitan Opera house. Samuel Barber wrote the role in his new opera *Anthony and Cleopatra* for her; however, the opera did not enjoy great success. In 1955 she was Flora Tosca in Puccini's *Tosca* shown on NBC-TV's nationally televised "Opera Workshop," becoming the first African American to appear in opera on television. Emerging in the 1950s as a major artist, Price was the first modern black soprano to achieve international fame.

Sources: Encyclopedia of Black America, p. 707; Lee, *Interesting People,* p. 142; *Notable Black American Women,* pp. 874–78; Story, *And So I Sing,* pp. 100–14.

1967 ◆ **Charley Pride** (1939–) became the first black singer with the Grand Ole Opry. His interest at first was in baseball; at age 16 he left his home state of Mississippi to seek employment with the now-defunct Negro American Baseball League. He was pitcher-outfielder with the Memphis Red Sox, later played with the Birmingham Black Barons, and in 1961 played in the majors with the Los Angeles Angels. Opry star Red Foley heard Pride sing country music in 1963 and encouraged him to go to Nashville, where he charmed RCA Records and entered the country music field. The white audience at his first major concert in 1967 did not know his race until he appeared on stage. His recording "Just Between Me and You" launched him into super-stardom and made him a number one country music attraction. In 1971 Pride was the first African American named Entertainer of the Year and Male Vocalist of the Year in the field of country music. In May 1994 he was honored as a Pioneer Award recipient during the Country Music Awards.

Sources: Current Biography, 1975, pp. 329–32; *Ebony Success Library,* vol. 2, pp. 212–15; Southern, *Biographical Dictionary of African-American and African Musicians,* p. 314.

1968 ◆ **Henry Lewis** (1932–) conducted the New Jersey Symphony Orchestra, becoming the first black conductor of a leading American symphony orchestra. In 1972 he was engaged by the Metropolitan Opera to conduct *La Bohème* and became the first African American to conduct in that house.

Sources: Encyclopedia of Black America, p. 505; Southern, *Biographical Dictionary of African-American and African Musicians,* pp. 244–45.

1977 ◆ Chuck Berry's song "Johnny B. Goode" and Blind Willie Johnson's 1927 recording "Dark Was the Night, Cold Was the Ground" were the first by African Americans to be sent out of the solar system. The space ship *Voyager I* was sent into outer space with a copper phonograph record containing greetings in a hundred languages, Bach's Concerto No. 2, "Johnny B. Goode," and "Dark Was the Night, Cold Was the Ground" on the chance that aliens might find it. **Chuck (Charles Edward Anderson) Berry** (1926–) was the first African American to receive four Special Commendation Awards from Broadcast Music, Inc. (BMI) in 1981. His first song, "Mabelline," received wide attention, and "Roll Over Beethoven" became one of his best-known songs. Blind Willie Johnson (?–1950), gospel singer and guitarist, was born in Marlin, Texas, and blinded at age seven. He sang at Baptist Association meetings and rural churches near Hearne, Texas, accompanying himself on the guitar. He made several recordings of exceptionally high quality between 1927 and 1930 and strongly influenced other gospel singers. After the Depression Johnson returned to street singing.

Sources: Cohn, and others, *Nothing But the Blues,* pp. 119–26; *Current Biography, 1977,* pp. 57–60; *Essence* 24 (May 1993), p. 40; *Jet* 60 (21 May 1981), p. 62; *New Grove Dictionary of American Music,* vol. 2, p. 577; Southern, *Biographical Dictionary of African-American and African Musicians,* p. 33.

1979 ◆ **Ray Charles** (Ray Charles Robinson, 1930–) was the first person of any race to perform before the Georgia Assembly. He was blinded by glaucoma when he was about six. Charles formed a trio in 1950, but the next year he formed a larger and more successful rhythm and blues group. He made a number of records, including "Georgia on My Mind," which set new sales records in 1959. It is said that Charles developed the concept of soul, merging

Michael Jackson

gospel, rhythm and blues, and popular music into a completely new form.

Sources: Current Biography, 1965, pp. 59–62; Southern, *Biographical Dictionary of African-American and African Musicians,* p. 68.

The first two rap records were "King Tim III (Personality Jock)," recorded by the Fatback Band, a Brooklyn group, and "Rapper's Delight," by the Sugar Hill Gang, with a New Jersey-based label. Bronx-style rapping began in 1976 but was not recorded until 1979.

Source: Split Image, p. 112.

1981 ♦ **James Cleveland** (1931–1991), minister, gospel singer, pianist, composer, arranger, choir director, and recording artist, was the first black gospel artist to receive a star on Hollywood's Walk of Fame. He was accompanist for the Caravans and the Roberta Martin Singers and later formed the James Cleveland Singers and the Southern California Community Choir. In 1968 Cleveland founded and was national president of Gospel Music Workshop of America. Known as the "Crown Prince of Gospel," he received four Grammy awards.

Sources: Ebony Success Library, vol. 1, p. 71; Heilbut, *Gospel Sound,* pp. 233–47; *Who's Who Among Black Americans, 1992-93,* p. 1595.

1982 ♦ **Max (Maxwell Lemuel) Roach** (1924–) was the first black drummer inducted into the Percussive Art Society. A founding member of Bebop and a member of Dizzy Gillespie's 1945 quintet, which gave the name to the music, he pioneered in exploiting the drums as both melodic and rhythmic instruments.

Sources: Feather, *Encyclopedia of Jazz,* p. 398; *Jet* 63 (20 December 1982), p. 21; Southern, *Biographical Dictionary of African-American and African Musicians,* p. 322; Southern, *The Music of Black Americans,* pp. 476–77.

1983 ♦ **Michael Jackson's** album *Thriller* was the first to produce five top singles: "The Girl Is Mine," "Billie Jean," "Beat It," "Wanna Be Startin' Somethin'," and "Human Nature." The *Guinness Book of Records* certified *Thriller,* for which Jackson (1958–) won eight Grammy Awards, as the best-selling album of all time. *Guinness* also cites Jackson for winning the most awards (seven) at the American Music Awards in 1984.

Sources: Jet 81 (November 18, 1991), p. 60; *Who's Who Among Black Americans, 1992–1993,* p. 724.

1984 ♦ Trumpeter and bandleader **Wynton Marsalis** (1961–) was the first black instrumentalist to simultaneously receive Grammy awards as best classical and jazz soloist. Born in New Orleans into a musical family, Marsalis was trained in both jazz and classical traditions. He made his first LP in 1981.

Sources: Hornsby, Jr., *Milestones in Twentieth Century African-American History,* p. 343; *Negro Almanac,* p. 1217.

1986 ◆ **Aretha Franklin** (1942–), the "Queen of Soul," was the first black woman selected for induction into the Rock 'n' Roll Hall of Fame and Museum. As a child she sang gospel in the church pastored by her father, a noted evangelist and singer, and later joined the quartet directed by James Cleveland. She turned to blues in the 1960s, and in 1967 two of her albums sold more than 1 million copies each. Franklin won four Grammy awards between 1967 and 1969.

Sources: Encyclopedia of Black America, p. 393; *Jet* 71 (13 October 1986), p. 54; *Notable Black American Women,* pp. 364–68.

Aretha Franklin

1987 ◆ **Ice-T** (born Tracy Marrow, c. 1957–) released the first "gangster rap" album, *Rhyme Pays,* which helped fuel a huge explosion in the popularity of rap music during the late 1980s. The album was also the first to carry voluntary warning labels of explicit lyrics. In 1991 Ice-T produced his fourth straight gold record, *O.G. Original Gangster.* The following year he formed a punk-metal band called Body Count and released an album by the same name featuring the song "Cop Killer." This highly controversial song led to boycott threats against Warner Communications (the song's publisher) and, ultimately, to Ice-T's voluntary withdrawal of it from the album.

1988 ◆ **Cab (Cabell) Calloway III** (1907–) was the first black winner of the ASCAP Duke Award. He was an important big-band leader of the 1930s and 1940s and played the role of Sportin' Life in *Porgy and Bess* in 1952.

Sources: Bogle, *Toms, Coons, Mulattoes, Mammies, and Bucks,* pp. 131–32; *Jet* 74 (30 May 1988), p. 36; Southern, *Biographical Dictionary of African-American and African Musicians,* pp. 61–62.

1989 ◆ The first black woman vice-president of a major record company, Atlantic Records, was **Sylvia Rhone** (1952–). In 1991 she was named co-president and chief executive officer of East-West Records America, her own Atlantic label.

Source: Contemporary Black Biography, vol. 2, pp. 194–95.

1992 ◆ The first black pianist to win the Naumburg Competition for young musicians was **Awadagin Pratt.** A student at Peabody Institute in Baltimore, Maryland, Pratt received $5,000, two major residencies with national arts organizations, and 40 concert and recital appearances.

Source: Jet 82 (1 June 1992), p. 22.

Performing Arts

Circus • Comedy • Dance • Radio • Theater

Circus

1966 ♦ The first black showgirl with Ringling Brothers Circus was **Toni Williams** (1943–) of Reading, Pennsylvania. Since then she has formed a trapeze act on her own.

Sources: Alford, *Famous First Blacks*, p. 71; *Essence*, 8 (March 1978), pp. 56, 58, 60.

1977 ♦ **Bernice Collins** (1957–) was the first black woman clown with Ringling Brothers.

Source: *Essence* 8 (March 1978), p. 58.

Comedy

1901 ♦ **Bert (Egbert Austin) Williams** (1873–1922) was the first African American to record with Victor Talking Machine Company. Between 1901 and 1903 he recorded 15 titles, primarily show tunes or comedy routines that he had done on stage. In 1910 he was the first African American to receive feature billing in the Ziegfield Follies and remained with them until 1919. He and George Nash Walker (1873–1911) formed a successful dance-comedy team that reached New York City in 1896. The most famous of the early black comedians, Williams & Walker appeared in numerous all-black musicals between 1899 and 1909 and became known for their characterizations: Walker as a dandy (a vain man, concerned mainly about clothes and appearances) and Williams as an outlandishly dressed blackface comic. In 1914 Williams became the first African American to star in a movie, *Darktown Jubilee*. The film is said to have caused a race riot when it was shown in Brooklyn. It was Williams's only movie. Williams's trademark was

Moms Mabley

the song "Nobody," which he wrote and sang. He is regarded by many as the greatest black vaudeville performer in American history.

Sources: *Dictionary of American Negro Biography*, pp. 653–54; Emery, *Black Dance*, pp. 211–13; *Encyclopedia of Black America*, p. 857; Johnson, *Black Manhattan*, pp. 104–8.

1960 ◆ Jackie "Moms" Mabley (1894–1974) became the first black comedienne to have a best-selling record. For many years she was the only black woman comic in the country and was the first to become widely recognized. Mabley traveled on the vaudeville circuit, was a regular at the Apollo in Harlem, made several recordings, and appeared in Broadway shows, on television, and in films.

Sources: *Current Biography, 1975*, pp. 216–64; Lee, *Interesting People*, p. 56; *Notable Black American Women*, pp. 688–90.

Dance

1845 ◆ Master Juba (William Henry Lane, c. 1825–1852) was the first black dance star. He took his stage name from the African dance the juba. In 1845 Lane won the title "King of All Dancers." He toured with three white minstrels, receiving top billing, and garnered acclaim for his 1848 performance in London.

Sources: Emery, *Black Dance*, pp. 185–90; Thorpe, *Black Dance*, pp. 42–44.

1923 ◆ In October 1923 *Running Wild* was the first black show to introduce the Charleston to nonblack audiences. After being featured on a white show in 1926, the dance achieved worldwide popularity second only to the black-inspired Tango, which came to Europe and America from Argentina. A third black dance to achieve wide success in the 1920s was the Black Bottom, which reached New York in *Dinah* at Harlem's Lafayette Theater in 1924. Both the Charleston and the Black Bottom were theatrical adaptations of dances known to African Americans in the South for a decade or more.

Sources: Emery, *Black Dance*, pp. 226–28; Johnson, *Black Manhattan*, pp. 189–90.

1932 ◆ Hemsley Winfield (1906–1934) was the first black ballet dancer. He choreographed and performed with his own company in the

Metropolitan Opera's production of Louis Gruenberg's *The Emperor Jones.* This was a one-time exception to the rules—management did not list the dancers in the program. The next black dancer did not appear with the company until 1951. Winfield's mother was a playwright, and he made his debut in one of her plays, *Wade in the Water* (1926). He became a dancer and a pioneer in black concert dance, organizing the Negro Art Theater Dance Group. This group gave its first concert on April 29, 1931, and appeared in Hall Johnson's *Run Little Chillun* in 1933.

Sources: Emery, *Black Dance,* pp. 242–43, 320; Thorpe, *Black Dance,* pp. 112–14.

1951 ◆ **Janet Collins** (1923–) was the first black prima ballerina at the Metropolitan Opera Company, a position that she held for three years. She made her debut in *Aida* and is known for her choreography and her dance instruction.

Katherine Dunham

Sources: Emery, *Black Dance,* pp. 320–22; *Encyclopedia of Black America,* p. 279; *Negro Almanac,* p. 1429; *Notable Black American Women,* pp. 210–11.

1958 ◆ The first black dancer in the country to become a member of a classical ballet company, the New York City Ballet, was **Arthur Mitchell** (1934–). Mitchell studied at New York's High School of Performing Art and at the School of American Ballet. He founded the Dance Theatre of Harlem as a school of dance—especially classical ballet—for children of all races. The first black classical ballet company in the United States, the Dance Theatre made its debut at the Guggenheim Museum of Art in New York City. In 1988 the company became the first black cultural group to tour the Soviet Union under the renewed cultural exchange program.

Sources: Emery, *Black Dance,* pp. 279–84; *Encyclopedia of Black America,* p. 564; *Jet* 74 (23 May 1988), p. 56; Garrett, *Famous First Facts About Negroes,* p. 44.

1963 ◆ **Katherine Dunham** (1910–) was the first black choreographer to work at the Metropolitan Opera House. Dunham incorporated her training in anthropology and her study of African and West Indian dances into her own techniques and dance instruction.

Sources: Emery, *Black Dance,* pp. 251–60; *Notable Black American Women,* pp. 296–301; Thorpe, *Black Dance,* pp. 124–30.

Alvin Ailey

1984 ◆ The Alvin Ailey Dance Theater was the first black modern dance troupe to perform in the Metropolitan Opera House. Founded in 1958 by Alvin Ailey (1931–1989), the troupe has performed before more than 15 million people throughout the world. In 1961 Ailey unveiled his best-known work, "Revelations," which is based on his childhood experiences in black Baptist churches.

Sources: Emery, *Black Dance,* pp. 272–79; Hornsby, Jr., *Chronology of Twentieth Century African-American History,* pp. 432–33; *Jet* 66 (23 July 1984), p. 13; Thorpe, *Black Dance,* pp. 131-35.

Radio

1929 ◆ The Harlem Broadcasting Corporation was established, becoming the first black radio venture of its kind. It operated its own radio studios at Lenox Avenue and 125th Street in Harlem, leased time on local radio outlet WRNY, and operated an artist bureau for black radio talent.

Source: *Split Image,* p. 185.

1933 ◆ The first black hero to be heard on network radio was **Juano Hernandez** as *John Henry: Black River Giant* in a series broadcast on CBS.

Source: *Split Image,* p. 187.

1945 ◆ WSM, located in Nashville, Tennessee, provided the first clear-channel broadcasting oriented to African Americans in the South. Its success spurred the growth of this kind of radio programming throughout the South. The late-night programs had white announcers.

Source: (Nashville) *Tennessean,* 20 February 1992.

1948 ◆ **Hal Jackson** (1922–) was the first black announcer and disc jockey on WOOK in Washington, D.C., when the station changed to a black format. Known as the dean of broadcasting, he was also the first black master of ceremonies of a network jazz show, the first African American to host an interracial network jazz show, the first black host of an international network television presentation, and the first minority inducted into the National

Association of Broadcasters' Hall of Fame. Jackson founded the Miss Black Teenage America Pageant (now the Miss United States Talented Teen Pageant).

Sources: Split Image, p. 212–13; Tenth Anniversary, Candace Awards (program), 22 June 1992.

1949 ◆ WDIA in Memphis, Tennessee, a white-owned radio station, became the first to have all black-oriented programming. The station hired **Nat D. Williams** (?–1983), who became the first black disk jockey in the South, and the first black announcer in the South to play popular rhythm and blues records on the air. On October 21, 1948, the station launched *Tan Town Jamboree,* its first black show, making it the first all-black format radio station. Memphis became a center for blues broadcasting. Blues master "B. B." (Riley) King (1925–) was on WDIA with his band, and in 1949 KWEM in West Memphis, Arkansas, featured Howlin Wolf (Chester Burnett, 1910–1975) and his band.

Sources: Jet 65 (5 December 1983), p. 18; Southern, *The Music of Black Americans,* p. 493; *Split Image,* pp. 209–10; (Nashville) *Tennessean,* 29 February 1992.

1954 ◆ **W. Leonard Evans, Jr.** (1915–), publisher of the black radio trade magazine *Tuesday,* founded the National Negro Network. The first black radio network, it began programming on January 20, 1954, and was carried on 40 stations. Juanita Hall starred in the first program, a soap opera titled *The Story of Ruby Valentine.*

Sources: Encyclopedia of Black America, p. 378; *Negro Almanac,* p. 1429; *Split Image,* p. 226.

Theater

1821 ◆ The African Theater Company of New York City was the first black theatrical company. Henry Brown formed the group, which lasted until at least 1823, when a playbill announced a benefit performance for Brown. The company's building was destroyed by disorderly whites that same year.

Sources: Bergman, *The Chronological History of the Negro in America,* pp. 117–18; Emery, *Black Dance,* p. 180; Johnson, *Black Manhattan,* pp. 78–80; Southern, *Biographical Dictionary of African-American and African Musicians,* p. 178.

1823 ◆ In June 1823 *The Drama of King Shotaway* was the first play by a black to be produced in the United States. Written by West Indian Henry Brown and produced by the African Company, the play—no copy of which has survived—featured actor and singer James Hewlett.

Source: Southern, *The Music of Black Americans,* p. 120.

Ira Frederick
Aldridge

1826 ◆ The first black actor to gain international fame was **Ira Frederick Aldridge** (1805–1867), one of the leading Shakespearean actors of the century. He attended the African Free School No. 2 in New York City until he was about 16 and then left home. From 1821 to 1824 Aldridge worked with the African Theater Company in New York City and later moved to Europe, where he studied briefly at the University of Glasgow in Scotland. His first professional engagement in London was in October 1825 with the Coburg Theatre. For three decades his fame on the continent exceeded his high standing in England. Aldridge won acclaim for his portrayal of many roles, but was best known for his portrayal of Othello.

Sources: Dictionary of American Negro Biography, pp. 8–9; *Encyclopedia of Black America,* pp. 96–97; Johnson, *Black Manhattan,* pp. 80–87.

1865 ◆ **Charles "Barney" Hicks** organized the first permanent black minstrel company, the Georgia Minstrels. Black entertainers had appeared in troupes as early as the 1840s, and an all-black company, Lew Johnson's Plantation Minstrel Company, was formed in the early 1860s. Organized in Indianapolis, Indiana, the celebrated Georgia Minstrels' tours included performances in Germany and Great Britain. Hicks faced great difficulties in dealing with white theater managers and sold his rights in 1872 to Charles Callender. The troupe was then known as Callender's Georgia Minstrels.

Sources: Johnson, *Black Manhattan,* pp. 89–93; Southern, *The Music of Black Americans,* p. 229; Thorpe, *Black Dance,* p. 48.

1891 ◆ *The Creole Show,* an all-black production in New York City with a white promoter, John Isham, was the first minstrel show to introduce black women into the cast. In the finale Dora Dean and Charles Johnson introduced the first theatrical cake walk, derived from the old plantation chalk-line walk.

It also is one of the first shows in which black performers did not wear black face.

Sources: Emery, *Black Dance,* pp. 207–9; Johnson, *Black Manhattan,* pp. 95–96; Thorpe, *Black Dance,* pp. 28–29, 53.

1897 ◆ *Oriental America* was the first black show to play on Broadway and the first to break away from burlesque entertainment. The production followed the minstrel pattern, but the after-piece was a medley of operatic selections. It did not enjoy a long run.

Sources: Emery, *Black Dance,* pp. 208–9; Johnson, *Black Manhattan,* pp. 96–97; Thorpe, *Black Dance,* p. 55.

1898 ◆ *A Trip to Coontown* was the first black musical comedy. In a break with the minstrel tradition, it had a cast of characters involved in a story from beginning to end. The show was written and produced by Robert "Bob" Cole (c. 1863–1911), a composer, dancer, singer, musician, and actor. The first black show to be organized, produced, and managed by African Americans, it ran for three seasons after its April 1898 debut in New York.

Sources: Dictionary of American Negro Biography, pp. 121–22; *Encyclopedia of Black America,* p. 530; Johnson, *Black Manhattan,* p. 102; Southern, *The Music of Black Americans,* p. 297.

1905 ◆ **Frederick Douglass O'Neal** (1905–1992), stage, movie, and radio actor, was the first black president of the Actor's Equity Association and later the first black international president of the Associated Actors and Artists of America.

Sources: Current Biography, 1946, pp. 438–40; *Encyclopedia of Black America,* pp. 655–56; *State of Black America, 1993,* p. 295.

1905 ◆ The Pekin Theater in Chicago was the first black-owned theater in the United States. Founded by Robert Mott (?–1911), the theater was important not only for stage productions but also for its concert series. The Pekin Stock Company was the first black repertory company in this century. The theater ceased operation in 1916.

Sources: Dictionary of American Negro Biography, p. 261; Southern, *The Music of Black Americans,* p. 291.

1915 ◆ **Anita Bush** (1883–1974) organized the Anita Bush Players and became the first black woman to organize a professional black stock dramatic company in the United States. Her company was also the first stock company in New York since the African Players of 1821. The players opened at the Lincoln Theater in New York City on November 15, 1915, with *The Girl at* *the Fort.* They had a short but successful run and by December 27, 1915, had transferred to the larger Lafayette Theatre, where they became the Lafayette Players.

Sources: Black Women in America, pp. 205–6; Kellner, *The Harlem Renaissance,* p. 63; *Notable Black American Women,* pp. 142–43.

1917 ◆ Black actors in serious drama first won the attention of mainstream audiences and critics on April 5, 1917, when three one-act plays written for African Americans were presented at the Garden City Theater. The author, Ridley Torrence, was white, but this production marked the first serious use of black life on a commercial stage. A folk comedy, a tragedy, and a religious play broke stereotypes that had imprisoned black actors.

Sources: Bergman, *The Chronological History of the Negro in America,* p. 384; *Encyclopedia of Black America,* p. 532; Johnson, *Black Manhattan,* pp. 175–78.

1920 ◆ **Charles Sidney Gilpin** (1878–1930) was the first African American to star in a major American play, Eugene O'Neill's *The Emperor Jones.* He has been called "the first modern American Negro to establish himself as a serious actor of first quality." In 1896 Gilpin began traveling with vaudeville troupes, a practice which he followed for two years. In 1907 he joined the Pekin Stock Company of Chicago as a dramatic actor, and in 1916 joined the Lafayette Theater Company in Harlem. Gilpin played the lead in *The Emperor Jones* from 1920 to 1924, winning the Spingarn Award in 1921 for his theatrical accomplishment.

Sources: Bergman, *The Chronological History of the Negro in America,* pp. 284, 400; *Dictionary of American Negro Biography,* pp. 261–62; Johnson, *Black Manhattan,* pp. 182–85; Kellner, *The Harlem Renaissance,* pp. 137–38; *Negro Almanac,* p. 1140.

1933 ◆ The first folk opera by an African American to reach Broadway was *Run, Little Children,* by **(Francis) Hall Johnson** (1888–1970). It ran 126 performances. Hall was one of the most successful choral directors of his time and had been choral director of *Green Pastures* in 1930.

Sources: Robinson, *Historical Negro Biographies,* pp. 211–12; Southern, *Biographical Dictionary of African-American and African Musicians,* pp. 207–8; Southern, *The Music of Black Americans,* pp. 411–13.

1939 ◆ **Ethel Waters** (1896–1977), as Hagar in *Mamba's Daughters,* became the first black woman to perform the leading role in a dramatic play on Broadway. She made her first public appearance when she was five years old as a singer in a church program. Waters appeared in nightclubs and vaudeville and in 1927 made her Broadway debut in *Africana.* When she toured in *As Thousands Cheer* (1934), she became the first black person to co-star with white players below the Mason-Dixon line. Her greatest role came in 1940 when she appeared on stage in *Cabin in the Sky;* she appeared in the movie version in 1943. From 1957 to 1976 she toured with evangelist Billy Graham and achieved wide recognition for the gospel hymn "His Eye Is on the Sparrow." In 1950 Waters was the first African American to star in a scheduled comedy program on television. She appeared in *Beulah* on ABC on October 3, taking over the role played by Hattie McDaniel (1895–1952) on the radio. Waters's health only enabled her to film a few episodes.

Source: Encyclopedia of Black America, p. 724; Negro Almanac, p. 1162; Notable Black American Women, p. 1225; Southern, Biographical Dictionary of African-American and African Musicians, p. 393.

1943 ◆ **Paul Robeson** (1898–1976) was the first African American to play Othello on an American stage with a white cast. The son of a former slave, he was born in Princeton, New Jersey, and graduated from Rutgers University and Columbia University School of Law. At Rutgers he was an All-American athlete and was elected to Phi Beta Kappa. Robeson developed an international career on stage and in film, as well as in concert, and became a recording star. His work with the Progressive Party, the Council on African Affairs, the National Negro Congress, the left-wing unions of the CIO, and his early call for a militant black movement made him a hero in Communist and third world countries and led the U.S. State Department to revoke his passport.

Paul Robeson

Sources: Duberman, Paul Robeson; Encyclopedia of Black America, p. 732; Hornsby, Jr., Milestones of Twentieth-Century African-American History, pp. 263–66; Lee, Interesting People, p. 57.

1959 ◆ **Lloyd Richards** (1923–), who directed Lorraine Hansberry's *Raisin in the Sun,* was the first black director of a straight play on Broadway. He was dean of the Yale School of Drama from 1979 to 1991.

Sources: Bergman, The Chronological History of the Negro in America, p. 562; Hornsby, Jr., Milestones in Twentieth-Century African-American History, p. 62; Jet 81 (18 November 1991), p. 12.

1965 ◆ **Ruby Dee** (1924–) was the first black actress to play major parts at the American Shakespeare Festival in Stratford, Connecticut, where she played Kate in *The Taming of the Shrew* and Cordelia in *King Lear.* Dee is known for her Broadway performances, which included the plays *A Raisin in* *the Sun* (1959) and *Purlie Victorious* (1961). She and her husband, Ossie Davis, share careers in television, stage, screen, and other public appearances and have been active in civil rights causes.

Sources: Black Women in America, pp. 313–15; *Current Biography, 1970,* pp. 107–10; *Encyclopedia of Black America,* p. 30; *Notable Black American Women,* pp. 260–62.

Politics

Local Offices • State Offices • Federal Appointments and Diplomacy
National Politics • Political Parties

Local Offices

1870 ◆ During Reconstruction in December 1870 **Robert H. Wood** was elected mayor of Natchez, Mississippi. He was possibly the first black mayor in the United States.

Sources: Bennett, *Before the Mayflower,* pp. 489, 629; *Ebony* (March 1982), p. 130.

1967 ◆ In September 1967 **Walter E. Washington** (1915–) was appointed the first mayor of Washington, D.C. In 1974 Washington became the first elected mayor of the city and went on to serve a second term.

Sources: Ebony Success Library, vol. 2, pp. 272–75; *Encyclopedia of Black America,* pp. 846–47; Hornsby, Jr., *Chronology of African-American History,* p. 131; *Who's Who Among Black Americans, 1992–1993,* p. 1466.

On November 13, 1967, **Carl Stokes** (1927–) was the first African American elected mayor of a major city, Cleveland, Ohio. Stokes and Richard G. Hatcher (1933–) were elected on the same day, but Hatcher was not sworn in until January 1, 1968, when he became the first black mayor of Gary, Indiana.

Sources: Ebony Success Library, vol. 1, p. 145 (Hatcher), p. 293 (Stokes); *Encyclopedia of Black America,* pp. 422–23 (Hatcher), p. 810 (Stokes); *Who's Who Among Black Americans, 1992–1993,* p. 622 (Hatcher), p. 1343 (Stokes).

1973 ◆ On April 16, 1973, **Lelia Smith Foley** (1942–) was elected the first black woman mayor in the United States when she became mayor of Taft, Oklahoma, a town of about 500. She served as mayor for 13 years.

Sources: Jet 60 (23 April 1981), pp. 61–62; Lee, *Interesting People,* p. 93; *Negro Almanac,* p. 429.

On October 16, 1973, **Maynard Holbrook Jackson** (1938–) was elected the first black mayor of Atlanta. Jackson was admitted to the Georgia bar in 1965 and ran for the U.S. Senate against Herman Talmadge in 1968. He lost by a small margin. Not only was Jackson the first black mayor of a major

Tom Bradley

southeastern city, he was also the youngest person ever elected mayor of Atlanta.

Sources: *Current Biography Yearbook*, 1976, pp. 193–96; *Ebony Success Library*, vol. 1, p. 169; *Encyclopedia of Black America*, p. 467; Hornsby, Jr., *Chronology of African-American History*, p. 209; *Who's Who Among Black Americans, 1992–1993*, p. 724.

Thomas Bradley (1917–) became the first black mayor of Los Angeles at a time when only 15 percent of the voters were African American. He was the first black elected official in the city upon his election to the Los Angeles city council in 1963. Between 1940 and 1961 he was a member of the police department, becoming the first African American to hold the rank of lieutenant. In 1982, while still mayor, Bradley became the first African American nominated by a major party (Democratic) as a candidate for governor. He announced his retirement as mayor in 1992.

Sources: *Contemporary Black Biography*, vol. 2, pp. 33–36; *Encyclopedia of Black America*, p. 189; *Jet* 82 (12 October 1992), pp. 4–5; *Negro Almanac*, p. 478; *Who's Who Among Black Americans, 1992–1993*, p. 144.

Coleman Young (1918–) was elected the first black mayor of Detroit on November 6, 1973. Young and Thomas Bradley, elected at the same time, were the first black mayors of cities with populations over 1 million. In 1968 Young was the first African American to serve on the Democratic National Committee.

Sources: *Encyclopedia of Black America*, p. 873; *Negro Almanac*, pp. 434–35; Hornsby, Jr., *Chronology of African-American History*, p. 211; *Who's Who Among Black Americans, 1992–1993*, p. 1584.

1976 ◆ **Unita Blackwell** (1933–), as head of Meyersville, was the first black woman mayor in Mississippi. She was a leading figure in the civil rights struggle and in the organization of the Mississippi Freedom Democratic Party in 1964. She became the first female president of the National Conference of Black Mayors in 1990. Blackwell was awarded a MacArthur Fellowship in 1992.

Sources: *Jet* 82 (6 July 1992), pp. 34–35; Lanker, *I Dream a World*, p. 50; (Nashville) *Tennessean*, 16 June 1992.

1977 ◆ **Ernest Nathan Morial** (1929–1989) was the first black mayor of New Orleans and served from 1977 until 1986. In 1954 Morial became the first black graduate of the Louisiana State University School of Law, and in 1965 he was the first black lawyer to work in the U.S. Attorney's office in Louisiana. In 1967 he became the first African American elected to the state legislature in this century and the first ever elected as a Democrat. He was the first black judge on the Juvenile Court of New Orleans. And in 1972 he became the first African American elected to the Louisiana Fourth Circuit Court of Appeals.

Sources: Ebony Success Library, vol. 1, p. 228; *Encyclopedia of Black America,* p. 568; Hornsby, Jr., *Chronology of African-American History,* p. 418; *Jet* 77 (15 January 1990), pp. 12–13; *Who's Who Among Black Americans, 1992–1993,* p. 1605.

1982 ◆ On May 6, 1982, **Loretta Thompson Glickman** (c. 1945–) became the first woman to head a city of more than 100,000 when she was elected mayor of Pasadena, California. She was elected by the city's board of directors.

Sources: Hornsby, Jr., *Chronology of African-American History,* p. 311; *Jet* 62 (24 May 1982), p. 13, 63 (31 January 1983), p. 38.

As mayor of Pagedale, Missouri, **Mary Hall** was head of the first all-black, all-women city administration.

Source: Jet 82 (24 May 1982), p. 13.

1983 ◆ **Harold Washington** (1922–1987) was the first black mayor of Chicago. He was re-elected in 1987 but died of a massive heart attack on November 25. Washington served as a member of the House of Representatives (1980–83) before he challenged the Democratic machine to win the mayoralty.

Sources: Bennett, *Before the Mayflower,* pp. 613, 618–19; Hornsby, Jr., *Chronology of African-American History,* p. 318–19, 354; *Jet* 64 (21 March 1983), p. 12; *Who's Who Among Black Americans, 1988,* p. 721.

1984 ◆ On January 2, 1984, **W. Wilson Goode** (1938–) became the first black mayor of Philadelphia. He won a second term in 1987.

Sources: Hornsby, Jr., *Chronology of African-American History,* p. 326; *Negro Almanac,* pp. 86, 88, 430; *Who's Who Among Black Americans, 1992–1993,* p. 535.

1989 ◆ On November 7, 1989, **David Dinkins** (1927–) was elected the first black mayor of New York; he took office in 1990. From 1956 on he has been active in Democratic party politics and was elected to the New York State Assembly in 1966. He held office as president of the city Board of Elections (1972–1973), city clerk (1975–1985), and Manhattan borough president (1986–1990) before he became mayor.

Sources: Hornsby, Jr., *Chronology of African-American History,* pp. 411–12; *Jet* 79 (22 January 1990), p. 4, 81 (18 November 1991), p. 62; *Who's Who Among Black Americans, 1992–1993,* p. 382.

P. B. S. Pinchback

Norman Blann Rice (1943–) was the first African American elected mayor of Seattle.

Sources: Fortune 126 (2 November 1992), cover and p. 43; Jet 77 (22 January 1990), p. 4; Who's Who Among Black Americans, 1992–1993, p. 1185.

1990 ♦ On November 6, 1990, **Sharon Pratt Dixon** (Kelly) (1944–) was elected the first black woman mayor of Washington, D.C., a first for a woman of any race.

Sources: Marketing (14 April 1992), p. 47; Notable Black American Women, pp. 278–80; Who's Who Among Black Americans, 1992–1993, p. 385.

1991 ♦ **Wellington E. Webb** (1941–) was the first black mayor of Denver. Active in both local and national politics, Webb was a state representative from 1973 to 1977 and was auditor of the city at the time of his election. He took office on June 30, 1991.

Sources: Jet 81 (18 November 1991) p. 66; State of Black America 1992, pp. 375, 377; Who's Who Among Black Americans, 1992–1993, p. 1479.

1992 ♦ **Dwight Tillery** (1948–) was the first black popularly elected mayor of Cincinnati. The two African Americans who held the office previously had been selected by the City Council.

Source: Ebony (March 1992), pp. 107, 110.

Willie W. Herenton (1940–) was elected the first black mayor of Memphis, Tennessee; he took office in 1992. Herenton taught in the elementary schools of the Memphis City School System and became the first black superintendent of the system in 1979.

Sources: Ebony 47 (March 1992), pp. 106, 108; State of Black America, 1992, pp. 383–84; Who's Who Among Black Americans, 1992–1993, p. 644.

1993 ♦ **Sharon Sayles Belton** (1951–) was elected the first African American and the first woman mayor of Minneapolis, Minnesota, in November 1993.

Source: Minneapolis Star Tribune, 3 November 1993; p. 1A.

State Offices

1866 ◆ **Charles Lewis Mitchell** (1829–1912) and Edward Garrison Walker (c. 1831–1910) of Massachusetts were the first African Americans elected to a state legislature.

Sources: Bennett, *Before the Mayflower,* p. 477; *Dictionary of American Negro Biography,* pp. 443–44 (Mitchell), 623 (Walker); *Negro Almanac,* pp. 16, 1425..

1868 ◆ **Oscar James Dunn** (c. 1821–1871) of Louisiana was the first black lieutenant governor. He was elected on April 22, 1868, and took office on June 13. Dunn may have been free born and was a music teacher before the Civil War. During his term as lieutenant governor he won a reputation for honesty. His sudden death after a violent two-day illness came at a moment when it seemed that he might become the Republican nominee for governor. The first black state treasurer, Antoine Dubuclet, was also named in the same election.

Crystal Bird Fauset

Sources: Bennett, *Before the Mayflower,* p. 481; *Dictionary of American Negro Biography,* pp. 204–5; Hornsby, Jr., *Chronology of African-American History,* pp. 41–42; Kane, *Famous First Facts,* p. 352.

The South Carolina General Assembly was the first state legislative body with a black majority when it met on July 6, 1868. There were 87 African Americans and 40 whites in the lower house. The whites, however, had a majority in the state senate, and in 1874 (near the end of Reconstruction) there was again a white majority in the house.

Sources: Bennett, *Before the Mayflower,* p. 629; Hornsby, Jr., *Chronology of African-American History,* p. 42.

1872 ◆ **Pinckney Benton Pinchback** (1837–1921) was the first black governor. He served as governor of Louisiana from December 9, 1872, to January 13, 1873, while Governor Henry Clay Warmoth faced impeachment proceedings. His election to the U.S. House of Representatives in 1872 was disputed, as was his election to the U.S. Senate in 1873. He became surveyor of customs in New Orleans about 1883. In the 1890s he moved permanently to Washington, D.C.

Sources: Dictionary of American Negro Biography, pp. 493–94; *Encyclopedia of Black America,* p. 677; Hornsby, Jr., *Chronology of African-American History,* p. 45; Kane, *Famous First Facts,* p. 290.

1882 ◆ **Edward (sometimes Edwin) P. McCabe** (1850–1920) was the first African American elected to state office outside the Deep South when he became state auditor of Kansas. McCabe moved to Oklahoma in 1889 and was one of the founders of Langston City, Oklahoma.

Sources: Dictionary of American Negro Biography, pp. 410–13; Encyclopedia of Black America, p. 83; Katz, The Black West, pp. 254–61.

1885 ◆ **Benjamin William Arnett** (1838– 1906) was the first African American to represent a majority white constituency in a state house of representatives. A bishop of the AME church, he represented Green County from 1885 to 1887. In 1864 Arnett was the first and, for a period, the only black teacher in Fayette County, Pennsylvania. As a legislator, Arnett helped erase discriminatory laws in Ohio. He remained especially influential through his friendship with William McKinley, Jr., who became president in 1897.

Sources: Dictionary of American Negro Biography, pp. 17–18; Kane, Famous First Facts, p. 347; Negro Almanac, p. 1425.

1920 ◆ **Walthall M. Moore** was the first African American elected to the Missouri legislature in modern times.

Source: Garrett, Famous First Facts About Negroes, p. 186.

1938 ◆ **Crystal Bird Fauset** (1893–1965) of Pennsylvania was the first black woman elected to a state legislature in the United States. Born in Maryland, Fauset worked for the Young Women's Christian Society, the American Friends Service Committee, and the Works Progress Administration (WPA) before going into politics. She resigned from the legislature after a year to return to the WPA. She continued a career of government service and active involvement in politics.

Sources: Black Women in America, pp. 410–11; Negro Almanac, pp. 25, 1426; Notable Black American Women, pp. 333–36.

1951 ◆ **Kermit Parker** was the first African American to qualify as a Democratic party primary candidate for the nomination for governor.

Source: Jet 65 (17 October 1983), p. 22.

1952 ◆ **Cora M. Brown** (1914–1972) was the first black woman in the United States to be elected to a state senate. Since the only previous woman senator in Michigan had been appointed, she was the first woman of any race elected to the Michigan senate. After supporting Eisenhower in the 1956 election, she was appointed special associate general counsel of the U.S. Post

Office Department on August 15, 1957, becoming the first black woman member of the department's legal staff.

Sources: Alford, *Famous First Blacks,* p. 45; Clayton, *The Negro Politician,* pp. 139–43; *Ebony* 22 (September 1967), pp. 27–28.

1958 ◆ **Robert Nelson C. Nix** (1905–) was the first black congressman from Pennsylvania. He held membership on the foreign affairs, post office, and civil service committees. Nix's son, Robert N. C. Nix, Jr., was the first African American to sit on a state Supreme Court bench since Reconstruction; he was inaugurated as chief justice of the Pennsylvania Supreme Court in 1984.

Sources: Dictionary of Black Culture, p. 331; Garrett, *Famous First Facts About Negroes,* p. 40; Hornsby, Jr., *Chronology of African-American History,* p. 327.

1960 ◆ On November 8, 1960, **Otis M. Smith** (1922–) became the first African American to win a statewide election since Reconstruction when he was elected auditor general of Michigan. He also was a Michigan State Supreme Court justice from 1961 to 1966. He was the first African American to serve in this capacity in any state since Reconstruction. Smith became a lawyer for General Motors in 1967, Smith was named head of the firm's legal staff in 1977. He held this post until his retirement in 1983.

Sources: Ebony 16 (March 1961), pp. 75–80, 33 (December 1977), pp. 33–42, 37 (March 1982), p. 130; *Ebony Success Library,* vol. 1, p. 286; *Encyclopedia of Black America,* p. 798; *Who's Who Among Black Americans, 1992–1993,* p. 1309.

1962 ◆ **Leroy Reginald Johnson** (1928–) of Georgia was the first African American elected to a southern legislature since Reconstruction. He served for 12 years.

Sources: Ebony 18 (March 1963), pp. 25–28, 30 (January 1975), p. 35; *Encyclopedia of Black America,* p. 475; Hornsby, Jr., *Chronology of African-American History,* pp. 113, 249; *Who's Who Among Black Americans, 1992–1993,* p. 763.

1967 ◆ **Barbara Charline Jordan** (1936–) was the first African American to sit in the Texas senate since 1883. In 1972 she became president pro tem of the senate, the first black woman to preside over a legislative body in the United States, and the first black to serve as acting governor of the state. Later that year, she was elected to the U.S. House of Representatives and became the first southern black congresswoman. Her reputation as one of the twentieth century's great orators was sustained by her keynote address to the 1976 Democratic Convention. Jordan decided in 1978 to retire from Congress.

She became the Lyndon B. Johnson Centennial Chair in National Policy Professor at the University of Texas at Austin.

Sources: *Black Women in America*, pp. 658–59; *Encyclopedia of Black America*, p. 480; *Negro Almanac*, p. 449; *Notable Black American Women*, pp. 609–12; *Who's Who Among Black Americans, 1992–1993*, p. 800.

Richard H. Austin (1913–) became the first black secretary of state in modern times when he assumed that position in Michigan. He was also the first black licensed certified public accountant in the state in 1941.

Sources: Alford, *Famous First Blacks*, p. 48; *Ebony* 26 (January 1971), p. 94; *Ebony Success Library*, vol. 1., p. 15; *Who's Who Among Black Americans, 1992–1993*, p. 51.

James Rankin Cowan (1916–) was the first African American in the United States appointed to a governor's cabinet as commissioner of health. He held the cabinet position from 1970 to 1974.

Source: *Ebony* 27 (April 1972), p. 96; *Ebony Success Library*, vol. 2, p. 81; *Who's Who Among Black Americans, 1992–1993*, p. 313.

Melvin H. Evans (1918–) was the first elected governor of the U.S. Virgin Islands. Evans had been appointed governor in mid-1969. Evans was also the first native-born governor. He was a physician who had served as assistant commissioner of health of the islands.

Sources: Alford, *Famous First Blacks*, p. 39; *Ebony* 26 (March 1971), pp. 105–8, 34 (March 1979), pp. 26; *Negro Almanac*, p. 1556.

Dorothy Mae Taylor was the first black woman elected to the Louisiana legislature. In 1986 she was elected the first councilwoman-at-large of New Orleans and was also the first woman to serve as acting mayor of the city.

Source: *Jet* 70 (28 July 1986), p. 20.

Vel R. Phillips (1924–) of Wisconsin was the first woman and the first African American to be elected to a statewide constitutional office, secretary of state. Her law degree from the University of Wisconsin in 1951 was also a first. She was the first African American elected to the Milwaukee Common Council (1956–71), the first African American elected to serve on the National Convention Committee of either party (1958), and the first black woman judge in the state (1972).

Sources: Clayton, *The Negro Politician*, pp. 132–37; *Ebony Success Library*, vol. 1, p. 246; Lee, *Interesting People*, p. 136; *Notable Black American Women*, pp. 848–51; *Who's Who Among Black Americans, 1992–1993*, p. 1122.

1990 ◆ On January 13, 1990, **Lawrence Douglas Wilder** (1931–) of Virginia became the first African American governor since Reconstruction. Previously he was Virginia's first black lieutenant governor. In 1969 Wilder became the first black state senator of Virginia since Reconstruction. In

September 1991 Wilder announced his intention to run for president of the United States.

Sources: Hornsby, Jr., and Straub, *African American Chronology*, p. 305; Hornsby, Jr., *Chronology of African-American History*, pp. 412, 420–21; *Negro Almanac*, p. 416; *Who's Who Among Black Americans, 1992–1993*, p. 1505.

Pamela Carter was the first black woman in the United States to be elected state attorney general and the first woman to be elected to the position in Indiana. Carter was also the second African American in Indiana elected to a statewide office. Dwayne Brown, elected state clerk of the courts in 1990, was the first.

Source: Jet 83 (23 November 1992), p. 58.

L. Douglas Wilder

Federal Appointments and Diplomacy

1865 ♦ **James Lewis** (1832–1914) was active in Reconstruction politics and was the first African American to receive an appointment from the federal government as inspector of customs for the Port of New Orleans. When the Union troops occupied New Orleans in 1862, Lewis abandoned the Confederate ship on which he was serving as a steward, raised two companies of black soldiers, and led the First Regiment of the Louisiana National Guard during the battle for Port Hudson. He was active in Louisiana politics and received several federal appointments.

Source: Dictionary of Black Culture, p. 270.

1924 ♦ **Clifton Reginald Wharton, Sr.** (1899–1990) was the first black American to pass the foreign service examination. Wharton entered the U.S. Foreign Service in 1925, functioning as third secretary to Monrovia, Liberia. Over the next 30 years he held posts in the Malagasy Republic, Portugal, and Romania; in 1958 he was the first African American to head a U.S. delegation to a European country, as minister to Romania.

Sources: Current Biography, 1990, p. 665; Garrett, *Famous First Facts About Negroes*, p. 7; Robinson, *Historical Negro Biographies*, p. 259.

1936 ♦ **Mary Jane McLeod Bethune** (1875–1955) was the first black woman to head a federal office. President Franklin D. Roosevelt appointed

Bethune to serve as director of the division of Minority Affairs of the New Deal's National Youth Administration (NYA). The NYA was founded in 1935 to provide job-training for unemployed youths and part-time work for needy students. (*See also* **Education: Honorary Degrees, 1946; Miscellaneous: Commemoratives and Monuments, 1974; Organizations: Civil Rights and Political Organizations, 1935.**)

Sources: Dictionary of American Negro Biography, pp. 41–43; *Notable Black American Women*, pp. 86–92; Robinson, *Historical Negro Biographies*, p. 163.

1944 ◆ **Ralph Johnson Bunche** (1904–1971) was the first black nondiplomatic official in the U.S. Department of State. Bunche was made divisional assistant, Division of Political Studies. In 1947 he transferred to the United Nations. He headed various divisions of the United Nations and mediated the end of the Arab-Israeli War in 1949—he was the highest ranking American at the United Nations. In 1950 he became the first black American to win the Nobel Peace Prize. (*See also* **Miscellaneous: Honors and Awards, 1950** and **1963.**)

Sources: Dictionary of Black Culture, p. 74; Garrett, *Famous First Facts About Negroes*, p. 185; Robinson, *Historical Negro Biographies*, p. 170.

1948 ◆ **Edward R. Dudley** (1911–) was the first black diplomat to receive the designation of ambassador. He was appointed ambassador to Liberia, where he served until 1953.

Sources: Dictionary of Black Culture, p. 144; Garrett, *Famous First Facts About Negroes*, p. 7; Robinson, *Historical Negro Biographies*, p. 186.

On August 7, 1954, **Charles H. Mahoney** (1886–1966) was confirmed by the Senate as the first black permanent member of the delegation to the United Nations.

Sources: Bennett, *Before the Mayflower*, pp. 550, 625; Garrett, *Famous First Facts About Negroes*, p. 192; *Who's Who in Colored America, 1950*, p. 350.

E. Frederic Morrow (c. 1909–) was the first black man to serve as a White House aide, under President Dwight D. Eisenhower. He wrote *Black Man in the White House* (1963).

Sources: Who's Who Among Black Americans, 1977, p. 651; *Who's Who in Colored America, 1950*, p. 385.

1960 ◆ **Andrew T. Hatcher** (1923–1992) was the first black presidential press secretary. President John Kennedy named Hatcher as associate press secretary on November 10, 1960, and for a time he was the highest-ranking black appointee in the executive branch of the federal government.

Sources: Hornsby, Jr., *Chronology of African-American History,* p. 111; Hornsby, Jr., *Milestones in Twentieth-Century African-American History,* p. 67.

1964 ◆ **Charlotte Moton Hubbard** was the first black deputy assistant secretary of state for public affairs. This was the highest permanent position held by a woman. Hubbard was later the first African American appointed to an important position with a television station.

Source: *Negro Almanac, 1976,* p. 1008.

Carl Thomas Rowan (1925–) was the first African American to head the U.S. Information Agency (1964–1965). He was deputy assistant secretary of state for public affairs (1961–1963), and from 1963 to 1964 he was ambassador to Finland. Tennessee-born, Rowan is a successful nationally syndicated columnist and journalist. He was the first African American to ever attend a meeting of the National Security Council.

Sources: *Contemporary Black Biography,* vol. 1, pp. 208–12; *Dictionary of Black Culture,* p. 385; Robinson, *Historical Negro Biographies,* p. 246.

1965 ◆ **Andrew Felton Brimmer** (1926–) became the first black member of the governing body of the Federal Reserve System. He joined government service as an assistant secretary for economic affairs at the Commerce Department.

Sources: *Contemporary Black Biography,* vol. 2, pp. 37–39; Garrett, *Famous First Facts About Negroes,* p. 163; *Negro Almanac, 1976,* pp. 345–46.

James Madison Nabrit, Jr. (1900–) was the first black American ambassador to the United Nations. President Lyndon B. Johnson appointed him U.S. deputy representative to the United Nations Security Council, where he served from 1965 to 1967. (*See also* **Education: College Administrators, 1960.**)

Sources: Bennett, *Before the Mayflower,* p. 574; Hornsby, Jr., *Chronology of African-American History,* p. 105; *Who's Who Among Black Americans, 1992–1993,* p. 1045.

1968 ◆ **Barbara M. Watson** (1918–1983) was the first black woman to serve as an assistant secretary of state. She began her career in the State Department in 1966.

Sources: Garrett, *Famous First Facts About Negroes,* pp. 163, 197; *Jet* 63 (7 March 1983), p. 12.

1970 ◆ **Samuel Riley Pierce, Jr.** (1922–) was the first African American to serve as a general counsel to the U.S. Treasury Department. In 1980 President-elect Ronald Reagan named Pierce secretary of Housing and

Patricia Roberts
Harris

Urban Development. He was the first and only black cabinet member in the Reagan administration.

Sources: Hornsby, Jr., *Chronology of African-American History*, p. 307; Hornsby, Jr., *Milestones in Twentieth-Century African-American History*, pp. 182, 307, 418; *Who's Who Among Black Americans, 1992–1993*, p. 1124.

Benjamin Lawson Hooks (1925–) was the first black commissioner of the Federal Communications Commission. He was a Baptist church minister and a founding member of the Southern Christian Leadership Council and was the executive secretary of the National Association for the Advancement of Colored People (NAACP; 1977–92). In 1986 Hooks received the NAACP Spingarn medal.

Sources: Hornsby, Jr., *Milestones in Twentieth-Century African-American History*, pp. 215, 489; *Who's Who Among Black Americans, 1992–1993*, p. 679.

Azie B. Taylor Morton (1936–) was the first black treasurer of the United States.

Sources: Kane, *Famous First Facts*, p. 675; *Who's Who Among Black Americans, 1992–1993*, p. 1030.

1976 ♦ **Patricia Roberts Harris** (1924–1985) became the first black woman cabinet member when President Jimmy Carter appointed her secretary of Housing and Urban Development in 1976. In 1965 she became the first black woman ambassador of an overseas post when President Lyndon B. Johnson appointed her ambassador to Luxembourg. Two years later she was named an alternate delegate to the United Nations. In 1971 she was elected to the boards of directors of IBM and Chase National Bank. The same year also became the first black to chair the credentials committee at a meeting of the Democratic National Committee.

Sources: Garrett, *Famous First Facts About Negroes*, p. 7; Hornsby, Jr., *Chronology of African-American History*, p. 280; Kane, *Famous First Facts*, pp. 31, 50; *Notable Black American Women*, pp. 468–72.

1977 ♦ **Andrew Jackson Young, Jr.** (1932–) was nominated by President Jimmy Carter as the first black U.S. ambassador to the United Nations (the position carried cabinet-level status). Five years earlier Young became the first black member of the House from Georgia since 1870. He was a leader in the civil rights movement and a close associate of Martin Luther

King, Jr. He later served as mayor of Atlanta (1982–1990) and ran unsuccessfully for governor of the state of Georgia. He is now co-chair of the Atlanta Committee for the Olympic Games.

Sources: Contemporary Black Biography, vol. 3, pp. 263–67; Hornsby, Jr., Chronology of African-American History, pp. 280, 282, 290, 305, 349, 409, 428; Who's Who Among Black Americans, 1992–1993, p. 1583.

1978 ♦ **Carolyn Robertson Payton** (1925–) was the first woman and first African American to head the Peace Corps.

Sources: Notable Black American Women, pp. 833–34; Who's Who Among Black Americans, 1992–1993, p. 1100.

1981 ♦ **Clarence M. Pendleton, Jr.** (1930–1988) was the first African American to chair the U.S. Civil Rights Commission.

Sources: Hornsby, Jr., Chronology of African-American History, p. 369; Hornsby, Jr., Milestones in African-American History, pp. 308, 379; Negro Almanac, p. 101; Who's Who in American Politics, 1987–1988, p. 136.

Ron Brown

Louis Wade Sullivan (1933–) was the first black cabinet member in President George Bush's administration, as Secretary of the U.S. Department of Health and Human Services. Sullivan was also the first dean and president of the Morehouse School of Medicine (1974–89).

Sources: Hornsby, Jr., Chronology of African-American History, p. 385; Who's Who Among Black Americans, 1992–1993, p. 1353.

1989 ♦ In 1989 **Ronald H. Brown** (1941–) was named chairman of the National Democratic Party—the first African American to hold this office. In 1993 Brown was confirmed as the first African American to hold the cabinet post of Secretary of Commerce. Brown was also the first black chief counsel of the Senate Judiciary Committee (1980).

Sources: Atlanta Constitution, 18 December 1992; Crisis 100 (March 1993), p. 16; Ebony 48 (May 1993), p. 62; Who's Who Among Black Americans, 1992–1993, p. 180.

1993 ♦ **Jesse Brown** (1944–) was the first African American ever confirmed to the cabinet as head of Veterans Affairs. Brown, executive director of

BLACKS ELECTED TO THE HOUSE OF REPRESENTATIVES IN THE NINETEENTH CENTURY

Representative	State	Years of Service
Joseph H. Rainey	South Carolina	1869–79
Jefferson F. Long	Georgia	1870–71
Robert C. Delarge	South Carolina	1871–73
Benjamin S. Turner	Alabama	1871–73
Robert B. Elliott	South Carolina	1871–75
Josiah T. Walls	Florida	1871–77
Alonzo J. Ransier	South Carolina	1873–75
James T. Rapier	Alabama	1873–75
Richard H. Cain	South Carolina	1873–75, 1877–79
John R. Lynch	Mississippi	1873–77, 1881–83
Jeremiah Haralson	Alabama	1875–77
John A. Hyman	North Carolina	1875–77
Charles E. Nash	Louisiana	1875–77
Robert Smalls	South Carolina	1875–79, 1881–87
James E. O'Hara	North Carolina	1883–87
John Mercer Langston	Virginia	1889–91
Thomas E. Miller	South Carolina	1889–91
Henry P. Cheatham	North Carolina	1889–93
George Washington Murray	South Carolina	1893–97
George H. White	North Carolina	1897–1901

BLACKS ELECTED TO THE SENATE IN THE NINETEENTH CENTURY

Senator	State	Years Served
Hiram Rhoades Revels	Mississippi	1870–71
Blanche K. Bruce	Mississippi	1875–81

Source: Negro Almanac, 1976, pp. 318–31.

Disabled American Veterans for more than 25 years, was an advocate for those who served in America's armed forces. He lost the use of his right arm while serving as a marine in the Vietnam War.

Sources: Atlanta Constitution, 18 December 1992; *Crisis* 100 (March 1993), p. 16; *Ebony* 48 (May 1993), p. 64.

1993 ♦ **Hazel O'Leary** (1938–) was the first black (and the first woman) Secretary of Energy. She acquired governmental experience under

presidents Gerald Ford and Jimmy Carter and was executive vice-president of Northern States Power Company of Minnesota at the time of her appointment.

Senator Hiram Revels (left) and representatives to the United States Congress, 1872.

Source: Ebony 48 (May 1993), p. 64.

Clifton Reginald Wharton, Jr., (1926–)was the first African American named deputy secretary of state. (*See also* **Education: College Administrators, 1970.**)

Source: Ebony 48 (May 1993), p. 62.

Alphonso Michael "Mike" Espy (1953–) was confirmed as the first black Secretary of Agriculture. In 1986 Espy became the first black congressman elected from Mississippi since Reconstruction.

Sources: Crisis 100 (March 1993), p. 16; *Ebony 48* (May 1993), p. 62; *Negro Almanac,* 388–89; *Who's Who Among Black Americans, 1992–1993,* p. 439.

National Politics

1868 ♦ **John Willis Menard** (1839–93) was the first African American elected to Congress. He was awarded his full salary but never seated. The committee on elections ruled that it was too early to admit a African American to Congress. He was appointed inspector of customs of the port of New Orleans. When he was allowed to plead his own case on February 27, 1969, he became the first African American to speak on the floor of the House.

Sources: Bennett, *Before the Mayflower,* p. 626; Garrett, *Famous First Facts About Negroes,* p. 29; Robinson, *Historical Negro Biographies,* pp. 99–100.

1869 ♦ **Ebenezer Don Carlos Bassett** (1833–1908) was the first black diplomat when he became minister resident to Haiti. From 1857 to 1869, prior to the appointment, he was principal of Philadelphia's Institute for Colored Youth. After completing his Haitian assignment (1877), he served for 10 years as a general consul from Haiti to the United States.

Sources: Dictionary of American Negro Biography, p. 32; Garrett, *Famous First Facts About Negroes,* pp. 46, 158; Robinson, *Historical Negro Biographies,* p. 49.

1870 ♦ **Hiram Rhoades (Rhodes) Revels** (1822–1901) was the first black U.S. senator. He was elected to fill the vacated seat of Confederate President Jefferson Davis on January 20, 1870. He was elected to the Mississippi state senate in 1869 and elected U.S. senator by the legislature. He served from February 21, 1870, to March 3, 1871. After serving in the Senate, he served as the first president of the newly founded Alcorn College for Negroes.

Sources: Bennett, *Before the Mayflower,* p. 487; *Dictionary of American Negro Biography,* pp. 523–24; Garrett, *Famous First Facts About Negroes,* p. 30; Robinson, *Historical Negro Biographies,* p. 116.

Joseph Hayne Rainey (1831–1887) was the first black congressman from South Carolina. He was sworn in on December 12, 1870, since he was elected to fill an unexpired term. He was a delegate to the state constitutional convention in 1868 and to the state senate in 1870. In 1874 Rainey was the first African American ever to preside over the House. He served in Washington, D.C., for four consecutive terms until 1879.

Sources: Bennett, *Before the Mayflower,* p. 488; Christopher, *America's Black Congressmen,* p. 33; *Dictionary of American Negro Biography,* p. 510; Garrett, *Famous First Facts About Negroes,* p. 32; Robinson, *Historical Negro Biographies,* p. 112.

1871 ♦ **Josiah Thomas Walls** (1842–c. 1905) was the first black congressman ever elected from the state of Florida, taking office on March 4, 1871. He was elected a Republican congressman-at-large in 1870 and re-elected twice, serving until 1876, when he was unseated for the second time. He served for a while in the post of superintendent of a farm on the campus of Tallahassee State College (later Florida Agricultural and Mechanical University).

Sources: Dictionary of American Negro Biography, pp. 629–30; Garrett, *Famous First Facts About Negroes,* p. 33; Robinson, *Historical Negro Biographies,* p. 139.

On February 1, 1871, **Jefferson Franklin Long** (1836–1900) was the first African American to speak in the House of Representatives as a congressman. Long was the second African American elected and the first (and only) one from Georgia during Reconstruction. He served from January 1871 to the end of the session on March 3, 1871.

Sources: Bennett, *Before the Mayflower,* p. 489; *Dictionary of American Negro Biography,* p. 405.

1872 ◆ In 1872 **Frederick Douglass** (1817–1895) was the first African American to be nominated as a vice-presidential candidate, by the Woman Suffrage Association convention. Six years earlier he was the first black delegate to a national political convention, that of the National Loyalists' Union party. Born a slave and named Frederick Augustus Bailey, Douglass's talent as an orator won him employment as a lecturer by the Anti-Slavery Society. His freedom was bought while he was on a lecture tour in England. From 1847 until his death he was a fearless leader of his race. During Reconstruction he demanded the vote for the freedman. He moved to the nation's capital and became the first African American to serve as recorder of deeds in 1881 and U.S. minister to Haiti in 1889. He published his classic autobiography in 1845. A second version appeared in 1855, and this work was again revised and enlarged under the title *The Life and Times of Frederick Douglass* in 1882. In 1888 Frederick Douglass was the first African American to be nominated as a presidential candidate, at the Republican convention. He received one vote. (*See also* **Civil Rights and Protest, 1842** and **Literature: Short Stories, 1853.**)

Sources: Dictionary of American Negro Biography, p. 181; Garrett, *Famous First Facts About Negroes,* p. 160; *Negro Almanac,* p. 290.

1873 ◆ **John Roy Lynch** (1847–1939) was the first black congressman from Mississippi. At the age of 24 he became speaker of the Mississippi House. He was elected U.S. congressman three times and served with distinction from 1873–77. He served the Republican party as state chairman of the executive committee (1881–89) and received federal appointments (1898–1911) as a reward. In 1884 Lynch was the first African American to preside over a national nominating convention held by a major political party. He was named temporary chairman of the Republican Party meeting in

Chicago. He also wrote an authoritative account of the post–Civil War period, *The Facts of Reconstruction,* in 1913.

Sources: *Dictionary of American Negro Biography,* pp. 407–9; Garrett, *Famous First Facts About Negroes,* pp. 19, 33–34, 43, 53; Robinson, *Historical Negro Biographies,* p. 98.

1874 ◆ **Blanche Kelso Bruce** (1841–1898) was the first African American elected to a full term in the U.S. Senate. Mississippi's second black senator, Bruce took his seat in 1875. A wealthy Mississippi farmer and a successful banker, Bruce was the only black senator to serve a full term until the mid-twentieth century. In 1878 Bruce presided over the Senate, the first African American to do so. In 1881 President Ulysses S. Grant appointed him register of the treasury.

Sources: *Dictionary of American Negro Biography,* pp. 74–76; Hornsby, Jr., *Chronology of African-American History,* p. 45, 50, 56; Robinson, *Historical Negro Biographies,* pp. 56–57.

1875 ◆ **John A. Hyman** (1840–91) was the first African American to serve the state of North Carolina as a U.S. congressman. He was elected to the 44th Congress. During his term he served on the Committee of Manufacturers. He held several federal appointments in North Carolina.

Sources: Garrett, *Famous First Facts About Negroes,* p. 35; *Paths Toward Freedom,* p. 160.

1888 ◆ **John Mercer Langston** (1829–1897) was the first black Virginian elected to the House of Representatives. Langston was also the first African American to win an elective office, as a member of the city council of Brownhelm, Ohio, in 1855. An active leader in the convention movement before the Civil War, he helped to organize the freedmen in the Negro National Labor Union. In 1868 President Andrew Johnson appointed him Inspector General of the Freedmen's Bureau. From 1869 to 1876 he was associated with Howard University (Washington, D.C.). President Rutherford B. Hayes appointed him minister to Haiti in 1877. Later Langston served as president of Virginia Normal and Collegiate Institute at Petersburg, Virginia (now Virginia State College). Elected to the U.S. Congress as a Republican in 1888, he was not seated until 1890 because the election was contested. He published a collection of addresses, *Freedom and Citizenship* in 1883, and his autobiography, *From the Virginia Plantation to the National Capitol* in 1894.

Sources: Christopher, *America's Black Congressmen,* p. 139; *Dictionary of American Negro Biography,* pp. 382–84; Garrett, *Famous First Facts About Negroes,* pp. 36–37, 63, 91; Hornsby, Jr., *Chronology of African-American History,* pp. 27–28, 55.

1929 ◆ Republican **Oscar Stanton DePriest** (1871–1951) was the first black congressman elected in the twentieth century and also the first from a

Northern state. He served three terms from the 21st Congressional District of Illinois. Born in Florence, Alabama, and reared in Kansas, he moved to Chicago and became active in real estate before entering politics. He blazed the trail for the return of African Americans to Congress.

Sources: Dictionary of American Negro Biography, pp. 173–74; Garrett, *Famous First Facts About Negroes,* p. 37; Hornsby, Jr., *Chronology of African-American History,* p. 76.

1934 ◆ **Arthur W. Mitchell** (1883–1968) was the first black Democratic congressman. He defeated Republican congressman Oscar DePriest of Illinois. He was an ardent civil rights advocate and, as a lawyer, won a significant Supreme Court case in 1941 involving interstate travel. Mitchell retired from Congress in 1942.

Sources: Clayton, *The Negro Politician,* pp. 54–55; Garrett, *Famous First Facts About Negroes,* p. 37; Gosnell, *Negro Politicians,* pp. 90–91; Hornsby, Jr., *Chronology of African-American History,* p. 89.

1944 ◆ **Adam Clayton Powell, Jr.** (1908–1972) was elected to Congress from Harlem, becoming the first black member of the House of Representatives from the East. He was one of the most flamboyant and controversial politicians of the twentieth century. As a freshman legislator Powell engaged in fiery debates with segregationists, fought for the end of discrimination at U.S. military bases, and sought—through the Powell amendment—to deny federal funds to any project where discrimination existed. This amendment eventually became part of the Flanagan School Lunch Bill, making Powell the first black congressman since Reconstruction to have legislation passed by both houses. In 1961 Powell became the first African American to chair the powerful Education and Labor Committee. Powell began his political career in 1941 as the first African American to serve as a member of the New York City Council.

Sources: Hornsby, Jr., *Chronology of African-American History,* pp. 92, 194, 224; *Negro Almanac, 1976,* pp. 326–27; Robinson, *Historical Negro Biographies,* pp. 238–39.

1949 ◆ On January 18, 1949, **William L. Dawson** (1886–1970) became the first African American to head a congressional standing committee in recent times, as chair of the House Expenditures Committee. He won election to Congress in 1942—the third northern black, and the second black Democrat, in the U.S. Congress. He served longer than any other African American (1941–70). In 1944 he was the first African American to be the vice-president of a major political party, the Democratic National Party.

Sources: Bennett, *Before the Mayflower,* p. 627; Clayton, *The Negro Politician,* pp. 67–85; Hornsby, Jr., *Chronology of African-American History,* p. 91; Robinson, *Historical Negro Biographies,* p. 181.

1952 ◆ **Charlotta A. Spears Bass** (1880–1961) was the first black woman to run for vice-president. She was the nominee of the Progressive Party.

Sources: Black Women in America, vol. 1, p. 93; *Notable Black American Women,* p. 61–64; *Who's Who in Colored America, 1928,* p. 23.

1954 ◆ **Charles C. Diggs, Jr.** (1922–) was elected to the House of Representatives, becoming the first black federal legislator from Michigan. His election marked the first time in the twentieth century that as many as three African Americans served in the House. Diggs was a founder and first head of the Congressional Black Caucus. In 1969 Congressman Diggs was the first African American to chair the Foreign Relations Subcommittee on Africa. In 1973 he became the first black congressman to head the Committee for the District of Columbia. He resigned his seat in 1980 after being convicted of mail and payroll fraud.

Sources: Garrett, *Famous First Facts About Negroes,* p. 40; Hornsby, Jr., *Chronology of African-American History,* p. 102; *Negro Almanac,* pp. 74, 77; *Who's Who Among Black Americans, 1977,* p. 238.

1966 ◆ **Edward W. Brooke** (1919–), running on the Republican ticket, was the first African American to be elected to the U.S. Senate since Reconstruction and the first ever elected by popular vote. In 1960 he became the first African American to be nominated to run for statewide office in Massachusetts. He lost this election, but in 1962 he was elected Massachusetts attorney general.

Sources: Contemporary Biography, 1967, pp. 40–43; Hornsby, Jr., *Chronology of African-American History,* pp. 113, 129, 264; Robinson, *Historic Negro Biographies,* p. 166.

Robert Clifton Weaver (1907–) was named Secretary of Housing and Urban Development by President Lyndon B. Johnson, becoming the first African American to serve in the cabinet of a president. Five years earlier he became the first black administrator of the Federal Housing and Home Finance Administration—at that time the highest federal post ever held by an African American. Weaver was also the first African American to hold cabinet rank in New York (1955).

Sources: Dictionary of Black Culture, p. 464; *Encyclopedia of Black America,* p. 849; Garrett, *Famous First Facts About Negroes,* p. 113; Hornsby, Jr., *Chronology of African-American History,* pp. 111, 126; Robinson, *Historical Negro Biographies,* pp. 257–58; *Who's Who Among Black Americans, 1992–1993,* p. 1478.

1968 ◆ **Shirley Chisholm** (1924–) was the first African American woman elected to the House of Representatives. In 1964 she was elected to the New York state legislature. Upon her entry into national politics she won a committee assignment on the veterans affairs committee. In 1972 Chisholm was the first black woman to seek nomination as the Democratic presidential candidate.

Sources: Black Women in America, vol. 1, pp. 236–38; Garrett, *Famous First Facts About Negroes*, p. 42; Hornsby, Jr., *Chronology of African-American History*, p. 133; *Notable Black American Women*, pp. 185–89.

Walter E. Fauntroy (1933–) was the first black nonvoting delegate to Congress from the District of Columbia. He worked closely with Martin Luther King, Jr., and was a coordinator of the 1963 march on Washington and the 1968 Poor People's Campaign.

Sources: Encyclopedia of Black America, p. 384; *Negro Almanac*, p. 389; *Who's Who Among Black Americans, 1992–1993*, p. 448.

Julian Bond (1940–) and **Channing E. Phillips** (1928–87) were the first African Americans proposed for president and vice-president at the same convention. Bond was an early member of the Student Nonviolent Coordinating Committee (SNCC) and communications direc-

Shirley Chisholm

tor of the organization. At the Democratic convention he was the first African American to be nominated from the floor of a major convention for the office of vice-president. After a few states voted, he withdrew, as he was too young to accept the nomination. Phillips was the first African American nominated for president at a major political convention in modern times. Phillips was a Congregationalist minister and active in Democratic politics.

Sources: Contemporary Black Biography, vol. 2, pp. 22–27 (Bond); *Dictionary of Black Culture*, p. 59 (Bond), p. 351 (Phillips); Garrett, *Famous First Facts About Negroes*, p. 163 (Phillips); Kane, *Famous First Facts*, p. 479 (Bond); *Who's Who Among Black Americans, 1977*, p. 710 (Phillips).

1971 ◆ **Louis Stokes** (1925–) was the first black member of the Appropriations Committee. Elected U.S. congressman from Ohio in 1968, Stokes received his legal training at John Marshall School of Law in Cleveland and had a private practice until his entry into politics. In 1983 Congressman Stokes became the first black member of the House Select Committee on Intelligence, and in 1985 the first black congressman to head the Program and Budget Authorization subcommittee of the House Permanent Select Committee on Intelligence.

Sources: Contemporary Black Biography, vol. 3, pp. 237–39; Hornsby, Jr., *Milestones in African-American History*, pp. 103, 493; *Negro Almanac*, p. 395.

1963 March on Washington

The Congressional Black Caucus (CBC) was formed as the first major group of black congressman to influence party politics and black-oriented legislation. The all-Democratic group, representing mainly northern big-city districts, was permanently headquartered on Capitol Hill with a director and staff. It was formally organized in 1971 and later included Republican members. Michigan congressman Charles C. Diggs, Jr., was founder and first head of the CBC.

Sources: Dictionary of Black Culture, p. 46; Hornsby, Jr., Milestones in Twentieth-Century African-American History, pp. 360, 404; Negro Almanac, pp. 380–82.

1973 ♦ **Cardiss Hortense Robertson Collins** (1932–) was the first black congresswoman from Illinois and the fourth black woman to serve in the

Jesse Jackson

Carol Moseley
Braun

Congress. In 1975 she became the first African American to chair the House Government Operations Subcommittee on Manpower and Housing. Born in Missouri and educated in Michigan and Illinois, Collins was elected to the House of Representatives to fill the seat left vacant by the death of her husband. She was the first woman to chair the Congressional Black Caucus. She was also the first black whip-at-large (1975).

Sources: Black Women in America, vol. 1, pp. 264–65; *Notable Black American Women,* p. 204; *Who's Who Among Black Americans, 1992–1993,* p. 290.

1974 ◆ **Charles Bernard Rangel** (1930–) was the first black member of the House Ways and Means Committee. In 1983 Rangel was the first black deputy whip in the House, a prestigious role in floor leadership. Rangel was elected to Congress in 1970 after a successful legislative career in New York state.

Sources: Hornsby, Jr., *Milestones in Twentieth-Century African-American History,* pp. 44, 103; *Negro Almanac,* p. 393–94; *Who's Who Among Black Americans, 1992–1993,* p. 1164.

1984 ◆ **William H. Gray III** (1941–) was the first black congressman to chair the House Budget Committee. Gray served in Congress from 1978 to 1991 and was also a member of the Democratic Congressional Steering Committee and the Committee on Foreign Affairs. In 1989 Gray was the first African American to serve as a majority whip in the House. In 1991 he gave up his political career to head the United Negro College Fund but Gray reentered politics less than two years later when President Bill Clinton appointed him special advisor on Haiti.

Sources: *Contemporary Black Biography,* vol. 3, pp. 77–80; Hornsby, Jr., *Milestones in African-American History,* p. 501; *Who's Who Among Black Americans, 1992–1993,* p. 552.

Jesse Louis Jackson (1941–), a Baptist minister and founder of Operation PUSH (People United to Serve Humanity), was the first black American to be a major candidate for the presidential nomination. He was a field director for the Congress of Racial Equality (CORE) and in 1967 was named by the Southern Christian Leadership Conference (SCLC) to head its Operation Breadbasket, which he helped found. In 1983 Jackson launched a major voter-registration drive among black Americans and toward the end of the year declared his candidacy for the Democratic presidential nomination. Jackson ran in a large number of Democratic primary elections in 1984, finishing a strong third to former Vice-President Walter Mondale and Senator Gary Hart. In 1987 Jackson again entered the race for the Democratic presidential nomination and finished second behind Massachusetts governor Michael Dukakis.

Sources: *Contemporary Black Biography,* vol. 1, pp. 108–12; Hornsby, Jr., *Milestones in Twentieth-Century African-American History,* pp. 122, 185, 247; *Negro Almanac,* 278–79; *Who's Who Among Black Americans, 1992–1993,* p. 722.

1988 ◆ **Lenora Fulani** was the first black woman to qualify for federal matching funds in a presidential election—and the first African-American (and woman) to appear on the presidential ballot in all 50 states. In 1992 Fulani was running on the National Alliance Party ticket and was on the ballot in 45 states.

Source: *Emerge* 4 (October 1992), p. 59.

1992 ◆ **Carol E. Moseley Braun** (1947–) was elected the nation's first black woman senator. She was active in Chicago legal circles and the state legislature and served as Cook County (Illinois) recorder of deeds/registrar of titles.

Sources: *Black Women in America,* vol. 1, pp. 162–64; *Crisis* 100 (March 1993), p. 7; *Jet* 83 (23 November 1992), p. 8; *Who's Who Among Black Americans, 1992–1993,* p. 1032.

Carrie Meek (1926–) became the first black woman to represent Florida in Congress. As a Florida state senator, she sponsored more than 30 bills and programs—ranging from education to small business to women's rights.

Sources: *Ebony* 48 (January 1993), p. 32; *Jet* 82 (28 September 1992), p. 34, 83 (23 November 1992), pp. 15, 52; *Who's Who in American Politics, 1987–1988,* p. 318.

1993 ◆ **Ronald V. Dellums** (1935–) became the first black chair of the House Armed Services Committee. In 1977 he became its first black member. A notable opponent of major military spending, he is nonetheless respected by military leaders and by more conservative members of the committee.

Sources: Ebony 48 (May 1993), p. 66; *Negro Almanac,* pp. 386–87; *Who's Who Among Black Americans, 1992–1993,* p. 372; *Who's Who in American Politics, 1987–1988,* p. 102.

Political Parties

1843 ◆ **Henry Highland Garnet, Samuel Ringgold Ward,** and **Charles B. Ray** were the first African Americans to participate in a national political gathering, the convention of the Liberty Party. Garnet (1815–82) pastored a New York Presbyterian church and preached a social gospel. At a Lincoln's birthday memorial, February 12, 1865, he became the first black man to preach in the rotunda of the Capitol to the House of Representatives. In 1843, at the Convention of Free Men in Buffalo, New York, he outlined a brilliant plan for a general slave strike. Ray (1807–86), one of the convention's secretaries, was a minister best known for his work as publisher of *The Colored American* and as president of the New York Society for the Promotion of Education Among Colored Children. Ward (1817–66), who led a prayer at the convention, was the leading black abolitionist before Frederick Douglass. His *Autobiography of a Fugitive Slave* was published in 1855.

Sources: Dictionary of American Negro Biography, pp. 252–53 (Garnet), 515–16 (Ray), 631-632 (Ward); *Dictionary of Black Culture,* pp. 181, 370, 460; Robinson, *Historical Negro Biographies,* pp. 82, 140.

Religion

AME Church • AME Zion Church • African Orthodox Church
African Union AME Church • African-American Catholic Church
Antioch Association of Metaphysical Science • Baptists
Black Christian Nationalist Church • Black Judaism • Catholics
Christian Church (Disciples of Christ) • Church of England
Congregationalists • Episcopalians • Holiness Churches
Interchurch Organizations • Islam • Lutherans • Methodists
Mormons • Nation of Islam • Peace Mission • Pentecostals
Presbyterians • Rastafarians • Spiritual Churches
Unitarian-Universalists • United Church and Science of Living Institute
United Church of Christ • United Methodists
United Society of Believers in Christ's Second Coming (Shakers)

African Methodist Episcopal (AME) Church

1799 ◆ **Richard Allen** (1760–1831) became the first black ordained deacon in the Methodist Episcopal church in 1799. In 1786 he established prayer meetings for blacks in Philadelphia. Resenting an effort by the white members of St. George's Methodist Episcopal Church to further segregate black members of the congregation, Allen and Absalom Jones led a walkout of blacks in 1787. The Free African Society, which seems to have been already organized as a mutual aid society, became the center of the congregation's worship. Jones entered the Protestant Episcopal ministry in 1794, but Allen remained a Methodist and organized Bethel Church that same year. When five black churches broke from the parent organization in 1816, Allen became the first bishop of the new African Methodist Episcopal (AME) Church. He is also one of the first black authors of a biography, *The Life Experiences and Gospel Labors of the Right Reverend Richard Allen,* and the compiler of the first black

Richard Allen

hymnal, *Collection of Spiritual Songs and Hymns Selected From Various Authors* (1801).

Sources: Dictionary of American Negro Biography, pp. 12–13; Directory of African American Religious Bodies, p. 242; Encyclopedia of Black America, p. 33; Smith, Climbing Jacob's Ladder, pp. 35–37, 60; Southern, The Music of Black Americans, pp. 75–79.

1816 ◆ On April 9 representatives of five Methodist congregations assembled at the Bethel Church in Philadelphia. Dissatisfied with the treatment of the black members of the Methodist Episcopal Church, they organized the AME Church. The representatives elected Daniel Coker (1780–1846) as their first bishop but he declined, perhaps because his light skin color caused dissension. Richard Allen (1760–1831) then became the first AME bishop. This denomination is currently the largest black Methodist group in the United States, with some 2.2 million members.

Sources: Dictionary of American Negro Biography, pp. 12–13 (Allen); 119–20 (Coker); Encyclopedia of Black America, p. 32; Lincoln and Mamiya, The Black Church in the African American Experience, p. 52; Smith, Climbing Jacob's Ladder, pp. 59–61.

1817 ◆ **Jarena Lee** (1783–?) was the first woman to preach in the AME church. In 1817 she rose in Bethel Church, Philadelphia, to give a spontaneous talk. Although never formally licensed to speak by the church, she began an extraordinary career as an evangelist. Lee and other women, including Juliann Jane Tillman, made a considerable impact on religious life as well as on the growth of their denomination.

Sources: Black Women in America, p. 707; Smith, Climbing Jacob's Ladder, pp. 64–65; Smith, Notable Black American Women, pp. 662–63.

1898 ◆ **Henry McNeal Turner** (1834–1915) was the first famous black churchman to declare that God is black. He said: "We had rather believe in no God, or ... believe that all nature is God than to believe in the personality of a God, and not to believe that He is a Negro." Turner was also the first black chaplain in the U.S. Army in 1863. Later, as a minister and bishop in the AME church, Turner supported black return to Africa.

Sources: Black Apostles, pp. 227–46; Encyclopedia of Black America, p. 820; Hornsby, Jr., Chronology of African-American History, pp. 66–67; Lincoln, The Black Church Since Frazier, p. 148.

African Methodist Episcopal (AME) Zion Church

Jarena Lee

1796 ◆ In New York City **Peter Williams, Sr.** (?–1823) a former slave and sexton of the John Street Methodist Church, organized the first African Chapel for Methodists in a cabinetmaker's shop owned by William Miller, a fellow member of the John Street Methodist Episcopal Church. Services were held there until a black church was completed in 1800. The church was the African Methodist Episcopal (AME) Zion Church, which became the mother church of the denomination in 1820. Despite his role in founding the church, Williams remained a member of the John Street Methodist Church, and his son, Peter, Jr., became a Protestant Episcopal priest.

Sources: *Dictionary of American Negro Biography*, pp. 660–62; Lincoln and Mamiya, *The Black Church in the African American Experience*, pp. 56–57; Smith, *Climbing Jacob's Ladder*, pp. 38–40.

1801 ◆ In New York City the first church of what would become the AME Zion Church was incorporated by Peter Williams, Sr., and Francis Jacobs. The building was completed in 1800. The church was initially pastored by a white minister supplied by the parent John Street Methodist Church. Complete independence came in 1820.

Sources: *Dictionary of American Negro Biography*, pp. 660–61; *Encyclopedia of American Religion*, vol. 1, p. 194; Lincoln and Mamiya, *The Black Church in the African American Experience*, pp. 50–52; Smith, *Climbing Jacob's Ladder*, pp. 38–40.

1820 ◆ On August 11 the African Methodist Zion and Asbury African Methodist churches, both of New York City, started their own separate AME Conference, still within the Methodist Episcopal church. The *Discipline* they adopted in September 1820 included the first and only open antislavery declaration by a Methodist church. With four other congregations from Pennsylvania, Connecticut, and New York, the conference held its first annual meeting on June 21, 1821. The denomination uses 1820 as its foundation date, although the break with the Methodist Episcopal Church did not become complete until 1824. The designation "Zion" was officially added to the name in

1848. It is currently the second largest black Methodist church, with some 1.2 million members in the United States.

Sources: Dictionary of American Negro Biography, pp. 616–17; Encyclopedia of Black America, pp. 35–36; Lincoln and Mamiya, The Black Church in the African American Experience, pp. 57–58; Smith, Climbing Jacob's Ladder, p. 63.

African Orthodox Church

1919 ◆ The movement that became the African Orthodox Church was organized on April 9, 1919, by **George Alexander McGuire** (1866–1934), who was consecrated its first bishop on September 28, 1921. In 1918 McGuire, an ordained Episcopal priest, was appointed the first chaplain-general and a spokesperson of the United Negro Improvement Society (UNIA) by

Henry McNeal Turner

Marcus Garvey. McGuire was disappointed in his hope that the African Orthodox church would become the official church of the UNIA, but he saw his church spread to Africa and the Caribbean before his death.

Sources: Baer and Singer, African-American Religion in the Twentieth Century, pp. 124–25; Dictionary of American Negro Biography, pp. 416–17; Directory of African American Religious Bodies, p. 126; Encyclopedia of American Religions, vol. 1, pp. 109–10.

African Union American Methodist Episcopal Church

1801 ◆ African Americans in Wilmington, Delaware, withdrew from Asbury Methodist Church and—under the leadership of Peter Spencer (1779–1843) and William Anderson—established Ezion Church. Because neither leader was ordained, Asbury Church appointed a white minister in 1812. Unable to keep control of the building in the ensuing legal dispute, the African Americans again withdrew and built another church, which was dedicated in 1813. Severing all ties with the Methodist Episcopal church, they formed the Union Church of Africans. The Union Church of Africans was the first all-black independent Methodist Church, and the mother church of one of the smaller black Methodist denominations, the African Union American

Methodist Episcopal church, which had about 6,500 members in 1988. The first annual conference was held in 1814 with three churches. The denomination refused to join the AME church in 1816.

Sources: Directory of African American Religious Bodies, p. 241; *Encyclopedia of American Religions,* vol. 1, pp. 194–95; Lincoln and Mamiya, *The Black Church in the African American Experience,* p. 48; Smith, *Climbing Jacob's Ladder,* pp. 58–59.

African-American Catholic Church

1990 ◆ **George Augustus Stallings, Jr.** (1948–) established the African American Catholic Church on May 13, 1990. He was its first bishop. Stallings broke with the Roman Catholic church over what he saw as its neglect of the spiritual needs of African Americans.

Source: Hornsby, Jr., *Chronology of African-American History,* p. 429.

Antioch Association of Metaphysical Science

1932 ◆ The Antioch Association of Metaphysical Science seems to be the first mainly black New Thought church. New Thought grows out of a Christian Science background and emphasizes healing through mental power. It has no connection with the current New Age movement. The Antioch Association was founded in Detroit by Lewis Johnson.

Sources: Baer and Singer, *African-American Religion in the Twentieth Century,* p. 200; *Encyclopedia of American Religions,* vol. 2, p. 886.

Baptists

1743 ◆ The first known black Baptist was **Quassey**, a member of the Newton, Rhode Island, church.

Source: Lincoln and Mamiya, *The Black Church in the African American Experience,* p. 23.

1758 ◆ The first known black Baptist congregation was the "Bluestone" African Baptist Church, located on the William Byrd plantation in Mecklenberg, Virginia. The church's nickname came from its location near the Bluestone River. (A claim for priority is also advanced for a congregation said to exist at Luneberg in 1756. The evidence is not clear cut, but all claims so far refer to Virginia and the decade of the 1750s.)

Sources: Baer and Singer, *African-American Religion in the Twentieth Century,* p. 16; Lincoln and Mamiya, *The Black Church in the African American Experience,* p. 23; Smith, *Climbing Jacob's Ladder,* p. 33; Wilmore, *Black and Presbyterian,* p. 41.

1773 ◆ The first black Baptist church under black leadership seems to have been formed in Silver Bluff, South Carolina. David George, a slave, became its first pastor. George Liele and, less probably, Andrew Bryan have also been associated with the church. The congregation seems to have been founded between 1773 and 1775. The present church was remodeled in 1920, and a cornerstone with the founding date of 1750 was put in place. Most historians believe this date is too early. In 1793 the congregation of some 60 persons, led by Jesse Galpin, moved to Augusta, Georgia, about 12 miles away.

c. 1775 ◆ **George Liele (Leile, Lisle)** (c. 1750-1820), the first known black Baptist missionary, was active before the Revolutionary War. Liele was born a slave in Virginia and became a convert after his master moved to Georgia. He was freed a short while before he began to preach. He preached in Savannah, Georgia, during the British occupation of the town from 1779 to 1782. Because British officers protected him against an attempt to reenslave him, he accompanied the withdrawal of the British troops to Jamaica. In 1784 he established the first black Baptist church on the island, in Kingston.

Sources: Dictionary of American Negro Biography, p. 397; Lincoln and Mamiya, *The Black Church in the African American Experience,* p. 23–24; Smith, *Climbing Jacob's Ladder,* pp. 32–33.

1806 ◆ The African Meeting House, also known as the Joy Street Baptist Church, Boston, Massachusetts, is the oldest surviving building constructed to serve as a black church. It housed the first black Baptist congregation in Boston, organized in 1805 by Thomas Paul, Sr. (1773–1831), who also founded the Abyssinian Baptist Church in New York City in 1809. On January 6, 1832, William Lloyd Garrison organized the Anti-Slavery Society in the church basement with the participation of prominent church members.

Sources: Baer and Singer, *African-American Religion in the Twentieth Century,* p. 26; Cantor, *Historic Landmarks of Black America,* pp. 70–71; *Dictionary of American Negro Biography,* pp. 482–83; Lincoln and Mamiya, *The Black Church in the African American Experience,* p. 25; Smith, *Climbing Jacob's Ladder,* pp. 48, 51–52.

1895 ◆ The National Baptist Convention, USA, held its first meeting in Atlanta, Georgia, on September 28, 1895. E. C. Morris was its first president. This remains the largest Baptist organization under the title National Baptist Convention, USA, Inc. The second largest is the National Baptist Convention of America, which split from the parent organization in 1915 in a dispute primarily about the control of the American Baptist Publication Society. The third largest is the Progressive National Baptist Convention, which broke away from the parent organization in 1961 over the issue of the churches' posture on civil rights.

Sources: Directory of African American Religious Bodies, pp. 229–32; Encyclopedia of Black America, pp. 163–64; Lincoln and Mamiya, The Black Church in the African American Experience, p. 28.

1983 ◆ As pastor of Mariner's Temple Baptist Church, Manhattan, **Suzanne Denise Johnson** (1957–) was the first African American and the first female pastor in the American Baptist Churches in the USA.

Sources: Essence (September 1983), p. 42; Jet 64 (13 June 1983), p. 25.

The South Carolina Baptist Educational and Missionary Convention authorized the ordination of women. This was the first state organization in the National Baptist Convention to do so.

Source: Jet 64 (30 May 1983), p. 26.

Black Christian Nationalist Church

1966 ◆ **Albert B. Cleage, Jr.** (1913–) preached a famous sermon at his independent and very activist Detroit church and became the first supporter of Black Theology to attract national attention. He later published two books presenting his position, *The Black Messiah* (1968) and *Black Christian Nationalism* (1972). The church maintains that Jesus was a black messiah and revolutionary sent to liberate blacks. The church building became known as the Shrine of the Black Madonna and the name was added to that of the church, which became Shrines of the Black Madonna Pan-African Orthodox Christian Church. In 1970 Cleage renamed himself Jaramogi Abebe Agyeman. By 1972 another name for the group was also in use: the Black Nationalist Church.

Sources: Baer and Singer, African-American Religion in the Twentieth Century, pp. 60–61, 126; Directory of African American Religious Bodies, pp. 128–29; Ebony Success Library, vol. 1, p. 70; Encyclopedia of American Religions, vol. 3, p. 156.

Black Judaism

1896 ◆ **William S. Crowdy**, a railroad cook, founded the Church of God and Saints of Christ in Lawrence, Kansas. The church mixes Judaism, Christianity, and black nationalism and is sometimes called the first black Jewish group. A principal belief is that blacks are the direct descendants of the lost tribes of Israel. A church with similar views is the Church of God (Black Jews), founded by Prophet F. S. Cherry, but the exact date of founding and current status of this church are unknown. The first black Jewish sect in New York City (which seems to have included some white Jewish members) arose in 1899, when Leon Richelieu (?–1964) established the Moorish Zionist Temple in Brooklyn.

Sources: Baer and Singer, *African-American Religions in the Twentieth Century,* pp. 50–51, 114–15; *Directory of African American Religious Bodies,* p. 131; *Encyclopedia of American Religions,* vol. 3, pp. 27, 152–53.

1968 ◆ The Original Hebrew Israelite Nation (also known as the Abeta Hebrew Cultural Center) is the first black American Jewish group to migrate to Israel. Formed in the 1960s by Ammi Carter (born G. Parker), the group was at first unsuccessful in establishing itself in Liberia and changed its goal to Israel. Some 1,500 members now live communally in Israel.

Sources: Baer and Singer, *African-American Religion in the Twentieth Century,* pp. 117–18; *Directory of African American Religious Bodies,* p. 133; *Encyclopedia of American Religions,* pp. 1291–92.

Catholics

1730 ◆ The Ursuline nuns of New Orleans, Louisiana, began instructing black Catholics in 1730. Catholic instruction for blacks was almost unknown in most places, and white Catholics were only somewhat better served.

Source: Raboteau, *Slave Religion,* p. 114.

1824 ◆ The first attempt to build a community of black nuns was the formation of a reserve group to the Sisters of Loretto in Loretto, Kentucky. This group consisted of three free black women whose names were not recorded. The attempt did not outlive the stay of the sponsoring priest, who soon left for Missouri.

Source: Davis, *The History of Black Catholics in the United States,* p. 98.

1829 ◆ On July 2, 1829, the first permanent order of black Catholic nuns, the Oblate Sisters of Providence, was founded in Baltimore, Maryland.

The order began through the efforts of a French priest, James Joubert, and four women of Caribbean origin—Elizabeth Lange, Rosine Boegues, Mary Frances Balas, and Mary Theresa Duchemin. This teaching order was formally recognized October 2, 1831. The sisters opened the first Catholic school for girls in 1843. The school survives today as Mount Providence Junior College, established in 1952. The second order was the Sisters of the Holy Family, founded in New Orleans in 1842 by Henriette Delille and Juliette Gaudin. That order was not officially recognized until after the Civil War.

Sources: Davis, *The History of Black Catholics in the United States,* pp. 99–105; *Encyclopedia of Black America,* p. 220; *Notable Black American Women,* pp. 813–14; Ochs, *Desegregating the Altar,* pp. 24–25; Smith, *Climbing Jacob's Ladder,* pp. 97–100.

1875 ◆ In February 1875 **James Augustine Healy** (1830–1900) became the first African American bishop. He was awarded the diocese of Portland, Maine, covering the states of Maine and New Hampshire. Healy entered the priesthood on June 10, 1854, when he was ordained in Paris, becoming the first American black ordained in the Catholic church. Two brothers followed him. All three had to study abroad. Alexander Sherwood was ordained for the diocese of Massachusetts. Patrick Francis (1834–1910) became a Jesuit. As bishop James Healy founded 60 parishes and 18 schools. (*See also* **Education: College Degrees, 1865**.)

Sources: Davis, *The History of Black Catholics in the United States,* pp. 147–51; *Dictionary of American Negro Biography,* pp. 301–2 (Eliza), 302–3 (James), 303–4 (Michael); 304–5 (Patrick); *Encyclopedia of Black America,* p. 423 (James); *Notable Black American Women,* pp. 479–81 (Eliza); Ochs, *Desegregating the Altar,* pp. 26–29.

1886 ◆ **Augustus Tolton** (1854–1897) celebrated his first mass in the United States at St. Mary's Hospital in Hoboken, New Jersey, on July 7, 1886. Although Tolton was not the first black priest, he was the first to be widely known and publicized. He seems to have believed himself the first, overlooking the Healy brothers.

Sources: Davis, *The History of Black Catholics in the United States,* pp. 152–62; *Dictionary of American Negro Biography,* pp. 596–97; Ochs, *Desegregating the Altar,* pp. 77–79, 94–95.

1891 ◆ **Charles Randolph Uncles** became the first black priest ordained in the United States, on December 19, 1891, in Baltimore, Maryland. (The four previous American blacks had all been ordained in Europe.)

Source: Ochs, *Desegregating the Altar,* pp. 81–82, 456.

1923 ◆ St. Augustine's Seminary was established in Bay St. Louis, Louisiana, by the Society of the Divine Word. This was the first separate semi-

nary to train black priests. The work of the seminary had begun two years earlier in Greenville, Mississippi.

Sources: Cantor, Historic Landmarks of Black America, p. 169; Davis, The History of Black Catholics in the United States, pp. 234–35; Ochs, Desegregating the Altar, p. 5-6, 271–72.

1953 ◆ On April 22, 1953, **Joseph Oliver Bowers** (1910–) became the
first black bishop consecrated in the United States since James A. Healy in
1875 and made bishop of Accra in the soon-to-be independent Ghana. He was
from the West Indies and a graduate of St. Augustine's Seminary. Later in
1953 he became the first black bishop to ordain black priests in the United
States.

Sources: Ebony (December 1957), p. 18, (August 1953), pp. 25–33; Ochs, Desegregating the Altar, pp. 422–23.

1966 ◆ On January 6, 1966, **Harold Robert Perry** (1916–1991) became
the first black Catholic bishop in the United States in this century to be consecrated for service in Africa. He was named auxiliary bishop of New Orleans,
Louisiana.

Sources: Current Biography 1966, pp. 311–12; Ebony (February 1966), pp. 62–70; Negro Almanac, 1989, p. 1330; Ochs, Desegregating the Altar, p. 446.

Eugene Antonio Marino (1934–)became the first black archbishop in the
United States and so only the second ordinary bishop (that is, a bishop who
heads a diocese). He served as auxiliary bishop in Washington, D.C., and
became archbishop of the Diocese of Atlanta.

Sources: Hornsby, Jr., Chronology of African-American History, p. 364; Jet 81 (18 November 1991), p. 57, 83 (5 April 1993), pp. 32–37; Negro Almanac, pp. 100, 1492; Who's Who Among Black Americans, 1992-1993, p. 913.

Christian Church (Disciples of Christ)

1853 ◆ **Alexander Cross,** a former slave from Kentucky, was the first
missionary of any race sent to Africa by this denomination.

Source: Encyclopedia of Black America, p. 226.

1982 ◆ **Cynthia L. Hale** became the first woman president of the mainly black National Convocation of the Disciples of Christ. Hale was chaplain at
the Federal Correctional Institute at Butner, Alabama.

Source: Jet 62 (30 August 1982), p. 24.

Church of England

1623 ◆ The first known black child baptized in the colonies was William, the son of Isabella and Anthony Johnson, at Jamestown, Virginia. It is possible that this father is the same Anthony Johnson who owned five servants and was granted 500 acres of land in 1651.

Sources: Blockson, *Black Geneology,* p. 46; Cantor, *Historic Landmarks of Black America,* p. 255; *Negro Almanac* (1976), p. 1041. Smith, *Ethnic Geneology,* pp. 346–47.

1743 ◆ The Society for the Propagation of the Gospel in Foreign Parts established in Charleston, South Carolina, the first known school to train black missionaries. Two blacks, Harry and Andrew, were in charge, and the school lasted until 1764, when Harry, who was the teacher, died. Andrew had been dismissed some time earlier.

Sources: Raboteau, *Slave Religion,* pp. 116–17; Smith, *Climbing Jacob's Ladder,* p. 28.

1968 ◆ **Coretta Scott King** (1927–) was the first woman of any race to preach at St. Paul's Cathedral, London, England.

Sources: Alford, *Famous First Blacks,* p. 21; *Notable Black American Women,* pp. 631–34.

Congregationalists

1693 ◆ Boston cleric **Cotton Mather** (1663–1728) drew up "Rules for the Society of Negroes" for a group of black people who were seeking to hold their own prayer meetings on Sunday evenings. These rules are the first known example of this kind of ethnic religious association.

Source: Smith, *Climbing Jacob's Ladder,* pp. 26-27.

1785 ◆ **Lemuel Haynes** (1753-1833) was the first black Congregational minister. Born in Connecticut, he never knew his black father, and his white mother refused to identify him. Haynes was very well educated by the man to whom he was bound as a servant. After serving in the Revolutionary army, Haynes was ordained in 1785 and became the pastor of a white congregation in Torrington, Connecticut. In 1818 he became pastor in Manchester, New Hampshire. He was the first black American to receive an honorary degree, in 1804, when Middlebury College, Vermont, gave him an honorary M.A. In April 1841 abolitionist Samuel Ringgold Ward (1817–c. 1866) also became minister of a white Congregationalist church located in South Butler, New

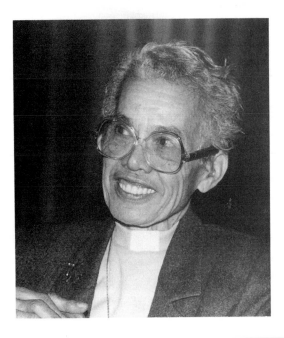

Pauli Murray

York. (*See also* **Education: Honorary Degrees, 1804,** and **Military: Revolutionary War, 1775.**)

Sources: *Dictionary of American Negro Biography*, pp. 300–301 (Haynes), pp. 631–32 (Ward); *Negro Year Book, 1913*, p. 115; Smith, *Climbing Jacob's Ladder*, p. 31.

1820 ◆ The Dixwell Congregational Church, New Haven, Connecticut, was the first all-black Congregational church. Francis L. Cardozo, who made a mark in South Carolina politics during Reconstruction, was one of its pastors. The number of black Congregationalists was quite small, but the influence of the denomination as a whole on black life was immense. Through the American Missionary Association, Congregationalists founded or supported some 500 schools in the South after the Civil War. These include such distinguished institutions as Fisk University (Tennessee), Atlanta Christian College (Georgia), Hampton Institute (Virginia), Tougaloo College (Missouri), and Dillard College (Louisiana).

Sources: *Encyclopedia of Black America*, p. 286; Gatewood, *Aristocrats of Color*, p. 288.

Episcopalians

1794 ◆ On July 17, 1794, the original Free African Society building in Philadelphia was dedicated as St. Thomas' African Episcopal Church, the first black Protestant Episcopal church. **Absalom Jones** (1746–1818) was ordained as the first black deacon in the denomination and became pastor of St. Thomas. He became the first black American priest in the denomination in 1804.

Sources: *Dictionary of American Negro Biography*, pp. 262–364; Lincoln and Mamiya, *The Black Church in the African American Experience*, pp. 51–52; Smith, *Climbing Jacob's Ladder*, pp. 36–37.

1819 ◆ On July 3, 1819, St. Phillip's African Church became the first black Protestant Episcopal church in New York City. Its leader was **Peter Williams, Jr.** (1780–1840), who became the second black American priest, on July 10, 1826.

Sources: Baer and Singer, *African-American Religion in the Twentieth Century*, p. 104; *Dictionary of American Negro Biography*, 660–61; *Encyclopedia of Black America*, p. 375; Smith, *Climbing Jacob's Ladder*, pp. 47–48, 50.

1885 ♦ **Samuel David Ferguson** became the first missionary bishop of the Protestant Episcopal church and thus the first black to sit in the American House of Bishops. His assignment was Liberia. The first suffragan bishops (auxiliary bishops who are given special missions) were not be elected until 1918, and the first diocesan bishop until 1970.

Sources: Encyclopedia of Black America, pp. 376–77; *Negro Almanac, 1989,* p. 1425.

1969 ♦ **John M. Burgess** (1909–) was elected presiding bishop of the Protestant Episcopal church. He was also elected bishop of the Diocese of Massachusetts, becoming the first

Barbara Harris

African American to head a diocese. He held that position from 1970 until his retirement in 1976.

Sources: Ebony (October 1960), pp. 54–58, (March 1982), p.128; *Ebony Success Library,* vol. 1, p. 50; *Encyclopedia of Black America,* pp. 199, 377; Toppin, *Biographical History of Blacks,* pp. 261–62; Wormley, *Many Shades of Black,* p. 331; *Negro Almanac,* p. 1326.

1977 ♦ On January 8, 1977, **Pauli Murray** (1910–1985) was the first woman ordained a priest in the Protestant Episcopal church.

Sources: Encyclopedia of Black America, p. 584; *Notable Black American Women,* pp. 783–88.

1989 ♦ **Barbara Harris** (1930–) became the first woman Anglican bishop in the world. On February 12, 1989, she was made an assistant bishop in the Diocese of Massachusetts. As a woman her election to a post held only by men from the time of St. Peter aroused the same controversy as the ordination of 11 women priests did in 1974. This earlier event encouraged Harris to prepare for the priesthood to which she herself was ordained in 1980.

Sources: Black Women in America, p. 537–38; Hornsby, Jr., *Chronology of African-American History,* p. 382; *Negro Almanac,* pp. 105–6; *Notable Black American Women,* pp. 462–66.

Holiness Churches

1886 ♦ The United Holy Church, established in Method, North Carolina, is known as the first black holiness church. It grew out of a revival conducted by Isaac Cheshier on the first Sunday in May. Early in this century it became a Pentecostal church.

Sources: Baer and Singer, *African-American Religion in the Twentieth Century,* p. 149; *Directory of African American Religious Bodies,* pp. 114, 250; *Encyclopedia of American Religions,* vol. 1, p. 443.

1929 ◆ Known as the "Happy Am I Evangelist," **Solomon Lightfoot Michaux** (1885–1968) of the Gospel Spreading Church, Washington, D.C., began radio broadcasts in 1929. After the purchase of a local station by the CBS network, he was the first African American to have a national and international audience on a regular basis. In 1934 he broadcast on Saturdays on the CBS radio network and internationally on shortwave to reach an audience estimated at 25 million people. He preached a mixture of holiness themes and positive thinking, and his church was related to the Church of God, Holiness. By 1941 his radio broadcasts were heard only in a few cities where he had congregations, but the broadcasts continued until his death.

Sources: Baer and Singer, *African-American Religion in the Twentieth Century,* pp. 155–57; *Dictionary of American Negro Biography,* pp. 432–33; *Encyclopedia of American Religions,* vol. 1, p. 223.

Interchurch Organizations

1972 ◆ **W. Sterling Cary** (1927–) became the first black president of the National Council of Churches in America on December 7, 1972. This distinguished Baptist minister was born in Plainfield, New Jersey, and was also a prominent political activist.

Sources: Ebony Success Library, vol. 1, p. 61; *Encyclopedia of Black America,* p. 219; Hornsby, Jr., *Chronology of African-American History,* p. 204; *Negro Almanac,* p. 1326; *Who's Who Among Black Americans, 1992–1993,* p. 244.

1984 ◆ **Philip R. Cousin** (1933–) was the first African American from a mainly black denomination to preside over the National Council of Churches. This African Methodist Episcopal (AME) minister has served with distinction as bishop and college president.

Sources: Jet 65 (30 January 1984), p. 24; *Who's Who Among Black Americans, 1992–1993,* p. 312.

1991 ◆ **Vinton R. Anderson** (1927–) was the first African American to be one of the seven presidents of the World Council of Churches. Anderson was a bishop of the AME church and was active in interchurch work for many years.

Sources: Jet 79 (1 April 1991), p. 29, 81 (18 November 1991), p. 66.

Maryann Coffey was the first African American and the first woman co-chair of the National Conference of Christians and Jews.

Source: Jet 80 (6 May 1991), p. 37.

Islam

1913 ◆ **Noble Drew Ali** (Timothy Drew, 1886–1929) formed the Moorish Science Temple in Newark, New Jersey. This was the first step to the appearance, or the reappearance, of various forms of black Islam. W. D. Fard, the founder of the Nation of Islam in the early 1930s, was originally a member of the Moorish Science Temple.

Sources: Baer and Singer, *African-American Religion in the Twentieth Century,* pp. 51, 60, 118–19; *Directory of African American Religious Bodies,* pp. 141–42; *Encyclopedia of American Religions,* vol. 3. p. 178.

Lutherans

1983 ◆ **Nelson W. Trout** (c. 1921–) was the first black elected bishop of the American Lutheran Church in America on June 17, 1983. He was named bishop of the South Pacific District in California.

Source: Hornsby, Jr., *Chronology of African-American History,* pp. 320–21.

1988 ◆ **Sherman G. Hicks** became the first black bishop of the Evangelical Lutheran Church in America.

Source: Jet 74 (23 May 1988), p. 12.

Methodists

1764 ◆ A slave named **Anne Sweitzer** (Aunt Annie) was one of the founding members of the first Methodist society in the colonies, organized in Frederick County, Maryland. Blacks were members of St. George's Methodist Church in Philadelphia, which dates to 1767. In 1776 a black servant called Betty would be a charter member of the John Street meeting, the first society in New York City.

Sources: Heritage and Hope, p. 24; Lincoln and Mamiya, *The Black Church in the African American Experience,* p. 50; Smith, *Climbing Jacob's Ladder,* pp. 33–35, 39.

1781 ◆ The first known black Methodist preacher was **"Black" Harry Hosier** (c. 1750–1806). His sermon "Barren Fig Tree" was delivered at Adams Chapel, Fairfax County, Virginia, in 1781, and was the first preached by a black to a congregation of Methodists. His sermon in 1784 at Thomas Chapel, Chapeltown, Delaware, was the first preached by a black to a white congregation.

Sources: *Encyclopedia of Black America*, pp. 511, 555; *Heritage and Hope*, pp. 50–51, 307; Lincoln and Mamiya, *The Black Church in the African American Experience*, p. 66; Smith, *Climbing Jacob's Ladder*, pp. 34–35.

1794 ◆ The African Zoar Church was organized as a mission church in Philadelphia. This was the first all-black church for persons who eventually stayed in the Methodist Episcopal church. The Zoar Church was incorporated in 1835.

Sources: *Encyclopedia of Black America*, pp. 32, 555; *Heritage and Hope*, p. 43; Smith, *Climbing Jacob's Ladder*, pp. 36, 44.

1858 ◆ **Francis Burns** (1809–1863) was the first black Methodist Episcopal missionary bishop. He served in Liberia for 24 years. In 1849 he was the first black to be designated a presiding elder for his work in Liberia. A second missionary bishop, John W. Roberts, was elected in 1866; a third, Isaiah B. Scott, in 1904; and a fourth, Alexander P. Camphor, in 1916. A regular bishop was not elected until 1920. The lack of leadership roles for African Americans in the denomination was one of the factors leading to black annual conferences, held officially from 1864 to 1939, and, in effect, dividing the denomination along racial lines.

Sources: *Encyclopedia of Black America*, pp. 555–57; *Heritage and Hope*, pp. 54, 67.

1870 ◆ **W. H. Miles** and **Richard H. Vanderhorst** were the first bishops of the Colored (now Christian) Methodist Episcopal Church. This denomination was formed by blacks leaving the Methodist Episcopal Church (South).

Sources: *Encyclopedia of American Religions*, vol. 1, pp. 195–96; Lincoln and Mamiya, *The Black Church in the African American Experience*, p. 62; Smith, *Climbing Jacob's Ladder*, pp. 123–24.

1920 ◆ **Robert E. Jones** (1872–1960) and **Matthew W. Clair, Sr.,** (1865–1943) were the first elected bishops of the United Methodist church for service in the United States. The denomination had elected its first black missionary bishop for service in Liberia in 1858.

Sources: *Encyclopedia of Black America*, p. 557; *Heritage and Hope*, pp. 87–88, 308, 314; *Negro Year Book, 1921–1922*, p. 16.

1936 ◆ **Laura J. Lange** was the first woman ordained a local elder in the Methodist Episcopal church. Lange was made a deacon in 1926. Not until 1956 was a black woman, Sallie A. Crenshaw, ordained an elder and admitted into full connection in an Annual Conference.

Source: Heritage and Hope, pp. 53, 155.

1984 ◆ **Leontine T. C. Kelly** (1920–) became the first woman bishop of a major denomination, the United Methodist church. She was consecrated July 20, 1984. In addition she was the first woman of any race to preach on the program National Radio Pulpit of the National Council of Churches. Made an elder in 1977, she had experience at both the local and the national level. Upon the retirement of the first (and only) woman bishop in the church, she was elected, and she supervised the California and Nevada conferences until her retirement in 1988.

Sources: Black Women in America, pp. 675; Heritage and Hope, p. 280; Notable Black American Women, pp. 621–26.

Leontine T. C. Kelly

Mormons

1836 ◆ **Elijah Abel** (?–1884) was the first African American to become an elder (priest) in the Mormon church, while the Mormons were headquartered in Nauvoo, Illinois. After the very early years of the church, a longstanding ban prevented black Mormons from advancing to the priesthood. This ban was abolished in 1978, and the church has since attracted a number of black members.

Sources: Cantor, Historic Landmarks of Black America, p.334; Encyclopedia of Black America, p. 1–2.

1978 ◆ **Joseph Freeman, Jr.** (1932–) became the first black priest (elder) in this century.

Sources: Cantor, Historic Landmarks of Black America, p. 334; Kane, Famous First Facts, p. 167; Negro Almanac, p. 1325.

Nation of Islam

1932 ◆ **Elijah Muhammad** (Elijah Poole, 1897–1975) established the Nation of Islam's Temple Number Two, the first temple in Chicago. When the movement's founder, W. D. Fard, disappeared in 1934, Elijah Muhammad became the Nation's leader. The movement grew under his leadership, especially in the late 1950s and the 1960s, in part due to the charismatic leadership of his principal lieutenant, Malcolm X (1925–1965). Malcolm X's suspension from the movement in 1963 marked the first major split in the organization. After Elijah Muhammad's death, Louis Farrakhan (1933–) formed a new Nation of Islam in 1978. The faction led by Wallace J. Muhammad (1933–) moved closer to orthodox Islam and renamed itself the American Muslim Mission.

Sources: Directory of African American Religious Bodies, pp. 139–40; Encyclopedia of American Religions, pp. 175–76, 179–80; Negro Almanac, 1989, pp. 1304–5, 1319.

Peace Mission

1914 ◆ It was about this year that **Father Divine** (George Baker, 1879–1965) first proclaimed himself God as he established his movement, Father Divine's "Kingdom" and Peace Mission. He was tried on a charge of insanity in a Valdosta, Georgia, court on February 27, 1914, on the grounds that his claim to be God was clearly bizarre. He was convicted but not imprisoned.

Sources: Dictionary of American Negro Biography, pp. 178–80; Directory of African American Religious Bodies, pp. 122–24; Watts, God, Harlem U.S.A., pp. 31–43.

Pentecostals

1906 ◆ From April 14, 1906, the preaching of **William J. Seymour** (1870–1922) at the Azusa Street Mission in Los Angeles began to shape the Pentecostal movement. The first major revival to stress the importance of speaking in tongues as evidence of baptism in the Holy Spirit, Seymour's gatherings drew both black and white audiences. C. H. Mason's experiences at the Azusa Street Mission in 1907 led him to make the practice central in the Church of God in Christ. In 1908 G. B. Cashwell introduced the practice he had learned from Seymour to the mainly white Church of God, USA. Pentecostalists soon split along racial lines. C. H. Mason's church was incorporated, however, and some white leaders of segregated congregations continued to be ordained by Mason for a few years in order to be legally recognized as ministers.

Sources: Baer and Singer, *African-American Religion in the Twentieth Century,* pp. 180–81; *Black Apostles,* pp. 213–25; *Directory of African American Religious Bodies,* pp. 250–51; *Encyclopedia of American Religions,* vol. 1, pp. xxxvii, 43, 45, 226, 231, 243–44; Lincoln and Mamiya, *The Black Church in the African American Experience,* p.79.

Presbyterians

1757 ◆ **Samuel Davis,** a white minister in Hanover County, Virginia, reported that he had baptized about 150 black people after 18 months of preaching to them. He began his activity in 1748. This is the first organized activity of Presbyterians among blacks. Davis would in time become the president of the College of New Jersey (Princeton).

Sources: Raboteau, *Slave Religion,* p. 129–30; Wilmore, *Black and Presbyterian,* p. 40.

1800 ◆ Black people participated in the Gasper River and Cane Ridge, Kentucky, camp meetings, which launched the Great Western Revival. The lead given by the Presbyterians was followed by other denominations, and camp meetings became important in the conversion of slaves. Many scholars maintain that the majority of blacks were not converted to Christianity until this second wave of revivalism was taken up by other denominations, principally the Baptists and Methodists, along with new denominations, such as the Campbellites (Disciples of Christ).

Sources: Baer and Singer, *African-American Religion in the Twentieth Century,* p. 6; *Directory of African American Religious Bodies,* pp. 5-6; *Encyclopedia of American Religions,* pp. xxix-xxxi; Raboteau, *Slave Religion,* p. 132.

1801 ◆ **John Chavis** (1763–1838) became the first black Presbyterian missionary in the South. Chavis was born free in North Carolina and fought in the Revolutionary War. By 1808 he set up a school where he taught Latin and Greek to both black and white students. The first known black person to have taught both races in the South, he was forced to give up his school and pulpit in 1831, after the Nat Turner revolt resulted in laws that barred blacks from teaching and preaching in North Carolina.

Sources: Dictionary of American Negro Biography, pp. 101–2; *Encyclopedia of Black America,* pp. 224, 704; Raboteau, *Slave Religion,* p. 135; Wilmore, *Black and Presbyterian,* p. 64.

1807 ◆ The first all-black Presbyterian church, First African, was organized in Philadelphia. It grew out of the work of **John Gloucester, Sr.** (c. 1776–1822), a freed slave from Tennessee.

Sources: Encyclopedia of Black America, p. 704; Smith, Climbing Jacob's Ladder, p. 44.

1818 ◆ **George M. Erskine** was the first slave in Tennessee to be licensed as a preacher by the Presbyterians. After buying his freedom and that of his wife and seven children, he went to Africa as a missionary. Only one other black Southerner is known to have been ordained by the church before the Civil War: Harrison W. Ellis in 1846. He was sent to Liberia as a missionary.

Source: Raboteau, Slave Religion, p. 207

1964 ◆ **Edler Garnet Hawkins** (1908–1977) was elected the first black moderator, or presiding officer, of the United Presbyterian church on May 21, 1964. Hawkins built his church from 9 black members to an integrated congregation of more than 1,000. He was also the first moderator of the church to visit the Roman Catholic pope.

Sources: Current Biography 1965, pp. 193–95; Ebony (September 1968), p. 66; Encyclopedia of Black America, p. 706.

1976 ◆ **Thelma Davidson Adair** (1921–) became the first black woman moderator of the United Presbyterian Church.

Sources: Afro-American (25 May 1976), p. 1; Encore (6 July 1979), p. 41; Jet 50 (1 July 1976), p. 9.

1989 ◆ **Joan Salmon Campbell** was the first black woman to head the Presbyterian Church (USA).

Sources: Ebony, (November 1989), pp. 100, 102, 104; Hornsby, Jr., Chronology of African-American History, p. 392; Jet 77 (26 June 1989), p. 17, (20 November 1989), p. 38.

Rastafarians

1935 ◆ **Haile Selassie** was crowned emperor of Ethiopia in 1935, the approximate date of the founding of the Rastafarian movement in Jamaica. The coronation of Selassie seemed to fulfill a 1927 prophecy by Marcus Garvey that the crowning of a king in Africa would be a sign that the end of black oppression by whites was near. Since about 1960 the group in the United States has grown to an estimated 3,000 to 5,000.

Sources: Directory of African American Religious Bodies, pp. 133–36; Encyclopedia of American Religions, vol. 3, pp. 156–57; Negro Almanac, 1989, p. 1319.

Spiritual Churches

1915 ◆ The first verifiable spiritual (formerly referred to as spiritualist) congregation is the Church of the Redemption in Chicago. It is possible that Mother Leafy Anderson established an earlier one in Chicago before she moved to New Orleans and established the first in that city, Eternal Life Spiritual Church, sometime between 1918 and 1921.

Source: Baer, *The Black Spiritual Movement,* p. 2.

1922 ◆ The first black spiritual denomination was the National Colored Spiritualist Association of Churches, formed in 1922 by a breakaway of black members from the mainly white National Spiritualist Association. William Frank Taylor and Leviticus Lee Boswell founded the largest present-day association of black spiritual churches, Metropolitan Spiritual Churches of Christ, in 1925.

Sources: Directory of African American Religious Bodies, p. 130; *Encyclopedia of American Religions,* vol. 2, pp. 270–71.

Unitarian-Universalists

1982 ◆ **Yvonne Reed Chappelle** was the first black woman ordained in the Unitarian-Universalist Church.

Sources: Black Scholar (January 1970), pp. 36–39; *Jet* 61 (11 February 1982), p. 32.

United Church and Science of Living Institute

1966 ◆ **Frederick J. Eikerenkoetter II** (c. 1935–), "The Rev. Ike," first founded his church in 1966. He began his ministry in the late 1950s as a Pentecostal but was shifting towards a New Thought position, a transition that would be complete by 1968. He rejected sin, taught that salvation must be achieved here and now, and praised material wealth.

Sources: Baer and Singer, *African-American Religion in the Twentieth Century,* pp. 64, 200–202; *Directory of African American Religious Bodies,* pp. 124–25; *Encyclopedia of American Religions,* vol. 2, p. 255.

United Church of Christ

1987 ◆ **Kwame Osei** was the first African American to head the Potomac Association Conference of the United Church of Christ in Washington, D.C.

Source: Jet 72 (27 July 1987), p. 38.

1991 ◆ **Denise Page Hood** became the first black woman to chair the Executive Council of the United Church of Christ.

Source: Jet 80 (5 August 1991), p. 10.

United Methodists

1968 ◆ In Cincinnati, Ohio, the First National Conference of Negro Methodists organized a black caucus for the denomination, Black Methodists for Church Renewal.

Sources: Baer and Singer, *African-American Religion in the Twentieth Century*, p. 106; *Directory of African American Religious Bodies*, pp. 204–5, 245; *Heritage and Hope*, pp. 209–10.

United Society of Believers in Christ's Second Coming (Shakers)

1859 ◆ **Rebecca Cox Jackson** (1795–1871) established the first largely black Shaker family in Philadelphia. Its existence in Philadelphia can be traced until at least 1908.

Sources: Black Women in America, pp. 626–27; *Notable Black American Women*, pp. 561–65.

Science, Medicine, and Invention

Atomic Energy Commission • Federal Employees • Hospitals
Inventions and Patents • Medical Agencies and Schools • Medicine
National Science Foundation • Nursing • Publications
Societies and Associations • Space

Atomic Energy Commission

1966 ♦ **Samuel M. Nabrit** (1905–) was the first black member of the Atomic Energy Commission. He became president of Texas Southern University in 1955. (*See also* **Education: College Administrators, 1960.**)

Sources: Current Biography Yearbook, 1963, pp. 295–97; *Encyclopedia of Black America,* pp. 611–12, 745; *Who's Who Among Black Americans, 1992–1993,* p. 1045.

Federal Employees

1864 ♦ **Solomon G. Brown** (1829–c. 1903) became the first black museum assistant at the Smithsonian Institution. With no formal education, he worked for Samuel F. B. Morse during the 1840s when the inventor was developing the telegraph system. In 1852 Brown succeeded Joseph Henry, an associate of Morse, as first secretary to the Smithsonian. He became a vital worker who prepared almost all of the illustrations for scientific lectures until 1887. In 1855 he may have been the first black American to deliver a public lecture on science when he gave a lecture on insects to the Young People's Club of the Israel A.M.E. Church in Washington, D.C.

Sources: Dictionary of American Biography, pp. 70–71; Simmons, *Men of Mark,* pp. 320–23.

Hospitals

1832 ♦ The Georgia Infirmary in Savannah, Georgia, founded by whites, was the first hospital and asylum established for the relief and protection of aged and afflicted blacks. It was chartered in 1832, and an organizational meeting was held on January 15, 1833.

Sources: Garrett, *Famous First Facts About Negroes*, p. 111; Kane, *Famous First Facts*, p. 309.

1881 ♦ **Charles Burleigh Purvis** (1842–1929) was the first black surgeon-in-chief to head a civilian hospital. He received the appointment to the Freedmen's Hospital in the nation's capital. (Alexander Augusta's appointment in 1865 was to Freedmen's when it was a military hospital.) He was the son of the prosperous abolitionist Robert Purvis and served in the army until 1869, when he became the assistant surgeon at Freedmen's and a faculty member at Howard University in Washington, D.C. When President James A. Garfield was wounded by an assassin's bullet in 1881, Purvis became the first and only black physician to serve the president of the United States when he was called to care for the fatally wounded chief executive. In 1897 he was appointed as the first African American to serve on the District of Columbia's Board of Medical Examiners.

Sources: *Dictionary of American Negro Biography*, p. 507; Morais, *The History of the Negro in Medicine*, p. 51.

Good Samaritan Hospital established in Charlotte, North Carolina, was the first privately run hospital exclusively for blacks in the United States.

Source: Randolph, *An African-American Album*, p. 84.

1891 ♦ Provident Hospital in Chicago, Illinois, was the first American hospital operated by black Americans. Founded by **Daniel Hale Williams,** Provident inspired the creation of similar hospitals around the country. Williams's aim was to establish a biracial hospital where black doctors and nurses could be trained and black patients could receive expert care without fear of racial bias. (*See* **Medicine, 1893.**)

Sources: *Dictionary of Black Culture*, p. 362; Morais, *The History of the Negro in Medicine*, p. 75.

1895 ♦ **Nathan Francis Mossell** (1856–1946) founded Philadelphia's first hospital primarily for black Americans, Frederick Douglass Memorial Hospital and Training School for Nurses. The Canadian-born physician was the first black graduate of the University of Pennsylvania when he received his M.D. in 1882 and, after a bitter struggle, was the first black physician admitted to the Philadelphia Medical Society in 1885. He studied at notable hospitals in

London before he attacked the problem of founding a hospital back in Philadelphia. An ardent civil rights activist, Mossell journeyed to Niagara Falls in 1905 with W. E. B. Du Bois as one of the organizers of the Niagara Movement, which led to the founding of the NAACP. Actor and singer Paul Robeson was Mossell's nephew.

Sources: Dictionary of American Negro Biography, pp. 457–58; *Dictionary of Black Culture*, p. 308; Morais, *The History of the Negro in Medicine*, p. 79.

Inventions and Patents

c. 1798 ◆ **James Forten, Sr.** (1766–1842) was the first black person to invent a sail-handling device, an invention that brought him considerable wealth. He became owner of a sail loft in 1798 and by 1832 was a rich businessman, who employed about 40 workers. His fortune enabled him to become one of the leading figures in the abolition movement.

Sources: Dictionary of American Negro Biography, pp. 234-35; *Dictionary of Black Culture*, pp. 166–67; James, *The Real McCoy*, pp. 33–35.

1821 ◆ **Thomas L. Jennings** (1791–1859) is believed to be the first black recipient of a patent, for a dry-cleaning process, on March 3, 1821. He was a tailor and dry cleaner in New York City and the founder and president of the Legal Rights Association, an abolitionist group. Henry Blair (1804–1860) of Glenross, Maryland, was long believed to be the first black to obtain a patent, for a corn planter, on October 14, 1834.

Sources: Haskins, Jim, Outward Dreams, pp. 4-5 (Jennings); James, *The Real McCoy*, p. 31; Katz, *Eyewitness: The Negro in American History*, pp. 98, 99, 139; *Negro Almanac*, pp. 1079–1424 (Blair).

1843 ◆ **Norbert Rillieux** (1806–1894) was the first person to revolutionize sugar production through a vacuum evaporating pan that delivered a superior product and reduced the industry's dependence on slave labor. Born a free black in New Orleans, Louisiana, Rillieux received a thorough education in mechanical engineering at the École Centrale in Paris, France. After demonstrating the practical effects of his invention in New Orleans and making a good deal of money, Rillieux returned to France in 1854 due to increasing restrictions on free blacks in Louisiana.

Sources: Dictionary of American Negro Biography, pp. 525–26; Haskins, *Outward Dreams*, pp. 26–33; James, *The Real McCoy*, pp. 41–43.

1848 ◆ **Lewis Temple** (1800–1854), a New Bedford, Massachusetts, blacksmith, was the first person to invent an improved model of the whaling

Elijah McCoy

harpoon used in the nineteenth century. He did not profit from it because he did not patent his new model, which was quickly adopted in the whaling industry.

Sources: Dictionary of American Negro Biography, pp. 582–83; Haskins, Outward Dreams, pp. 20–21; James, The Real McCoy, pp. 35–37; Negro Almanac, p. 1090.

1872 ◆ On July 2, 1872, **Elijah McCoy** (1843–1929) patented the original version of his lubricator for steam engines. This was the first in a series of 42 patents, most of which were designed to aid machine lubrication. McCoy was born in Canada, and after an apprenticeship in Edinburgh, Scotland, he moved to Michigan. His last patent was granted in 1920 for a graphite lubrication device.

Sources: American Speech 33 (December 1958), pp. 297–98; Dictionary of American Negro Biography, pp. 413–14; Flexner, I Hear America Talking, p. 291; Haskins, Outward Dreams, pp. 40–44; James, The Real McCoy, pp. 73–75.

1882 ◆ **Lewis H. Latimer** (1848–1928) patented the first cost-efficient method for producing carbon filaments for electric lights on June 17, 1882. His father, George, was an escaped slave whose capture led to the first of the highly publicized fugitive slave trials (1842) and prompted Frederick Douglass to publish his first article. Latimer made patent drawings for many of Alexander Graham Bell's telephone patents and worked for the United States Electric Lighting Company, where he made many innovations in the development of electric lighting and also supervised the installation of electric light plants in New York and Philadelphia. In 1884 he began to work for the Edison Electric Light Company and entered its legal department in 1890. From 1896 to 1911 he was head draftsman for the Board of Patent Control and then began to work as a patent consultant.

Sources: Dictionary of American Negro Biography, pp. 385–86; Haskins, Outward Dreams, pp. 49–52; James, The Real McCoy, pp. 96–99; Negro Almanac, p. 12.

W. B. Purvis of Philadelphia obtained his first patent on a paper bag device on April 25, 1882. Of the 16 patents he obtained by 1897, 11 were connected with the manufacture of paper bags. Most of the patents were sold to the Union Paper Bag Company of New York.

Sources: Journal of Negro History 2 (January 1917), p. 33; Twentieth-Century Negro Literature, pp. 403, 410; Work, Negro Year Book, 1925–1926, pp. 366–67.

1883 ◆ On March 20, 1883, **Jan Matzeliger** (1852–1889) patented the first successful shoe lasting machine. Matzeliger was born in Surinam of a Dutch father and a black mother. He developed his device while working in a shoe factory in Lynn, Massachusetts. The machine increased productivity nearly fourteen-fold over hand methods and thus revolutionized the industry.

Sources: Dictionary of American Negro Biography, pp. 429–30; James, *The Real McCoy,* p. 70–72; *Negro Almanac,* pp. 210, 1087.

On April 3, 1883, **Humpfrey H. Reynolds** was the first black inventor to patent an improved window ventilator for railroad cars, which was adopted on all Pullman cars. Since he received no payment from the company, Reynolds quit his job as a railroad porter and sued. He won $10,000.

Source: James, *The Real McCoy,* p. 72.

1884 ◆ **Granville T. Woods** (1856–1910) patented his first electric device, an improved telephone transmitter, on December 2, 1884. By 1900 Woods received 22 patents, most dealing

Jan Matzeliger

with electricity used in railway telegraphy systems and electric railways. A machinist, blacksmith, and locomotive engineer, he founded the Woods Electric Company in Cincinnati, Ohio, about 1884. He moved to New York in 1890 and patented an automatic air brake purchased by George Westinghouse in 1902. His inventions paved the way for the development of the electric street car. (*See also* **1904**.)

Sources: Dictionary of American Negro Biography, pp. 663–65; Haskins, *Outward Dreams,* pp. 47–49, 95–96; James, *The Real McCoy,* pp. 94–95; *Negro Almanac,* p. 1092.

1885 ◆ The first known black woman inventor may have been **Sarah E. Goode,** who patented a folding cabinet bed on July 14, 1885. However, because ethnic identity was not part of a patent application, historians continue to argue over who actually is the first black woman inventor. Another black woman, Ellen F. Eglin of Washington, D.C., may have been the first. In April 1890 Eglin invented a clothes wringer, though no patent was issued in her name. She sold the idea to an agent for $18 because she believed it would be impossible for a black woman to successfully market the device. As late as the early 1900s the claim to first black woman inventor belonged to Miriam E. Benjamin of Massachusetts, who patented a gong-type paging system on July 17, 1888. Her invention was adopted by the U.S. House of Representatives.

Sources: James, *The Real McCoy,* p. 67; Macdonald, *Feminine Ingenuity,* p. 172; *Twentieth Century Negro Literature,* p. 407.

1895 ◆ The U.S. Patent Office advertised its first special exhibit of the inventions of black inventors.

Source: James, *The Real McCoy,* p. 57.

1897 ◆ **Andrew J. Beard** (1849–1941) was the first black inventor to patent a coupling device for railroad cars. Although these devices were among the most popular subjects for patents—there were some 6,500 patents by 1897—Beard was able to sell his invention for some $50,000.

Sources: Alford, *Famous First Blacks,* p. 54; James, *The Real McCoy,* pp. 72–73; *Journal of Negro History* 2 (January 1917), p. 34.

1904 ◆ **Granville T. Woods** (1856–1910) and his brother Lyates patented the first of two improvements on railroad brakes on March 29, 1904. The second patent was issued on July 18, 1905. Both patents were then purchased by the Westinghouse Electric Company. (*See* **1884**.)

Source: *Journal of Negro History* 2 (January 1917), p. 32.

1912 ◆ **Garrett A. Morgan** (1875–1963) was the first black inventor to receive a patent for a safety hood and smoke protector. He demonstrated its worth in 1916 by rescuing workers trapped in a smoke-filled tunnel of the Cleveland, Ohio, waterworks. In 1923 he patented a three-way automatic traffic signal, which he sold to General Electric.

Sources: Cantor, *Historic Landmarks of Black America,* p. 352; *Dictionary of American Negro Biography,* p. 453; *Ebony* 48 (February 1993), p. 182 (portrait); James, *The Real McCoy,* pp. 91–93.

1913 ◆ **Henry Edwin Baker** (1859–1928), a black assistant examiner in the U.S. Patent Office, published the first separate list of black inventors, the *Negro Inventor.* Baker used his position in the patent office to discover and publicize the inventions of black inventors. (This was quite a formidable task, since race was not recorded on applications. Nevertheless, Baker tracked down the names of some 400 black inventors.)

Source: James, *The Real McCoy,* pp. 77–78.

1928 ◆ Marjorie Stewart Joyner (1896–) was the first black inventor to patent a permanent waving machine. Joyner was an employee of Madame C. J. Walker, to whose company the patent was assigned. She eventually became national supervisor of the Walker organization's chain of beauty schools. In 1945 she became a cofounder of the United Beauty School Owners and Teachers Association.

Sources: Macdonald, *Feminine Ingenuity,* pp. 297–301; *Who's Who Among Black Americans, 1992–1993,* p. 806.

1936 ◆ Percy Lavon Julian (1899–1975) was the first black chemist to be hired as a director of research by a major chemical manufacturing company, the Glidden Company of Chicago. He received 105 patents, 66 of which were assigned to this company. In 1954 he established his own company, Julian Laboratories. Among his many achievements in chemistry, Julian is linked with the creation of physostigmine (1935), used in treating glaucoma, and drugs related to cortisone.

Percy Julian

Sources: Ebony Success Library, vol. 2, pp. 150–53; Haber, *Black Pioneers of Science and Invention,* pp. 87–101; *Negro Almanac,* pp. 1084–85.

1940 ◆ Frederick McKinley Jones (1892–1961) was the first man to invent a practical refrigeration system for trucks and railroad cars. He received the patent on July 12, 1940. A native of Cincinnati, Ohio, he obtained a formal education to the sixth grade. By 1930 he succeeded as a self-taught manufacturer of movie sound equipment. The development of the refrigerating device marked a new direction for his efforts, and its success revolutionized the transportation and marketing of fresh foods. In 1991, 30 years after his death, he became the first black inventor honored with the National Medal of Technology.

Sources: Dictionary of American Negro Biography, p. 366; *Jet* 82 (20 July 1992), p. 24; *Negro Almanac,* p. 1084.

1969 ◆ George R. Carruthers (1940–) was the first black scientist to patent an image converter for detecting electromagnetic radiation. In 1964 Carruthers began working as a researcher for the Navy and then for the

National Aeronautics and Space Agency (NASA). NASA awarded him the NASA Exceptional Scientific Achievement medal for his work. He and another researcher developed the lunar surface ultraviolet camera/spectrograph, which was placed on the moon in April 1972 during the mission of *Apollo 16*.

Sources: *Ebony* 28 (October 1973), pp. 61–63; Haskins, *Outward Dreams*, pp. 83–84, 88; *Negro Almanac*, p. 1080; *Who's Who Among Black Americans, 1992-1993*, p. 234.

Medical Agencies and Schools

1876 ◆ Meharry Medical College was the first medical school founded solely for the education of blacks. Situated in Nashville, Tennessee, Meharry was part of the Central Tennessee College, founded in 1866 and maintained by the Freedmen's Aid Society. The school opened in 1876 with less than a dozen students. Its driving spirit was George W. Hubbard, who administered Meharry for 45 years.

Sources: *Dictionary of Black Culture*, p. 294; Morais, *The History of the Negro in Medicine*, p. 44.

1945 ◆ The first and only school of veterinary medicine in a black college or university was established at Tuskegee Institute in Alabama. Instruction began September 1, 1945. **Frederick D. Patterson** (1901-1988), veterinarian and then president of Tuskegee, founded the school. (*See also* **Miscellaneous: Organizations, 1944.**)

Sources: Bowles and DeCosta, *Between Two Worlds*, p. 131; *Jet* 72 (29 June 1987), p. 22; Tuskegee Institute, *Sixty-fifth Annual Catalog, 1946–1947*, p. 31.

1980 ◆ **Maurice C. Clifford** (1920–) was inaugurated as the first black president of the Medical College of Pennsylvania—the first at a mainly white college. Born in Washington, D.C., Clifford took his M.D. degree at Meharry Medical College in 1947.

Source: *Who's Who Among Black Americans, 1992–1993*, p. 276.

1993 ◆ **David Satcher** (1941–) was the first black appointed director of the Centers for Disease Control and Prevention in Atlanta, Georgia. Satcher, a genetics researcher, also served as president of Meharry Medical College in Nashville, Tennessee.

Sources: *Atlanta Journal and Constitution*, 21 August 1993; *Who's Who Among Black Americans, 1992–1993*, p. 1243.

Medicine

1667 ◆ **Lucas Santomee** was the first trained black physician in New Amsterdam.

Source: Encyclopedia of Black America, p. 670.

1706 ◆ **Onesimus** was the first black to introduce inoculation against smallpox to the American colonies. He revealed the practice to his master, Massachusetts minister Cotton Mather, who promoted it during the epidemic of 1721. There was considerable resistance to this life-saving procedure, and several of its supporters, including Mather, were threatened with mob violence. Inoculation was generally accepted by 1777.

Sources: James, *The Real McCoy,* p. 25; Morais, *The History of the Negro in Medicine,* p. 11.

1773 ◆ **James Durham** (Derham) was the first regularly recognized black physician in the United States. Born a slave in Philadelphia in the mid-eighteenth century his early masters taught him the fundamentals of reading and writing. He was owned by a number of physicians before 1773, when a Scottish doctor in New Orleans hired him to perform a variety of medical services. Durham bought his freedom in 1783 and then moved to Philadelphia, where he was praised by prominent local doctors. He returned to New Orleans and had a flourishing practice until 1801, when the city council restricted him because he was unlicensed and untrained.

Sources: Dictionary of American Negro Biography, pp. 205–6; Garrett, *Famous First Facts About Negroes,* p. 110; Morais, *The History of the Negro in Medicine,* pp. 5, 7–10.

1837 ◆ **James McCune Smith** (1811–1865) was the first black physician to obtain an M.D. degree. He studied at the African Free School in New York City and then, unable to pursue his education in the United States, he traveled to the University of Glasgow, Scotland, where he received his bachelor's, master's, and medical degrees. He became a very successful physician in New York, with a busy practice and two drug stores. He was also an avid abolitionist.

Sources: Dictionary of Black Culture, p. 410; Garrett, *Famous First Facts About Negroes,* p. 111; Morais, *The History of the Negro in Medicine,* p. 31.

1846 ◆ **David Ruggles** (1810–1849) erected the first building for hydropathic (water therapy) treatments in the United States. Known as the "water cure doctor," Ruggles operated his successful center in Northampton, Massachusetts, until his death. He was an active abolitionist, supporter of the Underground Railroad movement, and editor and publisher of *The Mirror of*

Susan McKinney
Steward

Liberty (1838). (*See also* **Business: Retailing, 1834.**)

Sources: *Dictionary of American Negro Biography*, pp. 536–37; Morais, *The History of the Negro in Medicine*, p. 23; *Negro Almanac*, p. 1012.

1847 ♦ **David J. Peck** was the first black to graduate from an American medical school, Rush Medical College in Chicago.

Sources: *Encyclopedia of Black America*, p. 671; Morais, *The History of the Negro in Medicine*, p. 30.

1863 ♦ **Alexander Thomas Augusta** (1825–1890) became the first black surgeon in the U.S. Army. In 1865 he became the first black physician to head any hospital in the United States when the newly created Freedmen Bureau erected buildings on the grounds of Howard University and established the Freedmen's Hospital, with Augusta in charge. (Formerly, freedmen were treated at Camp Barker.) In 1868 Howard University opened its own medical school, with Augusta as demonstrator of anatomy. He was the first black to receive an honorary degree from Howard University in 1869.

Sources: *Dictionary of American Negro Biography*, pp. 19–20; Garrett, *Famous First Facts About Negroes*, pp. 112–13; Morais, *The History of the Negro in Medicine*, p. 50.

1864 ♦ **Rebecca Lee (Crumpler)** (1833–?) was the first black woman awarded a medical degree. She completed a 17-week course to earn an M.D. from the New England Female Medical College in Boston. Lee established a long-lived practice in Richmond, Virginia, at the end of the Civil War.

Sources: *Black Women in America*, vol. 1, pp. 290–91; Garrett, *Famous First Facts About Negroes*, p. 112; Kane, *Famous First Facts*, p. 467; Morais, *The History of the Negro in Medicine*, p. 43.

1870 ♦ **Susan Maria Smith McKinney Steward** (1848–1918) was the first black woman to graduate from a New York state medical school. After graduating from New York Medical College for Women, she practiced in Brooklyn for more than 20 years. In 1873 she became the first black woman doctor to be formally certified. In 1888 Steward became the only woman at the time to undertake postgraduate study at the Long Island Medical School Hospital. She was a founder of the Women's Loyal Union of New York and Brooklyn, and in 1881 she co-founded the Women's Hospital and Dispensary in Brooklyn. Steward married a prominent AME minister, Theophilus Gould Steward, in 1896, and became the resident physician at Wilberforce University (Ohio).

Sources: Black Women in America, vol. 2, pp. 1109–12; Dictionary of American Negro Biography, pp. 569–70; Notable Black American Women, pp. 1077–79.

1872 ◆ **Rebecca J. Cole** (1846–1922) was the first black woman to establish a medical practice in Pennsylvania. Cole was also the first black graduate of the Female Medical College of Pennsylvania (1867) and practiced medicine for half a century in Philadelphia, Pennsylvania; Columbia, South Carolina; and Washington, D.C.

Sources: Black Women in America, vol. 1, pp. 261–62; Morais, The History of the Negro in Medicine, p. 43; Notable Black American Women, pp. 201-2.

1892 ◆ **Miles Vandahurst Lynk** (1871–1956) was the founder and original editor of the first black medical journal in the nation, *The Medical and Surgical Observer.* The first issue, dated December 1892, was 32 pages long. It was published regularly for 18 months. An 1891 graduate of Meharry Medical College, Lynk organized the Medical Department of the University of West Tennessee in Memphis in 1900.

Daniel Hale Williams

Sources: Dictionary of Black Culture, p. 279; Garrett, Famous First Facts About Negroes, p. 113; Morais, The History of the Negro in Medicine, p. 64.

1893 ◆ **Daniel Hale Williams** (1856–1931) performed the world's first successful heart operation on July 9, 1893. The open heart surgery took place at Provident Hospital in Chicago, which was founded by Dr. Williams in 1891. "Doctor Dan" was a founder and first vice-president of the National Medical Association and the first and only black invited to become a charter member of the American College of Surgeons in 1913. He was also the first black on the Illinois State Board of Health in 1889; in 1893 he was appointed surgeon-in-chief of Freedmen's Hospital, where he reorganized the services and established a nursing school. Williams's two abiding interests were the NAACP and the construction of hospitals and training schools for African American doctors and nurses. (*See* **Hospitals, 1891**.)

Sources: Dictionary of American Negro Biography, p. 654; Garrett, Famous First Facts About Negroes, p. 114; Morais, The History of the Negro in Medicine, p. 75.

1896 ◆ **Austin Maurice Curtis** (1868–1939) was the first black American on the medical staff of Chicago's Cook County Hospital. (Curtis became the first black to receive such an appointment in a nonsegregated hospital.) An 1891 graduate from Northwestern University, he was the first physician to intern with Daniel Hale Williams. He later succeeded Williams as head of Freedmen's Hospital in Washington, D.C., and taught at Howard University College of Medicine.

Sources: Dictionary of American Negro Biography, pp.153–54; *Dictionary of Black Culture,* p. 123; *Journal of Negro History* 25 (October 1940), p. 502; Morais, *The History of the Negro in Medicine,* p. 78.

1919 ◆ **Louis Tompkins Wright** (1891–1952) became the first African American appointed to a New York City municipal hospital, Harlem Hospital, where he served with distinction for more than 30 years. In 1945 he was the only black member of the American College of Surgeons. Wright was also a militant civil rights advocate and a prominent member of the NAACP. As chair of the board of the civil rights organization (1935–52), he was responsible for the establishment of a board committee on health. The association named him its Spingarn Medalist in 1940 for his work as a champion of human rights.

Sources: Dictionary of American Negro Biography, pp. 670–71; *Journal of the National Medical Association* 45 (March 1953), p. 130; Morais, *The History of the Negro in Medicine,* p. 106.

1940 ◆ **Charles Richard Drew** (1904–1950) was the first person to set up a blood bank. His research at the Columbia Medical Center in New York City led to the discovery that blood plasma could replace whole blood in transfusions. He established and administered the British blood bank from 1940 to 1941, then the American Red Cross project to collect and store blood. Drew was dropped from the American Red Cross project because he differed with Red Cross policy of refusing the blood of black donors. He asserted that there was no scientific difference between the blood of blacks and whites. His research was responsible for saving numerous lives during World War II. He was accorded the NAACP's Spingarn Medal as well as other tributes.

Sources: Bennett, Before the Mayflower, p. 534; *Dictionary of American Negro Biography,* pp. 190–92; Morais, *The History of the Negro in Medicine,* pp. 107–9.

1949 ◆ **William Augustus Hinton** (1883–1959) was the first black professor at Harvard Medical School. A world-renowned bacteriologist, he developed the Hinton test for syphilis and the Davis-Hinton tests for blood and spinal fluid. His book *Syphilis and Its Treatment* (1936) became an authoritative reference work. Hinton directed the Massachusetts Department of Public Health's Wassermann Laboratory from its establishment in 1915 until 1954.

Sources: Dictionary of American Negro Biography, p. 315–16; Garrett, Famous First Facts About Negroes, p. 114; Morais, The History of the Negro in Medicine, pp. 103–4.

1967 ◆ **Jane Cooke Wright** (1919–) was America's first black woman associate dean of a major medical school, New York Medical College. Wright received her medical degree from New York Medical College in 1945. She had appointments at Harlem Hospital and its Cancer Research Foundation and began teaching at New York Medical School in 1955.

Source: Notable Black American Women, pp. 1283–85.

1973 ◆ **John Lawrence Sullivan Holloman** (1919–) was the first black president of the New York City Health and Hospital Corporation. In 1963 Holloman led a physicians' picket line protesting racism within the medical profession.

Sources: Morais, The History of the Negro in Medicine, p. 162; Who's Who Among Black Americans, 1978, p. 427.

1984 ◆ **Levi Watkins, Jr.** (1944–) was the first black doctor to insert an automatic defibrillator (a device that corrects life-threatening heart rhythms). Watkins has been a cardiac surgeon at Johns Hopkins University Hospital since 1987.

Source: Who's Who Among Black Americans, 1992–1993, p. 1469.

National Science Foundation

1990 ◆ Physicist **Walter E. Massey** (1938–) was the first black to head the National Science Foundation. He has had a distinguished career, including being the first black president of the American Association for the Advancement of Science. In 1993 he was designated vice-president for academic affairs and provost of the University of California system.

Sources: Jet 83 (22 February 1993), p. 22; Negro Almanac, pp. 1086–87; Scientific American 266 (June 1992), pp. 40–41; Who's Who Among Black Americans, 1992–1993, p. 927.

Mary Elizabeth
Mahoney

Nursing

1863 ◆ **Susie King Taylor** (1848–1912) was the first black army nurse in U.S. history, serving with the 1st Regiment of the South Carolina Volunteers. Her Civil War memoirs, *Reminiscences of My Life in Camp* (1902), are the first and only continuous written record of activities of black nurses. Taylor was born a slave on a plantation near Savannah, Georgia.

Sources: Dictionary of American Negro Biography, p. 581; Garrett, *Famous First Facts About Negroes,* p. 147; *Notable Black American Women,* pp. 1108–13.

1879 ◆ **Mary Elizabeth Mahoney** (1845–1926) was the first black graduate nurse in the United States. In 1878 she entered the New England Hospital for Women and Children to begin a 16-month course. Of the 40 applicants in her class, only 3 remained to receive their diplomas, 2 white women and Mary Mahoney. The Mary Mahoney Medal was named in her honor by the American Nurses Association and is given every two years to the person making the most progress toward opening full opportunities in nursing for all.

Sources: Black Women in America, vol. 2, pp. 743–44; Garrett, *Famous First Facts About Negroes,* p. 148; Morais, *The History of the Negro in Medicine,* p. 70; *Notable Black American Women,* pp. 720–21.

1886 ◆ Spelman Seminary (now Spelman College) in Atlanta, Georgia, began the first nursing school for black women. Black Americans were forced to organize schools of their own for the training of nurses. As a result of the founding of all-black training schools, the number of African American graduate nurses steadily rose. The nursing school flourished until 1921.

Sources: Kane, Famous First Facts, p. 436; Morais, *The History of the Negro in Medicine,* p. 71.

1891 ◆ The first three black schools of nursing attached to hospitals were established in 1891 at Dixie Hospital in Hampton, Virginia; MacVicar Hospital, in connection with Spelman College in Atlanta, Georgia; and Provident Hospital Training School in Chicago. Alice M. Bacon, founder of Dixie Hospital, was connected with Hampton Institute, although her hospital was independent.

Sources: Morais, The History of the Negro in Medicine, p. 71; *Negro Education,* vol. 1, p. 176.

1936 ♦ Estelle Massey Osborne (1901–1981) was the first black director of nursing at City Hospital No. 2 (now the Homer G. Phillips Hospital Training School). Earlier she had been the first black nursing instructor at Harlem Hospital School of Nursing. In 1943, as the first black consultant on the staff of any national organization (in this case the National Nursing Council for War Service), she more than doubled the number of white nursing schools to admit blacks. In 1948 Osborne was the first recipient of an M.A. in nursing education from Teachers College of Columbia University. She was the first black member of the nursing faculty at New York University and also became the first black to hold office in the American Nurses Association.

Sources: Black Women in America, pp. 903–5; Encyclopedia of Black America, p. 90; Morais, The History of the Negro in Medicine, p. 255; Who's Who in Colored America, 1950, p. 402.

Publications

1792 ♦ **Benjamin Banneker** (1731–1806) was the first black man to issue an almanac and is commonly referred to as the first black American scientist. (His almanac series continued until 1797.) Banneker was born free in Maryland, where he became a tobacco farmer. As a result of his interest in mathematics and mechanics, he constructed a successful striking clock in about 1752. The clock, perhaps the first made in America, was still running at the time of his death. In 1787 a Quaker neighbor lent Banneker some books on astronomy and instruments, and he taught himself the skills necessary to produce his almanac. Banneker also helped survey the national capital. Although Banneker was unwell and could not work in the field, he did function as an assistant to George Ellicot in the survey of the 10-mile square of the District of Columbia, from early February to the end of April 1791.

Sources: Bedini, The Life of Benjamin Banneker, pp. 42–46, 103–36, 137–95; Bennett, Before the Mayflower, p. 649; Dictionary of American Negro Biography, pp. 22–25; James, The Real McCoy, pp. 96–99.

Title page of Benjamin Banneker's *Almanac*

1909 ♦ **Charles Victor Roman** (1864–1934) was the first editor of the *Journal of the National Medical Association.* Roman favored support of black institutions and believed black history should be written by blacks. He later directed health service at Fisk and taught at Meharry.

Sources: Dictionary of American Negro Biography, p. 532; *Encyclopedia of Black America,* pp. 735–36; Morais, *The History of the Negro in Medicine,* pp. 69–70.

Societies and Associations

1854 ♦ **John V. De Grasse** (1825–1868) was the first black physician to join a medical society. The Massachusetts Medical Society admitted him on August 24, 1854. He was one of the eight blacks who were commissioned as surgeons in the U.S. Army during the Civil War.

Sources: Dictionary of American Negro Autobiography, p.169; Morais, *The History of the Negro in Medicine,* p. 38.

1884 ♦ The Medico-Chirugical Society of the District of Columbia is the first black medical society. Its formation was the result of refusal of the white medical society to admit black physicians. Black physicians could not join their local American Medical Society branch until 1952. A national organization for blacks was formed in 1895, when the Medico-Chirugical Society was reactivated and incorporated. Although the society originally had white members, by 1920 it was entirely black.

Sources: Encyclopedia of Black America, p. 673; Gatewood, *Aristocrats of Color,* p 65; Morais, *The History of the Negro in Medicine,* pp. 57–58.

1895 ♦ The National Medical Association was formed in October 1895 in Atlanta, Georgia, during the Cotton States and International Exposition. The association was formed in reaction to the practices of mainly white associations. The American Medical Association did not urge all its local members to remove restrictive provisions until 1950. The first president of the black association was R. F. Boyd of Nashville, Tennessee.

Sources: Dictionary of Black Culture, pp. 320–21; *Encyclopedia of Black America,* pp. 633–34; Morais, *The History of the Negro in Medicine,* pp. 68–69.

Space

1983 ♦ On August 30, 1983, **Guion (Guy) S. Bluford, Jr.** (1942–) was the first black American astronaut to undertake a space flight. He participated in two more missions in space and totaled 314 hours in space before he retired from the program in 1993. He was the second black in space: a black Cuban had previously flown on a Soviet mission.

Sources: Contemporary Black Biography, vol. 2, pp. 19–21; *Ebony* 34 (March 1979), pp. 54–62; *Jet* 64 (22 August 1983), p. 2, (5 September 1983), pp. 20–22, 24; *Negro Almanac,* p. 1093; *Who's Who Among Black Americans, 1992–1993,* pp. 121–22.

1986 ◆ On January 20, 1986, **Ronald McNair** (1950–1986) was the first black astronaut killed during a space mission, when the space shuttle *Challenger* exploded during take-off.

Sources: Contemporary Black Biography, vol. 3, pp. 164–66; Hornsby, Jr., *Chronology of African-American History,* p. 340; *Negro Almanac,* p. 1094.

1987 ◆ **Frederick Drew Gregory** (1941–) was the first black astronaut to command a space shuttle. A nephew of the developer of blood plasma storage, Dr. Charles Drew, Gregory was also the first black American to pilot a space shuttle mission, in 1985.

Sources: Jet 77 (20 November 1989), p. 23, 80 (15 July 1991), p. 26; *Who's Who Among Black Americans, 1992–1993,* p. 563.

Mae C. Jemison

Mae C. Jemison (1956–) was named the first black woman astronaut. In 1992 she became the first black woman in space.

Sources: Contemporary Black Biography, vol. 1, pp. 113–14; *Jet* 82 (14 September 1992), cover, pp. 34–38; *Negro Almanac,* p. 1064; *Notable Black American Women,* pp. 571–73; *Who's Who Among Black Americans, 1992–1993,* p. 739.

Sports

Auto Racing • Baseball • Basketball • Bowling • Boxing • Cycling
Football • Golf • Hockey • Horse Racing • Horse Riding • Olympics
Rodeos • Tennis • Wrestling

Auto Racing

1963 ◆ **Wendell Oliver Scott** (c. 1921–1990) was the first and only black driver to win a NASCAR Winston Cup (then the Grand National) race. He was the first black driver since Rojo Jack to earn a national following. Scott began racing at Danville Fairgrounds Speedway in Danville, Virginia, and won more than 100 short-track Sportsman races as well as several state and track titles. He moved to NASCAR's premier division in 1961 where he made almost 500 starts. In summer 1964 Scott won a short-track race at Jacksonville, Florida. Injuries in a race at Talladega ended his career in 1973. The film *Greased Lightning,* starring Richard Pryor, is based on his life.

Sources: Ashe, *A Hard Road to Glory,* vol. 2, pp. 231–32; *Autoweek* 41 (7 January 1991), p. 55; *Jet* 79 (14 January 1990), p. 51.

1991 ◆ **Willy (Willie) T. Ribbs** (1956–) became the first African American ever to qualify for the Indianapolis 500.

Sources: Ashe, *A Hard Road to Glory,* vol. 3, pp. 232–33, 258; *Contemporary Black Biography,* vol. 2, pp. 196–99; *Road and Track* 44 (August 1993), pp. 130–32.

Baseball

1878 ◆ The first known black professional player was pitcher **John W. "Bud" Fowler** (c. 1858–?), whose real name was John W. Jackson. In April 1878, playing for a local team from Chelsea, Massachusetts, he defeated the Boston club of the National League in an exhibition game. Later Fowler also

PLAYERS FROM BLACK LEAGUES IN THE BASEBALL HALL OF FAME

1971	Satchel Paige
1972	Josh Gibson
1972	Walter "Buck" Leonard
1973	Monfors "Monte" Irvin
1974	James "Cool Papa" Bell
1975	William "Judy" Johnson
1976	Oscar Charleston
1977	Martin Dihigo
1977	John Henry "Pop" Lloyd
1981	Rube Foster
1982	Henry Aaron
1987	Ray Dandrige

Source: Total Baseball, pp. 311–12, 322, 329,338, 331, 341, 352, 354, 361–62, 376–77, 517–23.

became a second baseman, and his career as a semi-professional can be traced at least as late as 1891. He was the first of more than 70 black players on inter-racial teams in organized baseball during the nineteenth century until the last, Bert Jones, of Atchison in the Kansas State League, was forced out in 1899.

Sources: Chalk, *Pioneers of Black Sport,* pp. 5, 25–27; *Total Baseball,* pp. 548, 550; Young, *Negro Firsts in Sports,* pp. 16, 55–56, 206.

1884 ◆ **Moses Fleetwood Walker** (1857–1924) became the first black ball player in big league baseball when the Northwestern League Toledo team entered the American Association in 1884. In 1881 he was the first black college varsity baseball player and a member of the first Oberlin College varsity baseball team. In 1883 the bare-handed catcher signed with Toledo.

Sources: Ashe, *A Hard Road to Glory,* vol. 1, pp. 70–72; Kane, *Famous First Facts,* p. 104; *Total Baseball,* pp. 548–49; Young, *Negro Firsts in Sports,* pp. 16, 55, 73.

1901 ◆ **Charles Grant,** a second baseman, became the first black player in the American League (not yet a major league) under the name Charles Tokahama, claiming he was a full-blooded Cherokee. A former member of the black Columbia Giants, he played for the Baltimore Orioles until his true race was exposed.

Sources: Encyclopedia of Black America, p. 125; Kane, *Famous First Facts,* p. 104; *Total Baseball,* p. 550; Young, *Negro Firsts in Sports,* pp. 56–57, 61, 72, 149.

Satchel Paige

1920 ◆ Andrew "Rube" Foster (1879–1930), a former pitcher, organized the first successful black pro baseball league, the National Association of Professional Baseball Clubs, usually called the Negro National League, on February 13.

Sources: Ashe, *A Hard Road to Glory,* vol. 1, pp. 83–84; *Encyclopedia of Black America,* p. 125; *Total Baseball,* p. 552; Young, *Black Firsts in Sports,* pp. 58–62.

1947 ◆ Jackie (John Roosevelt) Robinson (1919–1972) joined the Brooklyn Dodgers as a third baseman to become the first African American in major leagues of the modern era. He played his first game against the Boston Braves at Ebetts field in Brooklyn on April 15, 1947, and in 1948 shifted to second base. Robinson probably received more racial insults in his career than any other person in history. In 1949 he became the first black batting champion and the first black American to receive the National League's Most Valuable Player Award. Robinson became the first African American enshrined in the Baseball Hall of Fame in 1952. Other black Americans who began playing in 1947 included Larry Doby for Cleveland, Dan Bankhead for Brooklyn, and Hank (Henry Curtis) Thompson and Willard Jessie Brown for Saint Louis. This same year Robinson and Bankhead became the first black players in a World Series.

Sources: Bennett, *Before the Mayflower,* p. 633; *Encyclopedia of Black America,* p. 126; Jones and Washington, *Black Champions Challenge American Sports,* pp. 96–101; *Total Baseball,* pp. 383–84, 503, 1412.

Dan (Daniel Robert) Bankhead (1920–1976), a member of the Brooklyn Dodgers, became the first black pitcher in the major leagues on August 26. Bankhead also joined fellow Dodger Jackie Robinson to become the first black players in a World Series the same year.

Sources: Ebony (May 1969), p. 110; *Negro Almanac,* pp. 1427–28; *Total Baseball,* p. 1586; Young, *Negro Firsts in Sports,* p. 207.

1948 ◆ Satchel (Leroy Robert) Paige (1900–1982) was the first black pitcher in the American League and the first African American to actually pitch in a World Series game. One of the best-known players in black baseball, he became the first black elected to the Baseball Hall of Fame for his career in the Negro leagues in 1971. At 59, the oldest man ever to pitch in the majors, he allowed just one hit.

Sources: Ashe, *A Hard Road to Glory,* vol. 2, p. 31, 38, 40; *Encyclopedia of Black America,* p. 126; *Total Baseball,* pp. 158, 376–77, 1871; Young, *Negro Firsts in Sports,* p. 207.

1953 ◆ **Roy "Campy" Campanella** (1921–1993) became the first black catcher to hit 20 or more homers in five successive seasons. He also had the most put-outs (807) and the most runs batted in (856). The first African American to be named the Most Valuable Player three times (1951, 1953, and 1955), Campanella was inducted into the Hall of Fame in Cooperstown, New York, in 1969. A 1958 automobile accident left the Philadelphia, Pennsylvania, native confined to a wheelchair.

Sources: Jet 84 (12 July 1993), pp. 14–17; *Negro Almanac,* p. 1428; *Total Baseball,* pp. 318–19, 1005; Young, *Negro Firsts in Sports,* pp. 213–14.

1955 ◆ **Elston Gene "Ellie" Howard** (1929–1980), an outfielder and catcher, became the first black player for the New York Yankees. In 1969 he became the first black coach in the American League, for the Yankees. He held this position until 1979. In the 1958 World Series he became the first African American to win the Babe Ruth Award, and in 1963 he was named Most Valuable Player in the American League, the first African American so honored.

Sources: Ashe, *A Hard Road to Glory,* vol. 2, p. 17; Jones and Washington, *Black Champions Challenge American Sports,* pp. 107, 149; *Total Baseball,* pp. 1193, 2155.

The first African American to pitch a no-hitter, and the first pitcher to have a no-hit game in 40 years, was **Samuel "Toothpick Sam" Jones** (1925–1971), in the game between the Chicago Cubs and the Pittsburgh Pirates held in Chicago on May 12.

Sources: Clark, *Sports Firsts,* p. 28; *Ebony* 14 (October 1959), p. 46; *Total Baseball,* p. 495, 1769.

1959 ◆ The first National League player to win the Most Valuable Player award two years in a row was **Ernie (Ernest) Banks** (1931–) of the Chicago Cubs. Also known as "Mr. Cub," he and second baseman Gene Baker formed the first black double-play combination in the major leagues. A "disaster on base," Banks produced four consecutive years of more than 40 home runs between 1957 and 1960.

Sources: Ashe, *A Hard Road to Glory,* vol. 2, pp. 19, 20, 25, 42, 271; *Encyclopedia of Black America,* p. 12; Jones and Washington, *Black Champions Challenge American Sports,* pp. 106–7, 149; *Total Baseball,* pp. 309–10, 946–47.

Hank Aaron

1962 ♦ The Chicago Cubs signed **John "Buck" O'Neil** (1911–) as coach, making him the first black coach on a major league baseball team. A notable first baseman in black baseball, he had served for several years as a scout.

Sources: Ashe, *A Hard Road to Glory*, vol. 1, p. 32; Bennett, *Before the Mayflower*, p. 637; Young, *Negro Firsts in Sports*, pp. 208–9.

Frank Robinson (1935–), playing for the National League Reds in 1961 and for the American League Orioles in 1966, was the first African American named the Most Valuable Player in both leagues. In 1966 he was also was the first black to win the triple crown—the most home runs, most runs batted in, and the highest batting average. Robinson became the first black manager of a major league baseball team when he was hired by the Cleveland Indians in 1975.

Sources: Bennett, *Before the Mayflower*, p. 636; Clark, *Sports Firsts*, p. 32; *Encyclopedia of Black America*, p. 128; Jones and Washington, *Black Champions Challenge American Sports*, pp. 107, 137, 148, 149, 151; *Total Baseball*, p. 383, 1411, 2146.

1972 ♦ The first person of any race to hit 30 or more home runs in 14 seasons was **Hank (Henry Louis) Aaron** (1934–). "Hammering Hank" hit 40 more in 1973. Playing for the Atlanta Braves on April 8, 1974, he hit his 715th home run in a game with the Los Angeles Dodgers to beat Babe Ruth's major league record. He retired in 1976 after 755 home runs—the most ever in the history of baseball—and became vice-president of player personnel for the Braves. In 1982 Aaron was elected into the Baseball Hall of Fame.

Sources: Alford, *Famous First Blacks*, p. 80; Ashe, *A Hard Road to Glory*, vol. 3, pp. 18–19, 268; *Total Baseball*, pp. 306, 924.

1980 ♦ **Sharon Richardson Jones** was named director of outreach activities for the Oakland Athletics, becoming the first black woman in major league baseball administration.

Source: Jet 81 (2 March 1992), p. 20.

Bill (William De Kova) White (1934–) was the first black president of a baseball league, the National League. He entered professional baseball in 1956 when he joined the New York Giants. White was named to the National

League All-Star team six times and served as a play-by-play broadcaster in the 1979 and 1980 seasons.

Sources: Contemporary Black Biography, vol. 1, pp. 243–45; Total Baseball, p. 1540.

1990 ◆ The first black woman assistant general manager of the Red Sox was **Elaine C. Weddington.**

Source: Jet 77 (26 February 1990), p. 52.

1991 ◆ **Rickey Henderson** (1958–) was the first African American to steal 939 bases in a career, surpassing Lou Brock. He already held the record for the most in one season. The first person of any race to steal 130 bases in one season under present counting methods was Maury (Maurice Morning) Wills (1932–), a Los Angeles Dodgers shortstop, who broke Ty Cobb's record of 96 stolen bases in a single season (1915) in 1962. His son Bump Wills was also an adept base stealer during his six year career (1977–82). Lou (Louis Clark) Brock (1939–) topped this record in 1974 with 118 and ended his career in 1976 with the all-time record of 938.

Sources: Ashe, A Hard Road to Glory, vol. 2, pp. 21, 26–27, 43; vol. 3, pp. 27–28, 43–44, 269; Current Biography, 1975, pp. 43–44 (Brock); Encyclopedia of Black America, p. 129; Jet 80 (20 May 1991), pp. 46–47; Jones and Washington, Black Champions Challenge American Sports, pp. 149–50, 151; Total Baseball, pp. 31, 316, 404, 1547.

Basketball

1923 ◆ The Rens, named after the team's home court, the Renaissance Casino in New York, was the first black professional basketball team. Founded and managed by Robert J. Douglas, the team ran up a record of 1,588 wins to 239 losses. They played from 1923 to 1939 and were the first black team in the Basketball Hall of Fame. On March 28, 1939, the Rens became the first black team on record to win a professional world's championship.

Sources: Chalk, Pioneers of Black Sport, pp. 83, 85–86, 88–89, 90–95; Encyclopedia of Black America, p. 129; Henderson, The Black Athlete, pp. 65–67; Young, Negro Firsts in Sports, pp. 80, 238.

1947 ◆ **Don (Donald Argee) Barksdale** (1923–1993) of UCLA was the first African American selected for All-American basketball honors. He was also the first black player on, and the first black captain of, the U.S. Olympic basketball team in 1948. Barksdale won an Olympic Gold medal. He and Jackie Robinson were the two black Americans in the London games. In 1947 Barksdale, of UCLA, was the first African American selected for the All-American basketball honors and the first black elected to the Helms all

Amateur Basketball Hall of Fame, in Culver City, California. Elected to the National Basketball Association's all-star game in 1953, Barksdale was also the first black to participate in that event.

Sources: Bennett, *Before the Mayflower,* p. 634; Jones and Washington, *Black Champions Challenge American Sports,* p. 89; Page, *Black Olympian Medalists,* pp. 162; Young, *Negro Firsts in Sports,* pp. 240, 279.

1950 ◆ **Chuck (Charles) Cooper** (?–c. 1984) of Duquesne University became the first African American drafted by a National Basketball Association (NBA) team, the Boston Celtics, in April. The New York Knickerbockers purchased Nathaniel "Sweetwater" Clifton, of Xavier University, from the Harlem Globetrotters in 1950, making him the second black player signed by the NBA.

Sources: Bennett, *Before the Mayflower,* p. 634; *Detroit Free Press,* 14 January 1992; *Encyclopedia of Black America,* p. 130; *Jet* 65 (20 February 1984), p. 51; Lee, *Interesting People,* p. 131; Young, *Negro Firsts in Sports,* p. 239.

The first African American to play in the NBA (October 21) was **Earl Lloyd** of West Virginia State College, a forward for the Washington Capitols. Although he was recruited later than Cooper and Clifton, he became the first to play (by one day) because of a quirk in NBA scheduling. Though Lloyd played 10 seasons with Washington, Syracuse, and the Pistons, his NBA statistics were modest. He was also the first black assistant coach and the first black chief scout in the NBA.

Sources: Detroit Free Press, 14 January 1992; *Encyclopedia of Black America,* p.131; Jones and Washington, *Black Champions Challenge American Sports,* pp. 89, 100; Young, *Negro Firsts in Sports,* p. 239.

1952 ◆ The Harlem Globetrotters team was founded, owned, and coached by Abe Saperstein of Chicago. Formed in Chicago, they were the first basketball club to make complete playing trips around the world. Mannie Jackson (1942–), a former Globetrotter, became the first African American to own the team in 1993.

Sources: Henderson, *The Black Athlete,* pp. 61, 64-65; *Jet* 84 (9 August 1993), pp. 49–51; Jones and Washington, *Black Champions Challenge American Sports,* pp. 57–58, 82, 83, 87–89, 110–11; Young, *Negro Firsts in Sports,* pp. 230–38.

1955 ◆ **Missouri "Big Mo" Arledge** of Philander Smith College in Arkansas was the first black woman All-American basketball player. The 5'10" player averaged 21 points a game.

Source: Young, *Negro Firsts in Sports,* p. 241.

1961 ◆ **Wilt (Wilton Norman) "Wilt the Stilt" Chamberlain** (1936–), then with the Philadelphia 76ers, was the first professional player to score more than 3,000 points in one season. In 1961–62 he scored 4,029 points and became the first player to score more than 4,000 points in a single season. Chamberlain was also the first African American to score 100 points in a single game.

Sources: Ashe, *A Hard Road to Glory,* vol. 2, pp. 67, 70–71, 299–300, 303; Chalk, *Pioneers of Black Sports,* pp. 114, 115, 116, 117; *Current Biography 1960,* pp. 85–86; Young, *Negro Firsts in Sports,* pp. 78–79, 239, 265.

1966 ◆ **Bill (William Felton) "Mr. Basketball" Russell** (1934–), while still a member of the Boston Celtics basketball team, was signed by the Celtics on April 18 to become the first black coach in the National Basketball Association and the first to coach a major, mainly white, professional team. He immediately produced a world championship team, a record which continued from 1968 to 1970. Called the greatest defensive player ever, Russell led the University of San Francisco to two NCAA championships, won a Gold Medal in the 1960 Olympics, and led the Celtics to eight consecutive world titles. As a college player, he played in one losing game, and at the end of 1955 the NCAA widened the foul lane from 6 feet to 12 feet because of his dominance at rebounds.

Sources: Ashe, *A Hard Road to Glory,* vol. 3, pp. 68–70; Bennett, *Before the Mayflower,* p. 636; *Encyclopedia of Black America,* pp. 130–31, 737; Jones and Washington, *Black Champions Challenge American Sports,* pp. 108–9, 137, 138; Page, *Black Olympian Medalists,* p. 132.

1972 ◆ The first black general manager in any sport was **Wayne Embry** (1937–) of the Milwaukee Bucks. He played as a center in the NBA for 11 years and was a five-time NBA all-star.

Sources: Alford, *Famous First Blacks,* p. 87; *Ebony* 30 (January 1975), p. 97, 28 (February 1973), pp. 74–80; *Sepia* 23 (December 1974), p. 62.

1973 ◆ The first black vice-president of the NBA was **Simon Peter Gourdine** (1940–). He held this position until 1972 and served as deputy commissioner from 1974 to 1981.

Sources: Alford, *Famous First Blacks,* p. 87; *Who's Who Among Black Americans, 1992–1993,* p. 543.

On April 3 **John Thompson** (1919–) of Georgetown University became the first black coach to win the NCAA Division I championship. The squad, led by Patrick Ewing, won over Houston 84–75. A former Boston Celtics player, Thompson joined the Georgetown Hoyas in 1972.

Sources: Ashe, *A Hard Road to Glory,* vol. 3, pp. 54, 63, 64, 80, 253; *Jet* 66 (16 April 1984), p. 52; *Time* (16 April 1984), p. 64.

Lynette Woodard (1959–) of the University of Kansas was the first woman to become a member of the Harlem Globetrotters.

Sources: Ashe, *A Hard Road to Glory,* vol. 3, pp. 64, 253; *Black Women in America,* vol. 2, p. 1282–83; *Jet* 73 (16 November 1987), p. 48, 77 (12 February 1990), p. 50; Page, *Black Olympian Medalists,* pp. 126, 163.

1989 ◆ The first black NBA team owners were **Bertram Lee** and **Peter Bynoe**, Chicago businessmen. On July 10 they purchased the Denver Nuggets for $65 million. (*See also* **Business: Manufacturing, 1990.**)

Sources: Hornsby, Jr., *Milestones in Twentieth-Century African-American History,* p. 409; *Jet* 76 (24 July 1989), p. 51; *Who's Who Among Black Americans, 1992–1993,* p. 212 (Bynoe).

Bowling

1993 ◆ **George Branham III** (1963–) became the first black bowler to win the Firestone Tournament of Champions. He won two championships in less than a month, including the Baltimore Open.

Source: Jet 84 (7 June 1993), p. 46.

Boxing

1902 ◆ **Joe Gans** (Joseph Gaines, 1874–1910) was the first American-born black to win a world crown (the lightweight), defeating Frank Erne in one round at Fort Erie on May 12. He was elected to the Hall of Fame in 1954.

Sources: Ashe, *A Hard Road to Glory,* vol. 1, pp. 28–30; Bennett, *Before the Mayflower,* p. 634; *Encyclopedia of Black America,* p. 132; *Encyclopedia of Boxing,* p. 51; Young, *Negro Firsts in Sports,* p. 225.

1908 ◆ **Jack (John Arthur) Johnson** (1878–1946) knocked out Tommy Burns on December 26 in Sydney, Australia, in the 14th round to become the first black heavyweight boxing champion. He lost only 5 of 97 fights. In 1954 Johnson was elected to the Hall of Fame.

Sources: Bennett, *Before the Mayflower,* p. 634; Chalk, *Pioneers of Black Sport,* 141, 144–48, 152–63; *Encyclopedia of Boxing,* pp. 65–66; Jones and Washington, *Black Champions Challenge American Sports,* pp. 25–27, 36–38.

1926 ◆ **Tiger (Theodore) Flowers** (1895–1927) became the first black middleweight champion of the world, defeating Harry Greb to win the title in New York City on February 26.

Sources: Bennett, *Before the Mayflower,* p. 634; *Encyclopedia of Boxing,* p. 48; Jackson and Washington, *Black Champions Challenge American Sports,* pp. 48, 60; Young, *Negro Firsts in Sports,* pp. 20, 29, 31, 226.

1937 ◆ The sole person to hold three championships and three world titles at once was **Henry "Hammering Hank" Armstrong** (1912–1988). During a 10-month period between 1937 and 1938 he won the featherweight, welterweight, and lightweight titles and challenged for the middleweight, fighting to a draw. Armstrong won 27 fights in 1937 alone, 26 by knockout. He lost the last of his three titles, the welterweight, in 1940.

Sources: Encyclopedia of Black America, p. 134; Encyclopedia of Boxing, p. 12; Jones and Washington, Black Champions Challenge American Sports, pp. 71–73; Young, Negro Firsts in Sports, p. 226.

1938 ◆ **Joe Louis** (Joseph Louis Barrow, 1914–1961) became the first African American of his rank to score a one-round knock-out when he defeated Max Schmelling on June 22, immediately becoming the first black national sports hero. He was the first black American to hold a boxing title 10 years or more, maintaining the title of world champion for almost 12 years. Universally loved, Louis fought Max Baer at New York on September 24, 1935, and became the first black fighter to draw a million-dollar gate. The following year he was the first African American to win *Ring* magazine's fight-of-the-year award. By 1949 Louis became the first black to defend his title successfully 25 times, and in 1954 he became the first black heavyweight elected to Boxing's Hall of Fame. Born in Alabama, this son of a sharecropping cotton farmer fought often as a child. At the age of eight he knocked out four boyhood tormentors, and by 1934 he turned professional. Now a folk hero, his success broke down many barriers to black participation in athletics in other areas.

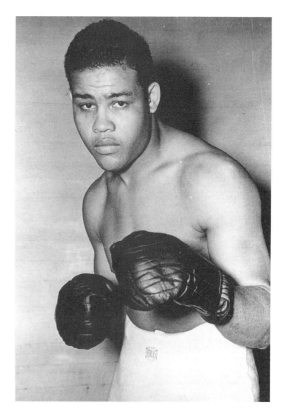

Joe Louis

Sources: Cantor, Historic Landmarks of Black America, pp. 24–25; Encyclopedia of Black America, p. 133; Young, Negro Firsts in Sports, pp. 98–114, 228–29.

1958 ◆ **Sugar Ray (Walker Smith) Robinson, Jr.** (1921–) became the first black fighter to hold the middleweight title on five separate occasions. In 202 professional fights, Robinson lost only 19 and was never knocked out.

Sources: Current Biography 1951, p. 526; Encyclopedia of Black America, pp. 111–12; Robinson, Historical Negro Biographies, p. 246.

1960 ◆ **Floyd Patterson** (1935–) became the first African American to regain the heavyweight title. Patterson lost his heavyweight title to Ingemar Johansson on June 26 and regained it nearly a year later when he knocked out Johansson in the fifth round. When he first won the championship, he was the youngest ever at 21 years of age. Patterson won an Olympic medal in 1952 and became the first black Olympic medalist to win a world title. Sonny Liston knocked him out in 2 minutes 6 seconds of the first round to win the title in 1962; in the rematch Patterson lasted 4 seconds longer.

Sources: Ashe, A Hard Road to Glory, vol. 2, pp. 90–92; Chalk, Pioneers of Black Sports, pp. 194–95, 198–99; Encyclopedia of Black America, p. 133; Encyclopedia of Boxing, p. 105.

1971 ◆ The first black boxers to draw a multimillion dollar gate were **Joe Frazier** (1944–) and **Muhammad Ali** (1942–), in their fight at Madison Square Garden on March 8. After 15 rounds Frazier won the match on points. The bout grossed some $20 million, and each fighter received $2.5 million.

Sources: Ashe, A Hard Road to Glory, vol. 3, p. 345; Chalk, Pioneers of Black Sports, pp. 204–8; Encyclopedia of Boxing, pp. 49–50, 199; Jones and Washington, Black Champions Challenge American Sports, pp. 160–61.

1978 ◆ **Muhammad Ali** (1942–) became the first to win the heavyweight title three times in the bout at the Louisiana Superdome in New Orleans on September 15. Ali won in a 13-round unanimous decision.

Sources: Ashe, A Hard Road to Glory, vol. 3, p. 100; Encyclopedia of Boxing, pp. 7–10; Kane, Famous First Facts, p. 508.

1987 ◆ The first African American to win boxing titles in five different weight classes was **Thomas "Hit Man" Hearns** (1958–). In 1977 he was national NAA light welterweight champion and national Golden Gloves welterweight champion. His titles include the vacant USBA welterwight title (March 2, 1980); the WBA welterweight title (August 2, 1980); the WBC junior middleweight title (December 3, 1982); the world middleweight title (April 15, 1985); and the WBC light heavyweight title (February 1987).

Sources: Ashe, A Hard Road to Glory, vol. 3, pp. 347–50; Negro Almanac, 1989, pp. 980–81; Who's Who Among Black Americans, 1992–1993, p. 633.

Cycling

1898 ◆ **Marshall W. "Major" Taylor** (1878– ?) was the first native-born black American to win a major bicycle race. He began as a trick rider for a local cycling shop and participated in a few amateur events. Taylor won his first professional start, a half-mile handicap held at Madison Square Garden, in spite of racism in cycling; his 121-point score made him the first black American champion in any sport. (Early boxing champion George Dixon was Canadian.) Toward the end of the year he compiled 21 first-place victories, 13 second-place berths, and 11 third-place showings. Taylor was known as the "fastest bicycle rider in the world" until his 1910 retirement.

Sources: Alford, *Famous First Blacks,* p. 97; Ashe, *A Hard Road to Glory,* vol. 1, pp. 54–57; *Encyclopedia of Black America,* p. 143; Young, *Negro Firsts in Sports,* pp. 177–78.

Football

1904 ◆ **Charles W. Follis** (1879–?) became the first black professional football player, for the Blues of Shelby, Ohio. The Blues were part of the American Professional Football League, formed in Ohio in this year, and a forerunner of the National Football League, which was formed in Canton, Ohio, in the summer of 1919, the year usually taken as the date of the beginning of modern professional football.

Sources: Ashe, *A Hard Road to Glory,* vol. 1, pp. 98, 99; Clark, *Sports Firsts,* p. 40; *Encyclopedia of Football,* pp. 18–23.

1916 ◆ **Frederick Douglas "Fritz" Pollard, Sr.** (1890–), a Brown University back, became the first African American to play in the Rose Bowl. Brown lost to Washington State 14–0. Pollard became the first black player and coach in professional football in 1919 when he joined the Akron Indians of the American Professional Football Association, which in 1921 became the National Football League. He coached the team to championship in 1920. In 1921 Paul Robeson (who later gained fame as an actor and singer) became one of Pollard's players. Pollard's career lasted through 1925. African Americans continued to play on professional teams until the end of the 1933 season and resumed play in 1946. His son Frederick Douglas Pollard, Jr., continued the family's athletic tradition by playing football for North Dakota and winning a bronze medal for the high hurdles in the 1936 Olympics.

Sources: Ashe, *A Hard Road to Glory,* vol. 1, pp. 100–02; Bennett, *Before the Mayflower,* p. 634, 636; Chalk, *Pioneers of Black Sport,* pp. 216–20, 222–23; Jones and Washington, *Black Champions Challenge American Sports,* pp. 40–41; Young, *Negro Firsts in Sports,* pp. 75–76, 146, 147, 250, 251.

1964 ◆ When **Buddy (Claude Henry Keystone) Young** (1926–) became the first director of player relations for the NFL, he was the first African American to hold an executive position with the league. In 1947 he became the first black to score a Rose Bowl touchdown, in the University of

Illinois vs. UCLA New Year's Day game. Young joined the AAFC New York Yankees in 1947 and eventually played for the Cleveland Browns from 1953 to 1955. His football jersey was retired by the Baltimore Colts in 1965, a first for a team.

Sources: Ashe, *A Hard Road to Glory,* vol. 3, p. 129; *Encyclopedia of Football,* p. 607; *Jet* 65 (25 January 1984), p. 53; Young, *Negro Firsts in Sports,* p. 279.

Kenny Washington of UCLA became the first black professional player to break the color barrier in place since 1933, when Joe Lillard of the Chicago Cardinals and Ray Kemp of the Pittsburgh Pirates were the last of the 13 African Americans who played in the National Football League between 1920 and 1933. Washington signed with the Los Angeles Rams of the National Football League on March 21. Other blacks who signed in that year were Woody Strode, with the Rams on May 7; and in the All-American Conference, Bill Willis on August 6, and Marion Motley on August 9, both with the Cleveland Browns. Washington played for the Rams through 1948. The last NFL team to be integrated was the Washington Redskins, which signed Bobby Marshall in 1962.

Sources: Ashe, *A Hard Road to Glory,* vol. 2, pp. 108–9, vol. 3, pp. 128–30; Bennett, *Before the Mayflower,* p. 635; *Encyclopedia of Football,* p. 592; Jones and Washington, *Black Champions Challenge American Sports,* pp. 79, 91; Young, *Negro Firsts in Sports,* pp. 144–46.

1953 ◆ The first black professional quarterback was **Willie Thrower**, a Michigan State graduate who signed with the Chicago Bears. Since the position was viewed traditionally as "white," Thrower played only a few downs and was active only one season. The first black quarterback to play professionally with any regularity was Marlin Briscoe in 1968 for the Denver Broncos, then in the American Football League.

Sources: Ashe, *A Hard Road to Glory,* vol. 3, p. 125, 143; Chalk, *Pioneers of Black Sports,* pp. 239–40; Clark, *Sports Firsts,* p. 50; *Encyclopedia of Football,* p. 583.

1958 ◆ **Jim (James) Nathaniel Brown** (1936–) was the first black athlete to win the Jim Thorpe Trophy. He is a football legend at his alma mater, Syracuse University, and played nine years with the Cleveland Browns. In the 1960s he also became the first African American to score 126 career touchdowns. He later became an actor, producer, sports commentator, and marketing executive.

Sources: Bontemps, *Famous Negro Athletes,* pp. 119–31; *Current Biography, 1964,* pp. 5–58; Henderson, *The Black Athlete,* pp. 200–204; *Historical Negro Biographies,* pp. 169–90; Toppin, *Biographical History of Blacks,* p. 259.

1961 ◆ **Ernie (Ernest) Davis** (1939– 1962), a Syracuse University running back, was cited as the first black player of the year and winner of the Heisman Trophy. Other early black Heisman winners were Mike Garrett in 1965, and O. J. Simpson in 1968. Davis was the first draft pick in both the NFL and the AFL, but he never played a moment of professional football since he was diagnosed with leukemia a few days before the college all-star game against the Green Bay Packers.

Sources: Ashe, *A Hard Road to Glory,* vol. 2, p. 12; Bennett, *Before the Mayflower,* p. 635; Henderson, *The Black Athlete,* pp. 203–4; Young, *Negro Firsts in Sports,* p. 281.

1965 ◆ **Emlen "The Gremlin" Tunnel** (1925–1975) was the first black coach in the National Football League. Tunnel had played for the New York Giants from 1948 to 1958 and the Green Bay Packers from 1959 to 1961. During his career he played in nine Pro Bowls and was an All-Pro four times. He was signed as assistant defensive coach by the New York Giants on May 1. In 1967 he became the first African American elected to the professional Hall of Fame.

Sources: Ashe, *A Hard Road to Glory,* vol. 3, pp. 130–31, 355–56; Bennett, *Before the Mayflower,* p. 635, 637; *Encyclopedia of Football,* p. 586.

1971 ◆ **Alan Cedric Page** (1924–), during his career with the Minnesota Vikings, became the first defensive player in the history of the NFL to receive the Most Valuable Player Award. After Page retired from football he launched a second career as an attorney. On November 3, 1992, he became the first African American elected to the Minnesota Supreme Court. Page was inducted into the National Football Hall of Fame in 1988.

Sources: *Encyclopedia of Football,* p. 529; Hornsby, Jr., *Milestones in Twentieth-Century African-American History,* p. 502.

1973 ◆ On September 16, **O. J. (Orenthal James) Simpson** (1947–) of the Buffalo Bills was the first African American to rush 250 yards in one game. In his years with the NFL he set records for running the most games in a season with 100 yards or more (11 in 1973), the most rushing attempts in a season (332 in 1975), and the most yards gained rushing in a single game (273 in 1976). Simpson played in the Pro Bowl in 1972, 1974, 1975, and 1976. The San Francisco native graduated from the University of Southern California, where he ran for 3,295 yards, scored 34 touchdowns, and led the Trojans to a national championship. In 1968 he received the Heisman Trophy, was named Rose Bowl Football Player of the Year, and received the Walter Camp Award, the Maxwell Award, and the *Sporting News* college player of the year award. Simpson was named NFL Player of the Decade in 1979 and was named to the

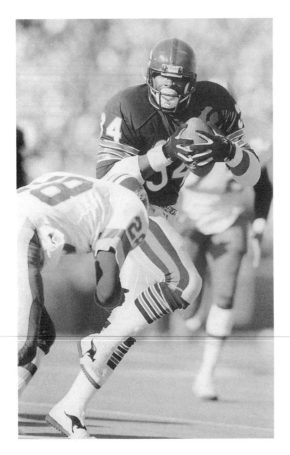

Walter Payton

College Football Hall of Fame (1983) as well as the Pro Football Hall of Fame (1985). He became a sports commentator and actor.

Sources: Encyclopedia of Football, p. 327; Great Athletes, vol. 16, pp. 2341–43; Negro Almanac, p. 970; Who's Who Among Black Americans, 1992–1993, p. 1284.

1986 ◆ **Walter Jerry Payton** (1954–) was the first black player to gain more than 20,000 yards. The number-one draft choice of the Chicago Bears in 1974 set NFL records for the most rushing touchdowns (110), most all-purpose running yards (21,803), most rushing yards (16,726), most seasons with at least 1,000 rushing yards (10), and set a new NFL record for the most rushing yards in a game (275 in 1977). He led the NFC in rushing 5 times, and in 2 games rushed 200 or more yards. His career ended on January 10, 1988, with a total of 16,726 rushing yards. Payton graduated from Jackson State University, where he set an all-time NCAA record of 66 touchdowns, scored 464 total points, and set 9 school records. He was named College Player of the Year and an All-American. Payton's uniform number 34 was retired by the Bears.

Sources: Great Athletes, vol. 14, pp. 1968–71; Jet 71 (27 October 1986), p. 52; Who's Who Among Black Americans, 1992–1993, p. 1101.

1987 ◆ **Bo Jackson** (1962–), then a pro baseball player for the Kansas City Royals, stunned sports fans by announcing in July that he had signed a five-year, $7.4 million contract with the Los Angeles Raiders. He thus became the first modern athlete to pursue careers in two pro sports. In 1989 Jackson became the first player in the history of the NFL to rush for 90 yards or more on two separate carries. Jackson was released from the Royals shortly after he suffered a hip injury in a January 1991 NFL playoff game. He later signed with the Chicago White Sox and then announced, in the fall of 1991, that he was retiring from football to concentrate on baseball. Jackson is equally well known for his "Bo Knows" commercials for the Nike athletic footwear manufacturer.

Sources: Harris, Biography Today, 1992, pp. 203–8; Johnson, Bo Jackson: Baseball/Football Superstar, pp. 46–61.

1989 ◆ **Arthur "Art" Shell, Jr.** (1946–) became the first black head coach in modern NFL history when he was appointed coach of the Los Angeles Raiders. (The first was Fritz Pollard in 1923.)

Sources: Contemporary Black Biography, vol. 1, pp. 219–20; *Sports Illustrated* (23 October 1989); *Jet* 77 (23 October 1989), p. 48, (26 February 1990), p. 48.

1991 ◆ The first black vice-president for labor relations of the National Football League was **Harold Henderson.** This was the league's third highest post, and Henderson became the highest ranking African American in the history of the NFL.

Source: Jet 80 (6 May 1991), p. 48.

Golf

1957 ◆ **Charlie (Charles) Sifford** (1922–) won the Long Beach Open on November 10 and became the first African American to win a major professional golf tournament. He also became the first black American to play in a major PGA tournament in the South at Greensboro, North Carolina, in 1961.

Sources: Ashe, *A Hard Road to Glory,* pp. 150–51, 154, 157; Bennett, *Before the Mayflower,* p. 635; *Encyclopedia of Black America,* p. 142; Jones and Washington, *Black Champions Challenge American Sports,* p. 116; Young, *Negro Firsts in Sports,* pp. 162–75, 281.

1967 ◆ **Renee Powell** was the first black woman on the Ladies' Professional Golf Association (PGA) tour. A native of Canton, Ohio, Powell won the USGA women's title in 1964.

Sources: Ashe, *A Hard Road to Glory,* vol. 3, p. 152; Spradling, p. 780.

1971 ◆ **Lee Elder** (1934–) became the first American to compete against whites in South Africa in the South African PGA Open. In 1974 he became the first black to qualify for the Masters Tournament and on April 10, 1975, teed off in Atlanta, Georgia, as the Master's first black entry. He became black America's first Ryder Cup Team member in 1979.

Sources: Alford, *Famous First Blacks,* p. 94; Ashe, *A Hard Road to Glory,* vol. 3, pp. 154, 156, 158; Bennett, *Before the Mayflower,* p. 635; Jones and Washington, *Black Champions Challenge American Sports,* pp. 147, 159.

1991 ◆ At 15, **Eldrick "Tiger" Woods** (1976–), of Cypress, California, was the first African American and the youngest person ever to win the U.S. Junior Amateur championship. With his participation in the Los Angeles Open in March 1992 he also became the youngest person ever to play in a Professional Golf Association tour event. He became the first two-time winner of the USGA Junior Amateur crown when he successfully defended his title in

Isaac Murphy

1992 at the championship in Milton, Massachusetts. Woods won his third consecutive U.S. Junior Amateur Golf Championship title in 1993, at the Waverly Golf Course and Country Club, Portland, Oregon. He is the only golfer ever to win three straight titles.

Sources: Jet 82 (31 August 1992), p. 47, 84 (30 August 1993), p. 46; *USA Weekend* (24–26 July 1992).

Hockey

1958 ♦ The first black professional hockey player was **Willie (William) Eldon O'Rhee,** of the National Hockey League's Boston Bruins. He played with the Bruins in their 3-0 win over the Montreal Canadiens in Montreal on January 18.

Sources: Ashe, *A Hard Road to Glory,* vol. 2, p. 222; Clark, *Sports Firsts,* p. 69; Kane, *Famous First Facts,* p. 301.

1981 ♦ The National Hockey League drafted its first black player, **Grant Fuhr.** He was picked in the first round and became the goalie for the world champion Edmonton Oilers.

Source: Ashe, *A Hard Road to Glory,* vol. 3, p. 222.

Horse Racing

1875 ♦ The first jockey of any race to win the Kentucky Derby was **Oliver Lewis,** who rode three-year-old Aristides in the first race in record time. Thirteen of the 14 jockeys in the first race were African American. In 1911 Jess Conley was the last black jockey from the United States to ride in a Derby.

1890 ♦ **Isaac Murphy** (Isaac Burns, c. 1861–1896), the first jockey of any race to win the Kentucky Derby three times, was considered one of the greatest race riders in American history: he won 44 percent of all the races he rode. His Derby record held until 1930. Murphy won the first in 1884 and the second in 1890, which made him the first jockey to capture Derby titles twice in a row. In 1884 he became the only jockey to win the Derby, the Kentucky Oaks, and the Clark Stakes in the same Churchill Downs meeting. In 1955

KENTUCKY DERBY BLACK JOCKEY WINNERS

Year	Jockey
1875	Oliver Lewis
1877	William "Billy" Walker
1880	George Lewis
1882	Babe Hurd
1884	Isaac Murphy
1885	Erskine Henderson
1887	Isaac Lewis
1890	Isaac Murphy
1891	Isaac Murphy
1892	Alonzo Clayton
1895	James Perkins
1896	Willie Sims
1898	Willie Sims
1901	Jimmie Winkfield
1902	Jimmie Winkfield

Sources: Ashe, *A Hard Road to Glory,* vol. 1, pp. 43–53, 129; Alford, *Famous First Blacks,* p. 95; Garrett, *Famous First Facts About Negroes,* pp. 77, 78–79, 185; *Encyclopedia of Black America,* pp. 138, 949.

Murphy was the first jockey voted into the Jockey Hall of Fame at the National Museum of Racing, Saratoga Springs, New York.

Sources: Ashe, *A Hard Road to Glory,* vol. 1, pp. 47–49; *Churchhill Downs News* (Black Expo Edition), 1980, p. 2; *Dictionary of American Negro Biography,* pp. 462–63; Young, *Negro Firsts in Sports,* pp. 49.

1899 ◆ The Kentucky Derby distance was trimmed from 1½ miles to 1¼ miles in 1896. **Willie (Willy) Simms** (1870–?) of Augusta, Georgia, was the first winner of the race at this distance. He won many of the best-known horse races in America, such as the Preakness Stakes (1898), Belmont Stakes (1893 and 1894), and the Champagne Stakes at Belmont in 1895. He was also the first American jockey on an American horse to win on the English track, and he became the first black American jockey to win international fame.

Sources: Ashe, *A Hard Road to Glory,* vol. 1, p. 49; Jones and Washington, *Black Champions Challenge American Sports,* p. 18; Young, *Negro Firsts in Sports,* pp. 52–53.

1971 ◆ **Cheryl White** (1954–) became the first woman jockey on June 15.

Source: Encyclopedia of Black America, p. 138.

Horse Riding

1990 ◆ **Donna Cheek** (1963–) became the first black member of the U.S. Equestrian Team. She was the first and only equestrienne to be inducted into the Women's Sports Hall of Fame.

> *Source: Jet* 79 (21 January 1991), p. 48.

Olympics

1908 ◆ **John Baxter "Doc" Taylor, Jr.** (1882–1908) became the first black winner of a gold medal in the Olympics won for the 4 x 400-meter relay in London. One of the first great black quarter-milers, Taylor was also the first black to win a gold medal as a United States team member. He died five months after winning the gold medal.

> *Sources:* Ashe, *A Hard Road to Glory*, vol. 1, pp. 63–64, 65–66; Page, *Black Olympian Medalists*, pp. 111–12, 149; Young, *Negro Firsts in Sports*, pp. 83–84.

1924 ◆ **William DeHart Hubbard** (1903–1976) became the first black in Olympic history to win an individual gold medal when he won the broad jump by leaping 24 feet 5½ inches on July 8. He set a new record on July 13, 1925, at Stagg Field in the NCAA championships where he leaped 25 feet 5⅛ inches. Although best known for his broad-jumps, he was also a sprinter, tying the world record of 9.6 seconds in the 100 yard dash.

> *Sources:* Ashe, *A Hard Road to Glory*, vol. 2, p. 79; Bennett, *Before the Mayflower*, p. 636; Page, *Black Olympian Medalists*, pp. 54, 149.

1930 ◆ **Thomas Edward "Little Eddie" Tolan** (1908–1967) ran in Evanston, Illinois, this year and was the first person officially credited with running 100 yards in 9.5 seconds. He set two Olympic records in the Los Angeles meet in 1932 and became the first black to win gold medals in both the 100- and 200-meter dash. In his career he won 300 races and lost seven.

> *Sources:* Alford, *Famous First Blacks*, p. 99; *Encyclopedia of Black America*, p. 139; Page, *Black Olympian Medalists*, pp. 116–17, 149; Young, *Negro Firsts in Sports*, pp. 84–85.

1932 ◆ **Ralph Metcalf** (1910–1978), while training for the Olympics, broke three world records on June 11—100 meters, 200 meters, and 220 yards. In 1934 he became the first man to win the NCAA doubles three times and the next year he became the only sprinter to win five times in a single event. In 1934–35 he was called the "world's fastest human." He and Jesse Owens were

Jesse Owens

the first blacks to win a gold medal for the 4 x 100-meter relay, which they ran in Berlin in 1936. Metcalf later became a U.S. Congressman.

Sources: Jones and Washington, *Black Champions Challenge American Sports,* pp. 67–68, 69, 70; Page, *Black Olympian Medalists,* pp. 82, 149; Young, *Negro Firsts in Sports,* pp. 84–85.

1936 ◆ **Jesse Owens** (James Cleveland Owens, 1913–1980), son of an Alabama sharecropper, ran with Ralph Metcalf and won the first gold medal for the 4 x 100-meter relay held in Berlin in 1936 and set both Olympic and world records. When he won a gold for the long jump, he set a record that remained unbroken for 24 years. He ran 200 meters in 20.7 seconds at the Berlin Olympics, then the fastest ever around a full turn. He tied the Olympic record for the 100-meter run at Berlin. Altogether he won four gold medals and set three records. Earlier, Owens ran in the Big Ten Championships in Ann Arbor, Michigan, on May 25, 1935, and set five world records and tied a sixth within 45 minutes. For his athletic achievement, his name was published in the record book for 40 years, showing that at the peak of his career he had won nine records in seven events and once held as many as 11 records. The world was stunned and his fame spread when Adolf Hitler refused to acknowledge Owens and the medals he had won in the Berlin Olympics. Later he was successful in business, as a speaker and youth worker. In 1976 he was the first black appointed by the Department of State as goodwill ambassador to the Olympic games. He was appointed to the United States Olympic Committee and in 1976 won the Presidential Medal of Freedom. Ohio State University, where he had studied, awarded him an honorary doctorate in 1972. In 1984 the Jesse Owens Memorial Monument was dedicated in his hometown, Oakville, Alabama.

Sources: Negro Almanac, p. 964–65; Page, *Black Olympian Medalists,* pp. 91–92, 149; Young, *Negro Firsts in Sports,* p. 98–105, 280.

John Woodruff (1915–) was the first black to win the 800-meter race in the Olympics. Since his time, no athlete has equalled his dominance of the 800-meter and half-mile run. He came to national attention in the 1936 Olympic sectional trials when he won this race. He won a gold medal in Berlin; that year he was also AAU champion. In addition to other titles, in 1940 he broke the American 800 record.

Sources: Alford, *Famous First Blacks,* p. 100; Jones and Washington, *Black Champions Challenge American Sports,* p. 70; Page, *Black Olympian Medalists,* pp. 126–27.

1948 ◆ **Alice Coachman (Davis)** (1923–) was the first black woman Olympic gold medal winner and the only American woman to win a gold medal in the 1948 Olympics in London. She took the gold for the high jump and set an Olympic record that held until two Olympiads later.

Sources: Encyclopedia of Black America, p. 143; *Notable Black American Women,* pp.193–95; Page, *Black Olympian Medalists,* pp. 23–24.

The first black heavyweight lifting champion in the Olympics was **John Davis.** He had thoroughly established himself in the field in 1941 when he set a record of 1,005 pounds for three lifts. Davis was Olympic champion again in 1952. Once called "the world's strongest man," he was the first weight lifter known to hoist 400 pounds over his head, a feat he accomplished in the 1951 National AAU senior championship in Los Angeles.

Sources: Alford, *Famous First Blacks,* p. 98; Young, *Negro Firsts in Sports,* pp. 184–85.

1956 ◆ **Milt (Milton) Gray Campbell** (1934–), one of the first great black decathletes, won 7,937 points and became the first African American to win the Olympic decathlon.

Sources: Ashe, *A Hard Road to Glory,* vol. 3, pp. 152, 183, 184, 516; *Encyclopedia of Black America,* p. 141; Henderson, *The Black Athlete,* p. 245; Jones and Washington, *Black Champions Challenge American Sports,* p. 115; Page, *Black Olympian Medalists,* p. 19.

Charles Everett Dumas (1937–), who won a gold medal at the 1956 Olympics at Melbourne with an Olympic record leap of 6 feet 11¼ inches, was the first man to break the 7-foot barrier, clearing 7 feet ⅝ inches at the Olympic finals trial at the Los Angeles Coliseum.

Sources: Ashe, *A Hard Road to Glory,* vol. 3, pp. 184, 516; *Negro Almanac,* p. 1429; Page, *Black Olympian Medalists,* p. 34.

1960 ◆ **Rafer Lewis Johnson** (1934–), winner of a silver medal for the decathlon at the 1956 Olympics and a gold medal for the same event at the 1960 Olympics, was the first African American to carry the American flag at an Olympic event: the opening ceremony at Rome in 1960. Johnson has served as national head coach for the Special Olympics.

Sources: Ashe, *A Hard Road to Glory,* vol. 2, pp. 184, 186; Henderson, *The Black Athlete,* p. 244; Page, *Black Olympian Medalists,* pp. 59–60.

Wilma Glodean Rudolph (1940–), born with polio that left her paralyzed in the left leg and unable to walk well until age 10, was the first woman to win three track gold medals in the Olympics. She ran in the 100-meter, 200-meter, and relay races, becoming also the first black woman winner of the 200-meter. She won a bronze medal as a member of the women's 4 x 100-meter relay team at the Melbourne Olympics in 1956. Her autobiography *Wilma* was made into a television film in 1977. Rudolph was one of five athletes and the

Wilma Rudolph

only track star honored in June 1993 at the first annual National Sports Awards held in Washington, D.C.

Sources: Ashe, *A Hard Road to Glory,* vol. 2, pp. 182, 185, 187, 189, 201; *Jet* 84 (12 July 1993), pp. 56–58; Kane, *Famous First Facts,* p. 45; *Notable Black American Women,* pp. 958–61; Page, *Black Olympian Medalists,* pp. 102–3.

1964 ◆ **Wyomia Tyus** (1945–) was the first athlete, male or female, to win an Olympic sprint title twice. She won a gold medal for the 100-meter run at the 1964 Olympics in Tokyo and a silver medal for the 4 x 100-meter relay at the same event. In 1968 she won the gold medal for the 100-meter run and the 4 x 100-meter relay in Mexico City. She set an Olympic and world record in the 100-meter run (the second time she had set a world rcord in the event) and helped set an Olympic and world record of 42.8 seconds in the latter event. In 1974 she joined the first professional track and field association. The state of Georgia elected her to its Athletic Hall of Fame in 1976.

Sources: Ashe, *A Hard Road to Glory,* vol. 3, pp. 188, 197, 201, 205, 514, 515, 518; *Guinness Book of Olympic Records;* Henderson, *The Black Athlete,* pp. 263–65; Page, *Black Olympian Medalists,* p. 118.

1972 ◆ **Willye Brown White (Whyte)** (1940–) became the first black woman to compete in five Olympic games. She won a silver medal for the long jump in 1956 and another silver for the 400-meter relay in 1964. She was also the first African American inducted into the Mississippi Hall of Fame in 1982.

Sources: Ashe, *A Hard Road to Glory,* vol. 3, p. 185; *Ebony* 18 (June 1963), pp. 115–20, 32 (August 1977), p. 62; Lee, *Interesting People,* p. 186.

1975 ◆ **Edwin Corley Moses** (1955–) is the only athlete to perfect the technique of taking 13 strides between the hurdles. This concentration on his event led to his being the first person to win 107 400-meter hurdle events in a row. His winning streak in the 400-meter intermediate hurdles began on September 2, 1977, in Dusseldorf, West Germany. The streak ended at the Madrid meet on June 4, 1987, when he was handed his first defeat in 10 years. Moses won a gold medal at Montreal in 1976 for the 400-meter hurdles and set a world and Olympic record of 47.64 seconds, which he lowered to 47.02 seconds when he set his fourth world record on August 31, 1983. He won a second gold medal in 1984 at Los Angeles for the 400-meter hurdle and a bronze, also for the 400-meter hurdles, in Seoul in 1988.

Sources: Ashe, *A Hard Road to Glory,* vol. 3, pp. 201–2, 204; Page, *Black Olympian Medalists,* pp. 85–86, 153, 154.

1984 ◆ **Carl (Frederick Carlton) Lewis** (1961–) was the first athlete to win four gold medals in a single Olympics since Jesse Owens. Lewis was influenced by Owens, whom he met at a school awards ceremony while in high school and who told him, "Dedication will bring its rewards." At the Los Angeles meet in 1984, Lewis won a gold medal each for the 100-meter run, the 200-meter run, the long jump, and the 4 x 100-meter relay. He continued to win other honors and to set records.

Sources: Ashe, *A Hard Road to Glory,* vol. 3, pp. 204–86; *Ebony* 39 (October 1984), p. 172; Page, *Black Olympian Medalists,* pp. 72–73, 154–56; *Sports Illustrated* (August 20, 1984).

Valerie Brisco-Hooks won a gold medal and set world records at the 1984 Olympics in Los Angeles for both the 200-meter run and the 400-meter run and became the first athlete to win at both distances. Running on the winning relay team that year, she tied Wilma Rudolph as winner of three gold medals in U.S. women's track and field events. She also received a silver medal for the 4 x 100-meter relay in the 1988 Olympics in Seoul.

Source: Ashe, *A Hard Road to Glory,* vol. 3, pp. 189, 205.

Cheryl De Ann Miller (1964–) was the first player, male or female, to be named to the Parade All-American basketball team for four consecutive years. She played in the 1984 Olympics in Los Angeles when the Americans won their first gold medal in women's basketball. Other black women on the U.S. team were Pam McGee, Lynette Woodard, Janice Lawrence, Cathy Boswell, and Teresa Edwards. She also led the U.S. team to gold medal victories in the World Championships and the Goodwill Games in Moscow, both in 1986.

Sources: Ashe, *A Hard Road to Glory,* vol. 3, pp. 54, 57, 64, 254; Page, *Black Olympian Medalists,* pp. 83–84, 163.

1988 ◆ **Debi Thomas** (1967–) was the first African American to win a medal (silver) in a Winter Olympics. In 1984 she was the first black skater on a World Team, and in 1985 she held U.S. and world figure skating championships.

Sources: Ashe, *A Hard Road to Glory,* vol. 3, pp. 224, 257; *Jet* 67 (25 February 1985), p. 54; *Who's Who Among Black Americans, 1992–1993,* p. 1381.

Jacqueline Joyner-Kersee (1962–) was the first U.S. woman to win the Olympic long jump and the first athlete in 64 years to win both a multi-event competition and an individual event in one Olympics. She won a silver medal for the heptathlon at the 1984 Olympics and a gold medal in 1988 for the heptathlon, setting an Olympic and world record. This year she became the only woman to gain more than 7,000 points four times in the heptathlon. Again in 1988 she won the gold for the long jump and set an Olympic record. She became the first woman ever to repeat as Olympic heptathlon champion in 1992 when she won the two-day, seven-event marathon. She has been called the world's fastest woman and the greatest female athlete. Born in East SaintLouis, she graduated from UCLA and in 1986 married Bob Kersee, her sprint coach. She was the first woman to receive *The Sporting News*'s Waterford Trophy, a prestigious annual award.

Sources: Black Women in America, pp. 667–69; *Current Biography, 1987,* pp. 293–96; *Epic Lives,* pp. 305–11; *Sports Illustrated* (27 April 1987).

Charles Lakes became the first black man to be a member of the U.S. Olympic gymnastics team.

Source: Jet 75 (5 September 1988), p. 48.

Jackie Joyner-Kersee

1992 ♦ The first black women gymnasts to compete on a U.S. Olympic team were **Dominique Dawes** and **Elizabeth Okino**, who were in the games in Barcelona, Spain.

Source: Jet 82 (17 August 1992), p. 48.

Anita Luceete DeFrantz (1952–) was the first African American elected to the executive board of the International Olympic Committee. She won a bronze medal for Rowing Eights in the Montreal Olympics in 1976, where she was the first black American to compete for the United States in Olympic rowing. An outspoken critic of the Olympian movement during the 1980 boycott, DeFrantz became only the second American athlete to receive the International Olympic Committee's Bronze Medal of the Olympic Order.

Sources: Ashe, *A Hard Road to Glory,* vol. 3, pp. 215–16; *Jet* 71 (9 February 1987), p. 51; *Jet* 72 (27 July 1987), p. 48, 82 (17 August 1992), p. 48; Page, *Black Olympian Medalists,* pp. 30–31.

Leroy Tashreau Walker (1918–) was the first African American to hold the four-year post of president of the U.S. Olympic Committee. The retired coach, who in 1976 was head coach of the U.S. Track and Field team at the Olympic Games in Montreal, is chancellor emeritus of North Carolina Central University.

Sources: Ebony 47 (August 1992), p. 7; *Jet* 83 (26 October 1992), p. 46; *Who's Who Among Black Americans, 1992–1993*, p. 1444.

Rodeos

1876 ◆ **Nat Love** (1844–?) was the only black American who claimed the title Deadwood Dick and so was the first known black rodeo champion. His account of his life is hard to verify, because none of the cowboys he worked with seemed to have ridden with other crews and records are lacking. Whatever the facts, the story makes interesting reading.

Sources: Durham and Jones, *The Negro Cowboys,* pp. 192–206; Katz, *Black People Who Made the Old West,* pp. 113–17; Katz, *The Black West,* 1993, pp. 150–52.

1887 ◆ **Pinto Jim** and **Bronco Jim Davis** are the first-known blacks to participate in a rodeo, in October in Denver, Colorado.

Source: Durham and Jones, *The Negro Cowboys,* p. 207.

1905 ◆ **Bill Pickett** (1860–1932) is generally credited with being the first person to develop a way of bulldogging, which made the act a spectacular performance. A black named Andy bulldogged in the 1870s; somewhat later, Sam Johnson did. When Pickett joined the 101 Ranch in 1900, his new technique involved biting the upper lip of the steer after the throw and raising his hands to show that he was no longer holding. The 101 Ranch put on its first major rodeo in 1905 and continued until the outbreak of World War I in 1914. Pickett was presented to King George V and Queen Mary after a special performance in that year. Pickett lived out his days on the 101 Ranch. On December 9, 1971, he became the first black elected to the National Rodeo Cowboy Hall of Fame.

Sources: Alford, *Famous First Blacks,* p. 68; *Crisis* 77 (November 1970), p. 388; Durham and Jones, *Negro Cowboys,* pp. 209–19; *Ebony* 33 (May 1978), pp. 58–62; Katz, *The Black West,* 1983, pp. 160–62.

1982 ◆ The first black World Rodeo champion was **Charles Sampson** of Los Angeles. The bullrider won the National Finals Rodeo in 1981, and the next year won the Winston Rodeo Series and was awarded the world title. He won the Sierra Circuit title in 1984, and for five consecutive years, 1981–85, qualified for the National Finals Rodeo.

Sources: Ashe, *A Hard Road to Glory,* vol. 3, p. 234; *Jet* 65 (20 February 1984), p. 40.

Tennis

1948 ◆ **Reginald Weir** (1912–) was the first African American to participate in the U.S. Indoor Lawn Tennis Association championship. He won his first match at the New York City event on March 11 and was eliminated on March 13.

Sources: Ashe, *A Hard Road to Glory,* vol. 2, pp. 61, 62, 64; Kane, *Famous First Facts,* p. 662; Young, *Negro Firsts in Sports,* pp. 184, 188.

1953 ◆ **Lorraine Williams** (1939–) became the first African American to win a nationally recognized tennis title when she won the junior girl's championship this year.

Sources: Bennett, *Before the Mayflower,* p. 635; *Ebony* 7 (June 1952), pp. 41–45, 9 (January 1954), p. 24; Young, *Negro Firsts in Sports,* p. 280.

Althea Gibson

1956 ◆ **Althea Gibson** (1927–) became the first African American to win a major tennis title when she won the women's singles in the French Open on May 26. She won the Wimbledon championship on July 6, 1957, when she also captured the women's singles, becoming the first African American to win these honors. She became the first black to win a major U.S. national championship on September 8, 1957, when she defeated Louise Brough at Forest Hills to win the women's singles. In 1991 she was the first black woman to receive the Theodore Roosevelt Award of the NCAA. In 1968 Gibson was the first African American inducted into the International Tennis Hall of Fame.

Sources: Ashe, *A Hard Road to Glory,* pp. 58, 64, 100; Bennett, *Before the Mayflower,* pp. 635; *Encyclopedia of Black America,* p. 141; *Notable Black American Women,* pp. 397–402.

1963 ◆ **Arthur Ashe** (1943–1993) was the first African American named to the American Davis Cup team. In 1961, the year he won the USLTA junior indoor title, another first, he was the first African American named to the U.S. Junior Davis Cup team. In 1968 he became the first black man to win a major tennis title, the national men's singles in the U.S. Lawn Tennis Association open tournament at Forest Hills. This was the first time the contest was open to professionals as well as amateurs. He became the first black man to win a singles title at Wimbledon in 1975. In 1983 he received a contract to produce the first complete book on African Americans in sports, *A Hard Road to Glory.* He was the first black man inducted into the International Tennis Hall of Fame in 1985. Ashe retired from active play after a mild heart attack on July 31, 1979. In 1993 Ashe died of AIDS acquired through a blood transfusion. In June 1993 President Bill Clinton honored his memory with the Presidential Medal of Freedom, awarded at the first annual National Sports Awards presentation in Washington, D.C.

Sources: Encyclopedia of Black America, p. 142; *Jet* 84 (12 June 1993), pp. 56, 58; Jones and Washington, *Black Champions Challenge American Sports,* p. 146.

1988 ◆ **Zina Garrison** (1963–) won a gold medal in doubles and a bronze in the singles, becoming the first black Olympic winner in tennis. She was also the first African American to rank in the top 10 on the women's professional tour.

Sources: Black Women in America, pp. 480–81; *Contemporary Black Biography,* vol 2, pp. 89–92; *Jet* 78 (23 July 1990), p. 51.

Wrestling

1992 ◆ The first black heavyweight wrestling champion was **Ron Simmons,** three-time All-American nose tackle at Florida State. He captured the World Championship Wrestling title for a first in the 60-year history of the sport.

Source: Jet 82 (21 September 1992), p. 50.

PICTURE CREDITS

SOURCES

Books:

Abdul, Raoul, *Blacks in Classical Music: A Personal History,* New York: Dodd, Mead, 1977.

Abramson, Doris E., *Negro Playwrights in the American Theatre, 1925-1959,* Books on Demand, 1969.

Alford, Sterling G., *Famous First Blacks,* New York: Vantage, 1974.

Archer, Jules, *They Had a Dream: The Civil Rights Struggle from Frederick Douglass to Marcus Garvey to Martin Luther King, Jr., and Malcolm X,* New York: Viking Children's Books, 1993.

Ashe, Arthur R., Jr., *A Hard Road to Glory,* 3 volumes, Washington, D.C.: Amistad Press, 1993.

Baer, Hans A., *The Black Spiritual Movement: A Religious Response to Racism,* Knoxville: University of Tennessee Press, 1984.

Baer, Hans A., and Merrill Singer, *African-American Religion in the Twentieth Century: Varieties of Protest and Accommodation,* Knoxville: University of Tennessee Press, 1992.

Barbeau, Arthur E., and Florette Henri, *The Unknown Soldiers: Black American Troops in World War I,* Philadelphia: Temple University Press, 1974.

Baskin, Wade, and Richard N. Runes, *Dictionary of Black Culture,* New York: Philosophical Library, 1973.

Bedini, Silvio A., *The Life of Benjamin Banneker,* Rancho Cordova, California: Landmark Enterprises, 1972; reprint, 1984.

Bennett, Lerone, Jr., *Before the Mayflower: A History of Black America,* Chicago: Johnson Publishing, 1987.

Black Americans in Defense of Our Nation, Washington, D.C.: Department of Defense, 1st edition, 1982; later edition, 1991.

The Black Perspective in Music, Cambria Heights, New York: Foundation for Research in the Afro-American Creative Arts, 1973.

Blackett, R. J., *Thomas Morris Chester, Black Civil War Correspondent: His Dispatches from the Virginia Front,* Baton Rouge: Louisiana State University Press, 1989.

Bogle, Donald, *Toms, Coons, Mulattoes, Mammies, and Bucks: An Interpretive History of Blacks in American Films,* New York: Continuum Publishing, 1989.

Bontemps, Arna Wendell, ed., *The Harlem Renaissance Remembered,* New York: Dodd, Mead, 1972.

Bowles, Frank Hamilton, and Frank A. DeCosta, *Between Two Worlds: A Profile of Negro Higher Education,* New York: McGraw-Hill, 1971.

Brawley, Benjamin G., *Negro Genius,* Biblo and Tannen Booksellers and Publishers, 1937; reprint, 1966.

Brelin, Christa, and William C. Matney, Jr., *Who's Who among Black Americans, 1992-1993,* Detroit: Gale, 1992.

Brown, Hazel P., *American Speech Sounds and Rhythm: Intermediate,* 3rd edition, Guilford, Connecticut: Audio-Forum, 1981.

Brown, Sterling., ed., *Negro Caravan,* Salem, New Hampshire: Ayer Company Publishers, 1917; reprint, 1969.

Brown, Hallie Q., *Homespun Heroines and Other Women of Distinction,* New York: Oxford University Press, 1992.

Burkett, Randall K., and Richard Newman, eds., *Black Apostles: Afro-American Clergy Confront the Twentieth Century,* Boston: G. K. Hall, 1978.

Cantor, George., ed., *Historic Landmarks of Black America,* Detroit: Gale, 1991.

Cederholm, Theresa, *Afro-American Artists: A Bio-Bibliographical Directory,* Boston: Boston Public Library, 1973.

Chalk, Ocania, *Pioneers of Black Sport: The Early Days of the Black Professional Athlete in Baseball, Basketball, Boxing, and Football,* New York: Dodd, Mead, 1975.

Chilton, John, *Who's Who of Jazz,* 4th edition, New York: Da Capo Press, 1985.

Christopher, Maurine, *America's Black Congressmen,* New York: Crowell, 1st edition, 1971; revised and expanded edition, 1976.

Clark, Patrick, *Sports Firsts,* New York: Facts on File, 1981.

Clayton, Edward Taylor, *The Negro Politician: His Success and Failure,* Chicago: Johnson Publishing, 1964.

Clayton, Xernona, and Hal Gulliver, *I've Been Marching All the Time: An Autobiography,* Marietta, Georgia: Longstreet Press, 1991.

Cohn, Lawrence, ed., *Nothing But the Blues,* New York: Abbeville Press, 1993.

Culp, Daniel W., ed., *Twentieth-Century Negro Literature,* Salem, New Hampshire: Ayer Company Publishers, 1902; reprint, New York: Arno Press, 1969.

Current Biography, Yearbooks, New York: H. W. Wilson, various volumes, 1940-1985.

Dannett, Sylvia G. L., *Profiles of Negro Womanhood,* multiple volumes, Yonkers: Educational Heritage, 1964-66.

Dates, Jannette L., and William Barlow, eds., *Split Image: African Americans in the Mass Media,* 2nd edition, Washington, D.C.: Howard University Press, 1993.

Davis, Sammy, Jr., Jane Boyer, and Burt Boyar, *Why Me?,* New York: Warner, 1990.

Davis, Cyprian, *The History of Black Catholics in the United States,* New York: Crossroad Publishing, 1990.

Du Bois, W. E. B., *Efforts for Social Betterment among Negro Americans,* Millwood, New York: Kraus Reprint, 1909.

Duberman, Martin B., *Paul Robeson: A Biography,* New York: Knopf, 1989.

Durham, Philip, and Everett L. Jones, *The Negro Cowboys,* Lincoln: University of Nebraska Press, 1965; reprint, 1983.

Ebony Success Library, Cincinnati: Southwestern, 1973.

Emery, Lynne, *Black Dance,* Pennington, New Jersey: Princeton Book Company, 1991.

Estell, Kenneth, ed., *African American Almanac,* 6th edition, Detroit: Gale, 1994.

Feather, Leonard, *Encyclopedia of Jazz,* New York: Da Capo Press, 1950; reprint, 1984.

Flexner, Stuart Berg, *I Hear America Talking: An Illustrated Treasury of American Words and Phrases,* New York: Van Nostrand Reinhold, 1976.

Foner, Jack D., *Blacks in the Military in American History: A New Perspective,* New York: Praeger, 1974.

Foner, Philip Sheldon, *Organized Labor and the Black Worker, 1619-1981,* New York: International Publishers, 1982.

Franklin, John Hope, and August Meier, eds., *Black Leaders of the Twentieth Century,* Champaign: University of Illinois Press, 1982.

Frazier, E. Franklin, and Eric C. Lincoln, *The Black Church since Frazier,* Schocken Books, 1974.

Gale Directory of Publications and Broadcast Media, 1993, Detroit: Gale, 1993.

Garrett, Romeo B., *Famous First Facts about Negroes,* Salem, New Hampshire: Ayer Company Publishers, 1972.

Gatewood, Willard B., *Aristocrats of Color,* William J. Thomas Braille Bookstore, 1992.

Gosnell, Harold F., *Negro Politicians: The Rise of Negro Politics in Chicago,* Books on Demand, 1967.

Gray, John., ed., *Blacks in Classical Music: A Bibliographical Guide to Composers, Performers, and Ensembles,* Westport, Connecticut: Greenwood, 1988.

Great Athletes, Pasadena: Salem Press, 1992.

Guinness Book of Olympic Records, New York: Bantam, various years.

Haber, Louis, *Black Pioneers of Science and Invention,* Orlando: Harcourt Brace, 1992.

Harris, Trudier, and Thadious M. Davis, *Dictionary of Literary Biography,* Volume 50: *Afro-American Writers before the Harlem Renaissance,* Detroit: Gale, 1986.

Harris, Laurie L., ed., *Biography Today: Profiles of People of Interest to Young Readers, 1992,* Detroit: Omnigraphics, 1993.

Haskins, Jim, *Outward Dreams: Black Inventors and Their Inventions,* New York: Walker and Company, 1991.

Heilbut, Anthony, *The Gospel Sound: Good News and Bad Times,* revised and updated edition, New York: Limelight Editions, 1985.

Herbert, Solomon, and George Hill, *Bill Cosby,* New York: Chelsea House, 1992.

Hine, Darlene C., Elsa B. Brown, and Rosalyn Terborg-Penn, eds., *Black Women in America: An Historical Encyclopedia,* Brooklyn: Carlson Publishing, 1993.

Holland, David., ed., *Encyclopedia Americana,* Danbury: Grolier, 1989.

Hornsby, Alton, Jr., *Milestones in 20th Century African-American History,* Detroit: Visible Ink Press, 1993.

Hornsby, Alton, Jr., ed. *Chronology of African-American History: Significant Events and People from 1400 to the Present,* Detroit: Gale, 1991.

Hornsby, Alton, Jr., and Deborah G. Straub, eds., *African American Chronology,* two volumes, Detroit: U•X•L, 1993.

Horton, James O., *Free People of Color: Inside the African American Community,* Washington, D.C.: Smithsonian Institution Press, 1993.

Hughes, Langston, and Arna Bontemps, *The Poetry of the Negro, 1746-1949,* Garden City: Doubleday, 1949.

Hughes, Langston, Milton Meltzer, and Eric C. Lincoln, *Pictorial History of Black Americans,* 5th edition revised, New York: Crown Publishing Group, 1983.

Jackson, Blyden, *A History of Afro-American Literature,* Baton Rouge: Louisiana State University Press, 1989.

James, Portia, *The Real McCoy: African-American Invention and Innovation, 1619-1930,* Washington, D.C.: Smithsonian Institution Press, 1990.

Johnson, James Weldon, *Black Manhattan,* Salem, New Hampshire: Ayer Company Publishers, 1940; reprint, 1968.

Johnson, Rick L., *Bo Jackson: Baseball/Football Superstar,* New York: Dillon Press, 1991.

Jones, Thomas J., ed., *Negro Education: A Study of the Private and Higher Schools for Colored People in the United States,* Salem, New Hampshire: Ayer Company Publishers, 1917.

Jones, Wally, and Jim Washington, *Black Champions Challenge American Sports,* New York: McKay Co., 1972.

Josey, E. J., ed., *The Black Librarian in America Revisited,* Metuchen, New Jersey: Scarecrow Press, 1994.

Joyce, Donald F., ed., *Gatekeepers of Black Culture: Black-Owned Book Publishing in the United States, 1817-1981,* Westport, Connecticut: Greenwood, 1983.

Kane, Joseph N., *Famous First Facts,* 4th edition, New York: H. W. Wilson, 1981.

Katz, William Loren, *Black Indians: A Hidden Heritage,* New York: Macmillan Children's Book Group, 1986.

Katz, William Loren, *The Black West,* revised edition, Seattle: Open Hand Publishing, 1987.

Katz, William Loren, *Eyewitness: The Negro in American History,* New York: Pitman, 1967.

Kellner, Bruce, ed., *The Harlem Renaissance: A Historical Dictionary for the Era,* Westport, Connecticut: Greenwood, 1984.

Klever, Anita, *Women in Television,* Philadelphia: Westminster Press, 1975.

Klotman, Phyllis R., *Frame by Frame: A Black Filmography,* Books on Demand, 1979.

LaBlanc, Michael L., ed., *Contemporary Black Biography,* volume 2, Detroit: Gale, 1992.

Lane, Roger, *William Dorsey's Philadelphia and Ours: On the Past and Future of the Black City in America,* New York: Oxford University Press, 1991.

Langstaff, John, and Ashley Bryan, *Climbing Jacob's Ladder: Heroes of the Bible in African-American Spirituals,* New York: Macmillan Children's Book Group, 1991.

Lanker, Brian, *I Dream a World: Portraits of Black Women Who Changed America,* New York: Stewart, Tabori, and Chang, 1989.

Lee, George L., *Interesting People: Black American History Makers,* Jefferson, North Carolina: McFarland and Company, 1989.

Lee, Irvin H., *Negro Medal of Honor Men,* New York: Dodd, Mead, 1967.

Lerner, Gerda, *Black Women in White America: A Documentary History,* New York: Random House, 1992.

Lewis, David L., *When Harlem Was in Vogue,* New York: Oxford University Press, 1989.

Lincoln, C. Eric, and Lawrence Mamiya, *The Black Church in the African American Experience,* Durham, North Carolina: Duke University Press, 1990.

Loewenberg, Bert James, and Ruth Bogin, eds., *Black Women in Nineteenth-Century American Life: Their Words, Their Thoughts, Their Feelings,* University Park: Pennsylvania State University Press, 1976.

Logan, Rayford W., and Michael R. Winston, eds., *Dictionary of American Negro Biography,* New York: Norton, 1983.

Low, A. W., and V. A. Clift, *Encyclopedia of Black America,* New York: McGraw-Hill, 1981.

MacDonald, Anne L., *Feminine Ingenuity: How Women Inventors Changed America,* New York: Ballantine, 1994.

Mason, Herman, Jr., *Going against the Wind: A Pictorial History of African-Americans in Atlanta,* Marietta, Georgia: Longstreet Press, 1993.

McDonnell, Patrick, Karen O'Connell, and Georgia R. De Havenon, *Krazy Kat: The Art of George Herriman,* New York: Harry N. Abrams, 1986.

Melton, J. Gordon, *The Encyclopedia of American Religions,* 5th edition, Detroit: Gale, 1992.

Morais, Herbert Montfort, *The History of the Afro-Americans in Medicine,* Cornwells Heights, Pennsylvania: Publishers Company, 1969.

Morton, David C., and Charles K. Wolfe, *DeFord Bailey: A Black Star in Early Country Music,* Knoxville: University of Tennessee.

Moses, Wilson J., *Alexander Crummell: A Study of Civilization and Discontent,* Amherst: University of Massachusetts Press, 1989.

Movies on TV and Videocassette, New York: Bantam, 1989.

Negro Almanac: A Reference Work on the African American, 5th edition, edited by Harry A. Ploski and James Williams, Detroit: Gale, 1989.

Ochs, Stephen J., *Desegregating the Altar: The Josephites and the Struggle for Black Priests, 1871-1960,* Baton Rouge: Louisiana State University Press, 1993.

Odd, Gilbert E., *Encyclopedia of Boxing,* Secaucus, New Jersey: Chartwell Books, 1983.

Orr, Jack, *Black Athlete: His Story in American History,* Scarsdale: Lion Books, 1969.

Page, James A., *Black Olympian Medalists,* Englewood, Colorado: Libraries Unlimited, 1991.

Payne, *Directory of African American Religious Bodies,* Washington, D.C.: Howard University Press, 1990.

Pederson, Jay P., and Kenneth Estell, eds., *African American Almanac,* Detroit: U•X•L, 1994.

Pelz, Ruth, *Black Heroes of the Wild West,* Seattle: Open Hand Publishing, 1989.

Penn, I. Garland, *Afro-American Press and Its Editors,* Salem, New Hampshire: Ayer Company Publishers, 1891; reprint 1969.

Perkins, George, Barbara Perkins, and Phillip Leininger, eds., *Benet's Reader's Encyclopedia of American Literature,* New York: HarperCollins, 1991.

Ploski, Harry A., and James Williams, eds., *Negro Almanac: A Reference Work on the African American,* 5th edition, Detroit: Gale, 1989.

Raboteau, Albert J., *Slave Religion: The Invisible Institution in the Antebellum South,* New York: Oxford University Press, 1978.

Read, Florence Matilda, *The Story of Spelman College,* Atlanta, 1961.

Richardson, Joe M., *History of Fisk University, 1865-1946,* Tuscaloosa: University of Alabama Press, 1980.

Robinson, Wilhelmina S., *Historical Negro Biographies,* New York: Publishers Company, 1978.

Rosenberg, Robert, *Bill Cosby: The Changing Black Image,* Brookfield, Connecticut: Millbrook Press, 1991.

Rush, Theressa G., Carol F. Myers, and Esther S. Arata, *Black American Writers Past and Present: A Biographical and Bibliographical Dictionary,* two volumes, Metuchen, New Jersey: Scarecrow Press, 1975.

Sadie, Stanley, ed., *The New Grove Dictionary of Music and Musicians,* 20 volumes, 6th edition, New York: Grove Dictionaries, 1980.

Scott, Emmett Jay, *Scott's Official History of the American Negro in the World War,* Washington, D.C.: War Department, 1919.

Shockley, Ann A., ed., *Afro-American Women Writers, 1746-1933: An Anthology and Critical Guide,* New York: NAL/Dutton, 1989.

Shoemaker, Dennis E., *Heritage and Hope: A People of Hope,* Reformed Church Press, Reformed Church in America.

Simmons, William J., *Men of Mark: Eminent, Progressive and Rising,* Salem, New Hampshire: Ayer Company Publishers, 1887; reprint, 1968.

Smith, Edward D., *Climbing Jacob's Ladder: The Rise of Black Churches in Eastern American Cities, 1740-1877,* Washington, D.C.: Smithsonian Institution Press, 1988.

Smith, Jessie Carney, ed., *Ethnic Genealogy: A Research Guide,* Westport, Connecticut: Greenwood, 1983.

Smith, Jessie Carney, ed., *Notable Black American Women,* Detroit: Gale, 1991.

Smythe, Mabel M., *The Black American Reference Book,* Englewood Cliffs, New Jersey: Prentice-Hall, 1976.

Sollors, Werner, Caldwell Titcomb, and Thomas A. Underwood, eds., *Blacks at Harvard: A Documentary History of African-American Experience at Harvard and Radcliffe,* New York: New York University Press, 1993.

Southern, Eileen, *Biographical Dictionary of Afro-American and African Musicians,* Westport, Connecticut: Greenwood Publishing Group, 1982.

Southern, Eileen, *Readings in Black American Music,* New York: Norton, 1983.

Southern, Eileen, *The Music of Black Americans,* 2nd edition, New York: Norton, 1983.

Spradling, Mary M., ed., *In Black and White,* two volumes, 3rd edition, Detroit: Gale, 1980.

The State of Black America, New York: National Urban League, 1976–.

Sterling, Dorothy, ed., *We Are Your Sisters: Black Women in the Nineteenth Century,* New York: Norton, 1984.

Story, Rosalyn M., *And So I Sing: African-American Divas of Opera and Concert,* Washington, D.C.: Amistad Press, 1990.

Thorpe, Edward, *Black Dance,* New York: Overlook Press, 1994.

Thum, Marcella, *Hippocrene U.S.A. Guide to Black America: A Directory of Historic and Cultural Sites Relating to Black America,* New York: Hippocrene Books, 1991.

Toppin, Edgar Allan, *A Biographical History of Blacks in America since 1528,* New York: McKay, 1971.

Treat, Roger L., *The Encyclopedia of Football,* 16th revised edition, Garden City: Doubleday, 1979.

Urban, Wayne J., *Black Scholar: Horace Mann Bond, 1904-1972,* Athens: University of Georgia Press, 1994.

Watts, Jill, *God, Harlem U.S.A.: The Father Divine Story,* Berkeley: University of California Press, 1992.

Westridge Young Writers Workshop Staff, *Kids Explore America's African-American Heritage,* Santa Fe: John Muir Publications, 1992.

Williams, Martin, *Jazz Masters of New Orleans,* New York: Da Capo Press, 1967.

Wills, David, and Richard Newman, *Black Apostles at Home and Abroad: Afro-Americans and the Christian Mission from the Revolution to Reconstruction,* Boston: G. K. Hall, 1982.

Wilmore, Gayraud S., *Black and Presbyterian: The Heritage and the Hope,* Philadelphia: Geneva Press, 1983.

Wilson, Charles R., *Encyclopedia of Southern Culture,* four volumes, New York: Doubleday, 1991.

Women in American Protestant Religion, 1800-1930, three volumes, New York: Garland, 1987.

Woodson, Carter G., *Education of the Negro Prior to 1861,* Salem, New Hampshire: Ayer Company Publishers, 1919; reprint, 1968.

Work, Nathan Monroe, ed., *Negro Year Book,* Tuskegee, Alabama, various years.

Wormley, Stanton L., and Lewis H. Fenderson, *Many Shades of Black,* New York: Morrow, 1969.

Yee, Shirley J., *Black Women Abolitionists: A Study in Activism, 1828-1860,* Knoxville: University of Tennessee Press, 1992.

Young, Andrew Sturgeon Nash, *Negro Firsts in Sports,* Chicago: Johnson Publishing, 1963.

Periodicals:

Various issues of the following periodicals were used in compiling *African American Breakthroughs:*

Alexander's Magazine
American Libraries
Atlanta Journal and Constitution
Autoweek
Black Ethnic Collectibles
Black Enterprise
Chicago Defender
Crisis
Detroit Free Press
Emerge
Encore
Essence
Fortune
Greensboro News and Record
Jet
Journal of the National Medical Association
Marketing
Minneapolis Star Tribune
Nashville Banner
Negro History Bulletin

New York
Opportunity
Parade
Road and Track
Scientific American
Sepia
Sports Illustrated
Tennessean (Nashville)
Time
USA Today
USA Weekend
U.S. News and World Report
Washington Post

INDEX